토플마스터

Jordan Jamie Green
Claire Park

Profreaders
Laura Joo
Jin Oh Bae

THE TOEFL iBT READING ACTUAL TEST

SERIES 1

2nd Edition

토플 Reading 30점 만점을 위한 최초 실전서 (총 9회분)

TOEFL
READING
ACTUAL
TEST

새롭게 시행된 New TOEFL iBT 완벽반영
TOEFL에 나오는 주요 토픽 별 실전 테스트 시리즈
토플전문강사가 직접 집필한 친절한 해설

HERMONHOUSE

토플마스터 TOEFL MASTER

THE TOEFL iBT
READING ACTUAL TEST
SERIES 1

발행 2022년 3월 31일 (초판1쇄)
　　　 2024년 10월 10일 (초판2쇄)

저자 Jordan Jamie Green · Claire Park
발행처 헤르몬하우스
발행인 최영민

기획 권주근
감수 Laura Joo · Jin Oh Bae

주소 경기도 파주시 신촌로 16
전화 031-8071-0088
팩스 031-942-8688
전자우편 hermonh@naver.com
출판등록 2015년 03월 27일
등록번호 제406-2015-31호
인쇄제작 미래피앤피

ISBN 979-11-91188-77-6　13740
정가 17,000원

About the Author

Jordan Jamie Green obtained a Master of Arts degree in TESOL (Teaching English to Speakers of Other Languages) and Applied Linguistics at the University of Central Lancashire, UK. Prior to this achievement, he completed a Bachelor of Arts degree in TESOL and Modern Languages at the same university. He has worked at several universities and world-renowned educational institutions in The United Kingdom, Spain, and China, and is now a professor in South Korea.

Jordan Jamie Green has over a decade worth of experience in materials development for language courses and assessments, including the ETS TOEFL test, IELTS exam, and TOEIC exam. He currently holds a perfect score of 120 for the ETS TOEFL test. His mission is to apply theoretical principles derived from linguistic research to the design of his educational materials, to help students excel in their language learning. Using corpora as a foundation of his materials design, he aims to present learners with authentic examples of English in all its forms and uses.

- Jordan Jamie Green

Now into her 13th year of teaching, Claire Park grew up in English-speaking countries, including New Zealand, Canada, and the United States. Such a diverse educational background motivated her to pursue a degree in International Studies (BA, Yonsei University), which became all the more valuable for an instructor who is capable of teaching a wide range of subjects, including TOEFL, SAT, AP and IB courses.

Her much knowledge and countless experiences in teaching strategic skills needed to excel in standardized tests are what inspired her to write this book.
Claire hopes to provide students who are studying English and other English tests with assistance during the course of their studies.

- Claire Park

Proofreaders

Laura has been engaged in EFL and ESL education for over 13 years in South Korea. Her specialty is English language test preparation including TOEFL and SAT. She pursues a student-centered learning by evaluating students' common mistakes and misconceptions regarding the author's word choices and sentence structures. She has built her reputation based on her lucid and easy explanations that brought outstanding test results on her students. Her long avid teaching experience and thorough analysis of existing TOEFL books and exams validate her role as the proofreader.

- Laura Joo

Jin Oh Bae has been involved in the education industry in Seoul, South Korea for the past twelve years; he spent seven years teaching the SAT and ACT to over 2,000 students and another seven teaching TOEFL to over 4,000 students. Jin's approach to teaching the TOEFL reading section was to think about the test from the perspective of the test maker; he analyzed around 60 TOEFL exams—focusing on question types, word choice, and common types of wrong answers—and developed tips and strategies for each question type. Thus, his insights about the ins and outs of the test make him an excellent candidate to proofread TOEFL reading exams.

- Jin Oh Bae

이 책의 구성과 특징

1. New TOEFL 변경사항과 최신 출제 경향/유형을 완벽히 반영

   2019년 8월부터 변경된 새로운 TOEFL 시험을 반영하여
   고득점을 목표로 하는 학습자를 위해서
   TOEFL 전문가들에 의한 실제 시험과 가장 유사한 문항으로 구성하였습니다.

   즉, 실제 시험과 동일한 문제 유형으로 구성하여 학습자들이 실전 감각을 익혀서
   시험에 효과적으로 대비할 수 있도록 했습니다.

2. **총 17회분의 Actual Test로 실전완벽대비(시리즈 1-9회분, 시리즈 2-8회분)**

   실전 테스트는 좋은 품질의 Test는 물론이고 동시에 일정 분량 이상의 양 또한 중요합니다.
   넉넉한 17회분으로 충분한 연습이 될 수 있도록 구성했습니다.

3. Actual Test를 TOEFL에서 자주 나오는 주요 토픽 별 Test로 묶어서
   부족한 부분부터 집중적으로 공략할 수 있도록 설계

   TOEFL에 자주 나오는 토픽, 즉 영어권 대학의 학습 현장에서 접할 수 있는 전공별 강좌에 대한
   주요 토픽들을 모두 담았습니다.

   총 17개 토픽에 대해서 체계적으로 토픽 별 학습이 가능하도록
   각 토픽 별 3개 Passage 즉 하나의 Actual Test로 강의를 만들었습니다.

4. TOEFL 전문 저자가 직접 꼼꼼하게 집필한 해설

   각 문제들이 ETS가 측정하는 TOEFL의 어떤 Question Types에 대해서
   묻는지 명시적으로 밝히고 각 문제들의 보기들이 왜 답이고 답이 아닌지를
   상세하게 설명하는 TOEFL 전문가의 노하우가 돋보이는 차별화된 해설입니다.

   해설에 본문의 어떤 문장/내용들이 어떻게 변형 (Paraphrase) 되었는지에 대한
   설명에 가장 포커스를 두어서 실력을 근본적으로 높일 수 있도록 설계하였습니다.

본 교재에 대한 인터넷 강의는 유학 전문 No.1 인터넷 강의 사이트인
마스터프렙(www.masterprep.net)에서 보실 수 있습니다.

TOEFL Scores 이해하기

Skill	Level
Reading	Advanced (24–30) High-Intermediate (18–23) Low-Intermediate (4–17) Below Low-Intermediate (0–3)
Listening	Advanced (22–30) High-Intermediate (17–21) Low-Intermediate (9–16) Below Low-Intermediate (0–8)
Speaking	Advanced (25–30) High-Intermediate (20–24) Low-Intermediate (16–19) Basic (10–15) Below Basic (0–9)
Writing	Advanced (24–30) High-Intermediate (17–23) Low-Intermediate (13–16) Basic (7–12) Below Basic (0–6)

New iBT TOEFL 시험 구성

Section	Time Limit	Questions & Task
Reading	54~72 분	지문 3~4개 각 지문당 10문제 30–40 문제 Read passages and respond to questions
Listening	41–57 분	대화 2~3개,각 5문제 강의 3~4개, 각 6문제 28–39 문제 Answer questions about brief lectures or classroom discussions
Break	10 분	
Speaking	17 분	4 개 과제 독립형 과제 1개 통합형 과제 3개 Talk about a familiar topic and discuss material you read and listened to
Writing	50 분	2 개 과제 Read a passage, listen to a recording, type your response Write an essay based on the given prompt

New iBT TOEFL Reading 영역 문제유형

Types of Questions

- 추론(Inference)
- 문장요약(Sentence Simplification)
- 정보찾기(Fact)
- 틀린 정보 찾기(Negative Fact)
- 어휘,동의어 찾기(Vocabulary)
- 문장 삽입(Sentence Insertion)
- 요약완성(Summary)
- 의도파악(Rhetorical Purpose)
- 글의 주제 찾기(Main Idea)

Contents

TOEFL

Reading
Actual Test

Actual Test
Psychology

Phobias

Fear is a basic human emotion that is felt by every human at some point in his or her life. This biochemical response occurs when humans are presented with some kind of imminent danger. Fear is a necessary part of human evolution; however, what happens when we fear *too much*? Psychologists identify a phobia as an intense and persistent fear about something which presents little or no danger at all. This could be an everyday object, place, or situation. While fear is a natural and proportionate response to danger, phobias are abnormal and often affect people's quality of life.

Phobias are irrational, as they pose no danger to an individual. For example, optophobia is the fear of opening one's eyes. More than just appearing irrational, this phobia could put one in danger. The second way in which phobias differ from fears is that phobias will affect the individual for an extended period. So, for example, if you found yourself standing on a golf course during a thunderstorm holding a golf club, you might have a very rational and understandable fear of being struck by lightning. On the other hand, consider someone with astraphobia. Astraphobia is the fear of thunderstorms. It is not just a fear of thunderstorms, but a prolonged and crippling anxiety surrounding them. Individuals with this phobia might think twice about leaving the house if they were to notice that the sky was dark.

What exactly causes a person to develop a phobia? Unfortunately, there is no precise answer – otherwise, phobias might be easier to treat. However, scientists believe that there are several factors which might lead to developing one. The first is a negative experience. It is possible that having a negative experience with an object or situation at a young age can develop into a phobia. For example, a young boy might wake up one night to find a spider crawling on his face. He will naturally be terrified and afraid. Most people would be afraid of spiders to some extent after such an event, but some individuals might develop arachnophobia, which is a continuing and intense anxiety related to anything to do with spiders and one of the world's most common phobias.

Another way in which phobias might develop is by being passed on to a younger child through his or her parents or caretakers. This transfer might be a result of genetics, learned behavior, or a mixture of the two. As is often the case, when we are discussing human behavior, it is not always possible to give a definite answer about why people act the way they do.

We have so far discussed what phobias are and some of their causes, but how are people with these conditions treated? There are several broad ways physicians treat those burdened by phobias. Obviously, treatment will have to be specific to the presenting case, but we can discuss these treatments here in general terms. Known as exposure therapy, this treatment involves exposing a patient to the phobia-inducing stimuli, starting with a stimulus that produces the lowest level of anxiety. Once the patient no longer feels anxious at this stimulus-exposure level, the patient is then exposed to stimuli that produce slightly higher levels of anxiety until the anxiety response is extinguished at all levels. For example, a woman with hydrophobia (a fear of water) might first be shown pictures of water. Next, she might be introduced to small amounts of water, like in a bathroom or kitchen sink. Later, she might be brought to a river and asked to step in it. The woman's fears gradually lose their hold on her as she eliminates her anxiety at each stage in the process.

Phobias

1 ➡ Fear is a basic human emotion that is felt by every human at some point in his or her life. This biochemical response occurs when humans are presented with some kind of imminent danger. Fear is a necessary part of human evolution; however, what happens when we fear *too much*? Psychologists identify a phobia as an intense and persistent fear about something which presents little or no danger at all. This could be an everyday object, place, or situation. While fear is a natural and proportionate response to danger, phobias are abnormal and often affect people's quality of life.

2 ➡ Phobias are irrational, as they pose no danger to an individual. For example, optophobia is the fear of opening one's eyes. More than just appearing irrational, this phobia could put one in danger. The second way in which phobias differ from fears is that phobias will affect the individual for an extended period. So, for example, if you found yourself standing on a golf course during a thunderstorm holding a golf club, you might have a very rational and understandable fear of being struck by lightning. On the other hand, consider someone with astraphobia. Astraphobia is the fear of thunderstorms. It is not just a fear of thunderstorms, but a prolonged and crippling anxiety surrounding them. Individuals with this phobia might think twice about leaving the house if they were to notice that the sky was dark.

1 According to paragraph 1, why does fear occur?

Ⓐ An individual's fear response is triggered by the possibility of a threat.

Ⓑ Fear is an unavoidable part of life.

Ⓒ A person encounters a stimulus that is immediately threatening.

Ⓓ Humans have evolved to fear abnormal phenomena.

2 In paragraph 2, the author states that optophobia

Ⓐ causes people to open their eyes in fearful situations

Ⓑ has the potential to put someone at risk

Ⓒ causes a rational and natural fear of opening one's eyes

Ⓓ is useful if one found oneself on a golf course

3 In paragraph 2, the author's description of astraphobia mentions which of the following?

Ⓐ It is a prolonged and crippling fear of thunderstorms.

Ⓑ It is a fear of thunderstorms.

Ⓒ It is quickly forgotten about.

Ⓓ It makes people think more than they want to.

4   In paragraph 3, what can be inferred about developing a phobia?

 Ⓐ Scientists' understanding of the causes of phobias is still developing.

 Ⓑ Those experiencing a traumatic event at a young age will unquestionably develop a phobia.

 Ⓒ Since treating phobias is a very difficult process, scientists are unable to determine the causes of phobias.

 Ⓓ Scientists have managed to pinpoint the exact reason people tend to develop a phobia.

5   In paragraph 3, the author uses the example of arachnophobia to

 Ⓐ highlight the fact that everyone thinks spiders are terrifying animals

 Ⓑ explain why a stressful childhood experience involving a spider might lead to developing a phobia

 Ⓒ express sympathy for individuals who are afraid of spiders

 Ⓓ emphasize that arachnophobia is one of the world's most common phobias

6   In paragraph 4, there is a missing sentence. The four letters (A, B, C, D) indicate where the following sentence could be added.

 However, what we do know is that degenerative changes to human behavior could be related to developing phobias in later years.

Where would the sentence best fit?

 Ⓐ Ⓑ Ⓒ Ⓓ

3 ➡ What exactly causes a person to develop a phobia? Unfortunately, there is no precise answer – otherwise, phobias might be easier to treat. However, scientists believe that there are several factors which might lead to developing one. The first is a negative experience. It is possible that having a negative experience with an object or situation at a young age can develop into a phobia. For example, a young boy might wake up one night to find a spider crawling on his face. He will naturally be terrified and afraid. Most people would be afraid of spiders to some extent after such an event, but some individuals might develop arachnophobia, which is a continuing and intense anxiety related to anything to do with spiders and one of the world's most common phobias.

4 ➡ **(A)** Another way in which phobias might develop is by being passed on to a younger child through his or her parents or caretakers. **(B)** This transfer might be a result of genetics, learned behavior, or a mixture of the two. **(C)** As is often the case, when we are discussing human behavior, it is not always possible to give a definite answer about why people act the way they do. **(D)**

7   In paragraph 5, the word 'burdened' is
    closest in meaning to
    (A) affected
    (B) afflicted
    (C) thwarted
    (D) irritated

8   In stating that 'treatment will be specific
    to the presenting case', the author means
    that
    (A) Doctors will treat all their patients with
        a phobia in the exact same manner.
    (B) It is possible to determine what a
        patient's phobia is when patients
        present themselves to the doctor.
    (C) Every case is different, and the
        treatment patients receive will depend
        upon their individual circumstances
        and needs.
    (D) Exposure therapy will be the
        most effective treatment for those
        presenting with a phobia.

9   What purpose does paragraph 5 serve as
    a whole?
    (A) It presents one method of treatment
        employed to patients with phobias.
    (B) It illustrates a concept of treatment
        that is widely studied today.
    (C) It compares two of the most practiced
        treatments.
    (D) It emphasizes the need to research
        more into phobia treatments.

5 ➡ We have so far discussed what phobias are and some of their causes, but how are people with these conditions treated? There are several broad ways physicians treat those burdened by phobias. Obviously, treatment will have to be specific to the presenting case, but we can discuss these treatments here in general terms. Known as exposure therapy, this treatment involves exposing a patient to the phobia-inducing stimuli, starting with a stimulus that produces the lowest level of anxiety. Once the patient no longer feels anxious at this stimulus-exposure level, the patient is then exposed to stimuli that produce slightly higher levels of anxiety until the anxiety response is extinguished at all levels. For example, a woman with hydrophobia (a fear of water) might first be shown pictures of water. Next, she might be introduced to small amounts of water, like in a bathroom or kitchen sink. Later, she might be brought to a river and asked to step in it. The woman's fears gradually lose their hold on her as she eliminates her anxiety at each stage in the process.

VIEW TEXT

REVIEW

HELP

BACK

NEXT

HIDE TIME 00:54:00

10 **Directions**: An introductory sentence for a brief summary of the passage is provided below. Complete the summary by choosing the THREE answer choices that express the most important ideas in the passage. Some sentences do not belong in the summary because they express ideas that are not presented in the passage or are minor ideas in the passage.

Drag your answer choices to the spaces where they belong. To remove an answer choice, click on it. To review the passage, click on **VIEW TEXT**.

Fear is distinct from phobia, and there are different factors involved in developing a phobia.

-
-
-

ANSWER CHOICES

A Optophobia is instant and can be perceived as an immediate threat to the individual.

B Phobias are prolonged and intense, unlike fear which is more of a universal emotion.

C Treatment for phobias is precise and easy to determine.

D Phobias might be caused by various factors such as childhood experiences, genetics, or conditioned behaviors.

E Usually, a phobia does not require any treatment and will resolve itself naturally over time.

F Phobias can be treated in various ways, but treatment must be designed precisely to meet each patient's needs.

Pavlovian Conditioning

In the 1890s, Pavlovian conditioning, also known as classical conditioning, was accidently discovered by the Russian physiologist Ivan Pavlov. He was conducting research concerning dog salivation in response to feeding. During his experiments, he inserted a small test tube into the cheek of each animal to measure saliva triggered by feeding. Pavlov thought the dogs would salivate when the food was delivered. Contrary to his assumption, he noticed his dogs salivated when they heard the feeding assistant's footsteps. In modern times, psychology has embraced his research, and it has become the foundation of behavioral conditioning.

Apparently, Pavlov didn't use a specific dog breed when conducting his digestive system experiments, so many of the animals were mutts or mongrels. As many as 30 canines were used in his classical conditioning tests before he got his surgical procedure correct. Because of the limitations of the Russian economy, Pavlov consistently employed thieves who regularly stole collared pets in their alleged collection of street dogs, to the consternation of the citizens near his laboratory. In the end, sadly, Pavlov's dogs were eaten during the siege of Leningrad, when Russians were starving during World War II. But to this day, Pavlov's dog experiments were critical in the discovery of one of psychology's most important concepts.

Since the time of Pavlov's dogs, numerous research studies have discovered classical conditioning to be an effective method in humans as well. In fact, it has been shown to treat unwanted thoughts and behaviors such as phobias, repulsion, nausea, rage, and sexual arousal. For example, conditioned nausea—the sight or smell of a particular food causing an upset stomach linked to some trauma from the past—can affect people greatly in their daily lives. Classical conditioning can eliminate this trauma by reconditioning the subject into thinking once again that the food doesn't provoke ill feelings.

Pavlov used classical conditioning to study reductionist behaviorism: a complex behavior that is broken down into smaller stimulus-response components. These smaller units can be managed more easily than larger ones. Behaviorism stresses the role of environmental influences in manipulating behavior to the near exclusion of native or inherited influences, and it becomes essentially a focus on learning as we learn new behaviors through classical conditioning. When humans are born, their minds are a blank slate, and psychological neuroses develop due to environmental factors and conditioning. During treatment of these negative conditions, the subject must go through three stages of conditioning.

Stage 1: Before Conditioning. In this phase, an unconditioned stimulus produces an unconditioned response in the subject. Basically, an environmental stimulus manufactures an unconditioned, or unlearned, response in behavior. This results in a natural response which has not been learned in the subject. This represents the "blank stage" process of conditioning that forms the psychological imprint. For example, seeing a dead animal might produce a response of revulsion. In another example, a food's aroma might create a hunger response. This stage also includes a person, object, or place known as a neutral stimulus, which doesn't produce a response until it is matched with an unconditioned stimulus.

Stage 2: During Conditioning. During this stage, a neutral stimulus is paired with an unconditioned stimulus. After this happens, the neutral stimulus becomes known as a conditioned stimulus. A conditioned stimulus must be presented to the subject before an unconditioned stimulus, instead of after it, or at least the same time for the conditioning to work. The conditioned stimulus acts as a signal for the unconditioned stimulus to take hold. Often, the unconditioned stimulus needs to be paired with the conditioned stimulus repeatedly in order for the subject to realize the two stimuli are associated.

Stage 3: After Conditioning. After Stage 2 is completed, the conditioned stimulus is paired with the unconditioned stimulus to generate a new conditioned response. For instance, an athlete who has been linked with a popular ad campaign appears more admirable. Also, a food that was eaten while a person had influenza now elicits a negative response. In the final stage, the association between the two stimuli asserts itself into the psychology of the subject, producing a new conditioned response. This completes the classical conditioning in the subject.

Pavlovian Conditioning

1 ➡ In the 1890s, Pavlovian conditioning, also known as classical conditioning, was accidently discovered by the Russian physiologist Ivan Pavlov. He was conducting research concerning dog salivation in response to feeding. During his experiments, he inserted a small test tube into the cheek of each animal to measure saliva triggered by feeding. Pavlov thought the dogs would salivate when the food was delivered. Contrary to his assumption, he noticed his dogs salivated when they heard the feeding assistant's footsteps. In modern times, psychology has embraced his research, and it has become the foundation of behavioral conditioning.

2 ➡ Apparently, Pavlov didn't use a specific dog breed when conducting his digestive system experiments, so many of the animals were mutts or mongrels. As many as 30 canines were used in his classical conditioning tests before he got his surgical procedure correct. Because of the limitations of the Russian economy, Pavlov consistently employed thieves who regularly stole collared pets in their alleged collection of street dogs, to the consternation of the citizens near his laboratory. In the end, sadly, Pavlov's dogs were eaten during the siege of Leningrad, when Russians were starving during World War II. But to this day, Pavlov's dog experiments were critical in the discovery of one of psychology's most important concepts.

---

1 According to paragraph 1, which of the following best explains how classical conditioning was discovered?

- (A) Russian researcher Ivan Pavlov observed an unexpected behavior in the subjects he was experimenting on.
- (B) Modern psychologists adapted Ivan Pavlov's experiments with dogs.
- (C) Ivan Pavlov assumed that the dogs he was experimenting on would salivate when they heard his assistant's footsteps.
- (D) Classical conditioning was founded by a Russian physiologist, Ivan Pavlov.

2 The word 'triggered' in the passage is closest in meaning to

- (A) dribbled
- (B) responded
- (C) activated
- (D) tripped

3 According to paragraph 2, which of the following is NOT true of Pavlov's dogs?

- (A) Many of the dogs were mixed street breeds, and some had owners
- (B) About three dozen dogs went through his surgeries until he got his procedure right
- (C) Many of the dogs were of a specific breed
- (D) Pavlov hired people to steal the dogs from the surrounding neighborhoods

4   According to paragraph 3, all the following are results of numerous research studies in classical conditioning EXCEPT:

    (A) Responses ranging from repulsion to rage are dealt with during the studies

    (B) Classical conditioning works for humans as well as for dogs

    (C) Conditioned nausea only affects people during the studies

    (D) The studies can eliminate trauma by reconditioning the subject

5   The word 'trauma' in the passage is closest in meaning to

    (A) test

    (B) mentality

    (C) situation

    (D) suffering

6   Which of the sentences below best expresses the essential information in the highlighted sentence in the passage? Incorrect choices change the meaning in important ways or leave out essential information.

    (A) Rather than focusing on intrinsic or inherited influences, behaviorism underscores the effect that the environment has on behavior and focuses on learning new behaviors through classical conditioning.

    (B) While behaviorism emphasizes environmental factors rather than native or inherited influences, classical conditioning focuses on learning new things.

    (C) Behaviorism no longer focuses on native or inherited influences but only on learning new behaviors through classical conditioning.

    (D) When we focus on learning, we can change our environmental, native, or inherited factors.

3 ➡ Since the time of Pavlov's dogs, numerous research studies have discovered classical conditioning to be an effective method in humans as well. In fact, it has been shown to treat unwanted thoughts and behaviors such as phobias, repulsion, nausea, rage, and sexual arousal. For example, conditioned nausea—the sight or smell of a particular food causing an upset stomach linked to some trauma from the past—can affect people greatly in their daily lives. Classical conditioning can eliminate this trauma by reconditioning the subject into thinking once again that the food doesn't provoke ill feelings.

4 ➡ Pavlov used classical conditioning to study reductionist behaviorism: a complex behavior that is broken down into smaller stimulus-response components. These smaller units can be managed more easily than larger ones. Behaviorism stresses the role of environmental influences in manipulating behavior to the near exclusion of native or inherited influences, and it becomes essentially a focus on learning as we learn new behaviors through classical conditioning. When humans are born, their minds are a blank slate, and psychological neuroses develop due to environmental factors and conditioning. During treatment of these negative conditions, the subject must go through three stages of conditioning.

More Available

7 The author mentions "hunger" in the passage as an example of which of the following?

    Ⓐ an unconditioned stimulus

    Ⓑ a neutral stimulus

    Ⓒ an unconditioned response

    Ⓓ a learned response

8 In the paragraph below, there is a missing sentence. Look at the paragraph and indicate (A, B, C and D) where the following sentence could be added to the passage.

All of these factors are integral in the first stage of conditioning.

Where would the sentence best fit?

    Ⓐ   Ⓑ   Ⓒ   Ⓓ

9 Why does the author mention 'neutral stimulus' in the passage?

    Ⓐ To explain why a conditioned stimulus must appear before an unconditioned response.

    Ⓑ To explain its role in a particular stage of conditioning.

    Ⓒ To emphasize the difference between a neutral stimulus and conditioned stimulus.

    Ⓓ To compare an unconditioned stimulus and a conditioned stimulus

5 ➡ Stage 1: Before Conditioning. In this phase, an unconditioned stimulus produces an unconditioned response in the subject. **(A)** Basically, an environmental stimulus manufactures an unconditioned, or unlearned, response in behavior. This results in a natural response which has not been learned in the subject. **(B)** This represents the "blank stage" process of conditioning that forms the psychological imprint. For example, seeing a dead animal might produce a response of revulsion. **(C)** In another example, a food's aroma might create a hunger response. This stage also includes a person, object, or place known as a neutral stimulus, which doesn't produce a response until it is matched with an unconditioned stimulus. **(D)**

6 ➡ Stage 2: During Conditioning. During this stage, a neutral stimulus is paired with an unconditioned stimulus. After this happens, the neutral stimulus becomes known as a conditioned stimulus. A conditioned stimulus must be presented to the subject before an unconditioned stimulus, instead of after it, or at least the same time for the conditioning to work. The conditioned stimulus acts as a signal for the unconditioned stimulus to take hold. Often, the unconditioned stimulus needs to be paired with the conditioned stimulus repeatedly in order for the subject to realize the two stimuli are associated.

7 ➡ Stage 3: After Conditioning. After Stage 2 is completed, the conditioned stimulus is paired with the unconditioned stimulus to generate a new conditioned response. For instance, an athlete who has been linked with a popular ad campaign appears more admirable. Also, a food that was eaten while a person had influenza now elicits a negative response. In the final stage, the association between the two stimuli asserts itself into the psychology of the subject, producing a new conditioned response. This completes the classical conditioning in the subject.

10 **Directions**: An introductory sentence for a brief summary of the passage is provided below. Complete the summary by choosing the THREE answer choices that express the most important ideas in the passage. Some sentences do not belong in the summary because they express ideas that are not presented in the passage or are minor ideas in the passage.

Drag your answer choices to the spaces where they belong. To remove an answer choice, click on it. To review the passage, click on **VIEW TEXT**.

Pavlovian conditioning was discovered by mistake but has become a well-embraced part of the field of behavioral science.

-
-
-

ANSWER CHOICES

A Pavlovian conditioning can be used to study behaviorism, which emphasizes the role environments can have on human mind and behavior.

B Up to 30 dogs were used in Pavlov's research on dogs before he performed surgery on them.

C Numerous research studies have discovered classical conditioning to be an effective method in humans because it can eliminate trauma by reconditioning the subject.

D In a particular phase in classical conditioning, a neutral stimulus must be repeatedly paired with an unconditioned stimulus before the neutral stimulus becomes a conditioned one.

E In one stage of classical conditioning, an unconditioned stimulus only needs to be paired with a conditioned stimulus once in order to elicit the neutral stimulus.

F Classical conditioning occurs in stages whereby the researcher pairs a neutral stimulus with an unconditioned stimulus until a conditioned response is achieved.

Addictions

The most perplexing human behaviors to psychologists can be attributed to chemical reactions occurring in the brain, in which dopamine plays a key role. Dopamine was actually synthesized in a laboratory in London by George Barger and James Ewens in 1910 before it was discovered in the human brain by Kathleen Montagu in 1957. Another important step in unlocking its role in the brain came a year later, when Arvid Carlsson and Nils-Åke Hillarp proved that dopamine functioned as a neurotransmitter.

Dopamine originates in the Ventral Tegmental Area (VTA) where it multiplies and is stored until released in response to an external stimulus. Leaving the VTA, it moves along two neural pathways in search of a receiving receptor in another part of the brain. The first of these is known as the Mesolimbic Dopamine Pathway, which starts in the VTA and is the primary dopamine producing region of the brain. This pathway is connected to the Nucleus Accumbens, which is the brain structure responsible for motivation and reward and where dopamine neurons are sent when we are rewarded. Subsequently, this causes dopamine levels to surge.

The second important neural pathway concerned with the reward system is the Mesocortical Dopamine Pathway. This pathway also starts in the VTA, but it sends neurons to the Frontal Cortex, which is activated when we experience a rewarding event. For this reason, it is considered part of the reward system. Interestingly, recent studies have found that dopamine may not be directly responsible for pleasure as was previously thought. Although its precise role in addiction is still undetermined, it was discovered that dopamine neurons were activated before we receive any reward. Scientists, therefore, hypothesize that dopamine plays a similar role in reward *seeking*.

Most researchers agree that there are two types of addiction. Behavioral addiction and chemical addiction. A behavioral addiction is one that does not offer any apparent reward other than the increase in dopamine in the brain. Two examples of this addiction are gambling and gaming disorder. A chemical addiction is one which involves the use of a substance. Examples include alcohol or nicotine addiction.

Dopamine is thought to affect the neurological biomechanisms for behavioral addiction by rewarding certain actions with the release of greater quantities of the hormone. Equally, the personal and environmental risk factors associated with substance addiction play a role in behavioral addiction. Individuals are 'rewarded' by a release of dopamine when they pursue certain activities. Gradually, they will come to associate these activities with the pleasure of dopamine release. Unfortunately, this 'dopamine rush' can occur with errant pursuits, and those with increased levels of dopamine in the brain could be at a higher risk of addiction because there are more dopamine hormones to flood their brains when dopamine is released.

Treatment for both types of addiction have some significant differences. The nature of chemical addiction means that those trying to recover from it will often suffer from withdrawal symptoms. These symptoms occur when the substance the individual was abusing has been removed. Therefore, medication is administered to help patients combat withdrawal symptoms and function normally in their daily lives. The treatment for behavioral addictions tends to focus more on rewiring the patient's neural pathways. If successful, this type of treatment can serve to instill in the patient new behaviors that are conducive to mental and physical well-being and less of a reliance on harmful habits to achieve the same feelings of motivation and pleasure.

1   According to the 1st paragraph, the author's description of dopamine mentions which of the following?

Ⓐ Dopamine causes perplexing behaviors in humans.

Ⓑ Dopamine was made in a laboratory before it was found in the human brain.

Ⓒ Dopamine's presence in the brain was substantiated by Arvid Carlsson and Nils-Åke Hillarp.

Ⓓ Dopamine causes chemical reactions to occur in the human brain.

2   According to paragraph 1, which of the following is NOT true of dopamine?

Ⓐ It plays a key role in chemical reactions in the brain.

Ⓑ It acts as a neurotransmitter.

Ⓒ It was created in a lab prior to being discovered in the human brain.

Ⓓ Its role in the brain was first discovered by George Barger and James Ewens.

3   Which of the following best expresses the essential information in the highlighted sentence in paragraph 2? Incorrect choices change the meaning in important ways or leave out essential information.

Ⓐ In response to external stimuli, dopamine is released from the Ventral Tegmental Area, an area in the brain where dopamine originates, proliferates, and remains.

Ⓑ The Ventral Tegmental Area responds to an external stimulus, originating and storing dopamine.

Ⓒ An external stimulus causes dopamine to move along neural pathways.

Ⓓ Released in response to external stimuli, the Ventral Tegmental Area produces and stores dopamine.

Addictions

1 ➡ The most perplexing human behaviors to psychologists can be attributed to chemical reactions occurring in the brain, in which *dopamine* plays a key role. Dopamine was actually synthesized in a laboratory in London by George Barger and James Ewens in 1910 before it was discovered in the human brain by Kathleen Montagu in 1957. Another important step in unlocking its role in the brain came a year later, when Arvid Carlsson and Nils-Åke Hillarp proved that dopamine functioned as a neurotransmitter.

2 ➡ Dopamine originates in the Ventral Tegmental Area (VTA) where it multiplies and is stored until released in response to an external stimulus. Leaving the VTA, it moves along two neural pathways in search of a receiving receptor in another part of the brain. The first of these is known as the Mesolimbic Dopamine Pathway, which starts in the VTA and is the primary dopamine producing region of the brain. This pathway is connected to the Nucleus Accumbens, which is the brain structure responsible for motivation and reward and where dopamine neurons are sent when we are rewarded. Subsequently, this causes dopamine levels to surge.

4   Which of the following is true about
     Mesocortical Dopamine Pathway?

     (A) It is initiated in the Ventral Tegmental
         Area.

     (B) It receives dopamine neurons from
         the Frontal Cortex and transfers them
         to the VTA.

     (C) It is the primary dopamine-producing
         pathway.

     (D) It may not be useful in explaining the
         cause of dopamine surge.

5   The word 'undetermined' in paragraph 3 is
     closest in meaning to

     (A) inoperable

     (B) unchanging

     (C) unknown

     (D) unstable

6   The author mentions 'gaming disorder' in
     paragraph 4 as an example of which of the
     following?

     (A) a type of gambling addiction

     (B) a treatment used for behavioral
         addictions

     (C) an addiction where the individual
         relies on a substance

     (D) a type of addiction in which the
         increase in dopamine is the only
         reward

3 ➡ The second important neural pathway
concerned with the reward system is
the Mesocortical Dopamine Pathway.
This pathway also starts in the VTA, but
it sends neurons to the Frontal Cortex,
which is activated when we experience a
rewarding rewarding event. For this reason,
it is considered part of the reward system.
Interestingly, recent studies have found that
dopamine may not be directly responsible
for pleasure as was previously thought.
Although its precise role in addiction is
stil undetermined, it was discovered that
dopamine neurons were activated before
we receive any reward. Scientists, therefore,
hypothesize that dopamine plays a similar role
in reward *seeking*.

4 ➡ Most researchers agree that there are
two types of addiction. Behavioral addiction
and chemical addiction. A behavioral addiction
is one that does not offer any apparent reward
other than the increase in dopamine in the
brain. Two examples of this addiction are
gambling and gaming disorder. A chemical
addiction is one which involves the use of
a substance. Examples include alcohol or
nicotine addiction.

7   According to paragraph 5, what can be inferred about the impact of dopamine on addiction?

(A) It is difficult to say with certainty why an individual develops an addiction.

(B) The greater the level of dopamine in the brain, the more pleasure an individual feels, which increases the likelihood the individual will develop an addiction.

(C) Dopamine is released only when we are engaged in harmful activities.

(D) Genetic factors influence addiction more than neurological factors.

8   According to paragraph 6, what is true about addiction treatment?

(A) Oftentimes, it is easy to treat chemical addicts by making them suffer from withdrawal symptoms.

(B) The nature of treatment for chemical and behavioral addiction is comparable.

(C) It is beneficial to provide medication when treating patients with chemical addiction.

(D) Making changes to neutral pathways is a type of treatment that can be harmful for patients with behavioral addictions.

9   Look at the four letters (A, B, C, D) that indicate where the following sentence could be added to paragraph 6.

Even when patients are mentally committed to beating the addiction, their bodies will still crave the missing dopamine high they have become accustomed to.

Where would it best fit?

(A)   (B)   (C)   (D)

5 ➡ Dopamine is thought to affect the neurological biomechanisms for behavioral addiction by rewarding certain actions with the release of greater quantities of the hormone. Equally, the personal and environmental risk factors associated with substance addiction play a role in behavioral addiction. Individuals are 'rewarded' by a release of dopamine when they pursue certain activities. Gradually, they will come to associate these activities with the pleasure of dopamine release. Unfortunately, this 'dopamine rush' can occur with errant pursuits, and those with increased levels of dopamine in the brain could be at a higher risk of addiction because there are more dopamine hormones to flood their brains when dopamine is released.

6 ➡ Treatment for both types of addiction have some significant differences. The nature of chemical addiction means that those trying to recover from it will often suffer from withdrawal symptoms. **(A)** These symptoms occur when the substance the individual was abusing has been removed. **(B)** Therefore, medication is administered to help patients combat withdrawal symptoms and function normally in their daily lives. **(C)** The treatment for behavioral addictions tends to focus more on rewiring the patient's neural pathways. **(D)** If successful, this type of treatment can serve to instill in the patient new behaviors that are conducive to mental and physical well-being and less of a reliance on harmful habits to achieve the same feelings of motivation and pleasure.

10 **Directions**: An introductory sentence for a brief summary of the passage is provided below. Complete the summary by choosing the THREE answer choices that express the most important ideas in the passage. Some sentences do not belong in the summary because they express ideas that are not presented in the passage or are minor ideas in the passage.

Drag your answer choices to the spaces where they belong. To remove an answer choice, click on it. To review the passage, click on **VIEW TEXT**.

Understanding the role that dopamine plays in human brains can shed light into its impact on addiction.

-
-
-

ANSWER CHOICES

A. Dopamine was created by two prominent scientists in the early 20th century in London.

B. After leaving the Ventral Tegmental Area, dopamine moves along the Mesolimbic Dopamine Pathway, which is connected to the Nucleus Accumbens.

C. Dopamine acts like a neurotransmitter, and its pathways consist of the Mesolimbic Dopamine Pathway and the Mesocortical Dopamine Pathway.

D. Scientists have come to understand that dopamine is important in reward seeking and is connected to addiction.

E. When it comes to addiction, dopamine release is associated with an increase in hormonal release.

F. Withdrawal symptoms are a common occurrence for those who are trying to overcome a chemical addiction.

TOEFL

Reading

Actual Test

Actual Test
Sociology

Suburbs

The suburbs that began to spring up all over the United States in the 1950s were hardly a new phenomenon. The word "suburb" dates back to the fourteenth century, and it has been applied to places in Europe since as early as the very beginnings of the industrial revolution. The name is derived from Latin—the prefix "sub" meaning "near to" and the root "urb" meaning "city." In modern usage, the term describes an outlying district of a city that is predominantly residential, but in the mid nineteenth century it took on a somewhat different meaning, referring to those areas of a city that had expanded beyond the original boundaries.

Following the end of the Second World War, there was a vast housing shortage in America. Millions of American servicemen had returned home, and it was estimated that no fewer than five million new homes would be required to accommodate these men who wished to settle down and start a family. The most straightforward and inexpensive solution was for developers to buy vast tracts of land that weren't too far from a city and construct an abundance of economically priced dwellings there. Keeping the homes relatively modest in size and building all of them to the same plan enabled these developers to save time and money, and building them within reasonable distance for someone looking to commute to a job in the city made these new suburbs the perfect choice for many American families.

By 1950, the number of Americans residing in the suburbs rocketed to around 40 million, with numbers surpassing 60 million barely a decade later. As people broke loose from cities, jobs followed suit, and this reduced the requirement for workers to commute to work. However, another factor appeared to cause the rapid rise of suburbs in America: the automobile. Back when suburbs were just beginning to take off, 40% of American households didn't own a mode of transport. Over the course of the following decade, having a car would become more than just a convenience—it would become an absolute necessity for modern life. As the population of the United States doubled, the number of cars on the road quadrupled. By 1970, over 95 percent of the American workforce was commuting by car. Half of the entire population relied on private vehicles as their sole means of transportation. Thus, the suburbs played a pivotal role in making cars such an integral component of life in America.

There's no denying that suburbs have shaped modern America. Millions of people left the cities to live the American Dream in the suburbs, but millions of people who didn't have the means to follow theirs were forced to stay behind. In some cities, entire neighborhoods were left virtually unoccupied. As the jobs relocated to the new industrial parks in the suburbs, life in many cities became intolerable. Living costs boomed, and crime rates followed that trend. Ironically enough, the exhausted cities have been given a recent boost by people from the suburbs moving back in. The struggling downtowns of many American cities are experiencing revitalization as people whose parents and grandparents fled decades before are returning.

Is America's love affair with the suburbs at an end? It's undeniable that over time many suburban communities have undergone changes that have made them indistinguishable from the cities to which they were initially attached, and while people have become increasingly disillusioned with life in the suburbs, there has been a great deal of positive change in cities. Improved public transportation, the construction of new residential buildings, and the re-emergence of a vibrant cultural scene have all helped to make cities attractive to young people again. Many of the jobs have also come back. These changes indicate that the suburbs of tomorrow will be strikingly different from those we know today.

Beginning ▲

Suburbs

1 ➡ The suburbs that began to spring up all over the United States in the 1950s were hardly a new phenomenon. **(A)** The word "suburb" dates back to the fourteenth century, and it has been applied to places in Europe since as early as the very beginnings of the industrial revolution. **(B)** The name is derived from Latin—the prefix "*sub*" meaning "near to" and the root "*urb*" meaning "city." **(C)** In modern usage, the term describes an outlying district of a city that is predominantly residential, but in the mid nineteenth century it took on a somewhat different meaning, referring to those areas of a city that had expanded beyond the original boundaries. **(D)**

2 ➡ Following the end of the Second World War, there was a vast housing shortage in America. Millions of American servicemen had returned home, and it was estimated that no fewer than five million new homes would be required to accommodate these men who wished to settle down and start a family. The most straightforward and inexpensive solution was for developers to buy vast tracts of land that weren't too far from a city and construct an abundance of economically priced dwellings there. Keeping the homes relatively modest in size and building all of them to the same plan enabled these developers to save time and money, and building them within reasonable distance for someone looking to commute to a job in the city made these new suburbs the perfect choice for many American families.

1 In paragraph 1, there is a missing sentence. Look at the paragraph and indicate (A, B, C and D) where the following sentence could best fit.

It was then that the mass exodus of people from the country to the city began in earnest.

(A)   (B)   (C)   (D)

2 According to paragraph 1, which of the following is true of suburbs?

(A) The word suburb is Latin and is from the era of The Roman Empire.

(B) In the 1800s, the word meant the parts of a city within the walls.

(C) Currently, the word refers to a part of the city on the outskirts that is mostly used for people's housing.

(D) Suburbs were first started to be built in the United States in the 1950s.

3 According to paragraph 2, which of the following is NOT true of America after World War II?

(A) There were not enough houses to meet the demand of the returning soldiers.

(B) The returning servicemen wished to have a home in which to raise a family.

(C) A minimum of five million new homes would be required to shelter the returning men.

(D) Developers bought land far from the cities in order to build affordable houses on it.

4   In paragraph 3, the author mentions '40% of American households didn't own a mode of transport' primarily to

  Ⓐ contrast early car ownership with car ownership in the 1970s as a factor that led to the increase of suburbs.

  Ⓑ explain that in the 1950s, people did not need a car to the extent they would in later decades.

  Ⓒ highlight the importance of the car to the people of America.

  Ⓓ stress the need for more extensive public transportation in the United States.

5   Which of the following can be inferred from paragraph 3 about the American population?

  Ⓐ They preferred to work in the suburbs and began to leave the cities.

  Ⓑ A large portion of the population did not have access to public transportation.

  Ⓒ Owning a car was a sign of prestige for American families, but not really a necessity.

  Ⓓ By 1970, there were more cars on the road than people in the workforce.

3 ➡ By 1950, the number of Americans residing in the suburbs rocketed to around 40 million, with numbers surpassing 60 million barely a decade later. As people broke loose from cities, jobs followed suit, and this reduced the requirement for workers to commute to work. However, another factor appeared to cause the rapid rise of suburbs in America: the automobile. Back when suburbs were just beginning to take off, 40% of American households didn't own a mode of transport. Over the course of the following decade, having a car would become more than just a convenience—it would become an absolute necessity for modern life. As the population of the United States doubled, the number of cars on the road quadrupled. By 1970, over 95 percent of the American workforce was commuting by car. Half of the entire population relied on private vehicles as their sole means of transportation. Thus, the suburbs played a pivotal role in making cars such an integral component of life in America.

6   Which of the following best expresses the essential information in the highlighted sentence in paragraph 4? Incorrect choices change the meaning in important ways or leave out essential information.

　Ⓐ Millions of Americans chose to pursue a better life by leaving the cities.

　Ⓑ Many Americans did not wish to move to the suburbs because the city was their dream location.

　Ⓒ The American Dream refers to living in the suburbs instead of the city.

　Ⓓ Those who could not afford the move to the suburbs were forced to stay in the cities.

7   In paragraph 5, the word 'disillusioned' is closest in meaning to

　Ⓐ shortsighted

　Ⓑ disenchanted

　Ⓒ discharged

　Ⓓ discouraged

8   In paragraph 5, the word 'strikingly' is closest in meaning to

　Ⓐ noticeably

　Ⓑ impactfully

　Ⓒ physically

　Ⓓ consciously

9   What does the author suggest about the changes of suburbs in paragraph 5?

　Ⓐ It is likely that suburb residents will outnumber city residents in the coming future.

　Ⓑ It is now impossible to estimate what the future will be like for suburbs and cities.

　Ⓒ American suburbs and cities are going through another phase in change.

　Ⓓ There has been an increase in the emergence of culture and better transportation in suburbs.

4 ➡ There's no denying that suburbs have shaped modern America. Millions of people left the cities to live the American Dream in the suburbs, but millions of people who didn't have the means to follow theirs were forced to stay behind. In some cities, entire neighborhoods were left virtually unoccupied. As the jobs relocated to the new industrial parks in the suburbs, life in many cities became intolerable. Living costs boomed, and crime rates followed that trend. Ironically enough, the exhausted cities have been given a recent boost by people from the suburbs moving back in. The struggling downtowns of many American cities are experiencing revitalization as people whose parents and grandparents fled decades before are returning.

5 ➡ Is America's love affair with the suburbs at an end? It's undeniable that over time many suburban communities have undergone changes that have made them indistinguishable from the cities to which they were initially attached, and while people have become increasingly disillusioned with life in the suburbs, there has been a great deal of positive change in cities. Improved public transportation, the construction of new residential buildings, and the re-emergence of a vibrant cultural scene have all helped to make cities attractive to young people again. Many of the jobs have also come back. These changes indicate that the suburbs of tomorrow will be strikingly different from those we know today.

10 An introductory sentence for a brief summary of the passage is provided below. Complete the summary by choosing the THREE answer choices that express the most important ideas in the passage. Some sentences do not belong in the summary because they express ideas that are not presented in the passage or are minor ideas in the passage.

Drag your answer choices to the spaces where they belong. To remove an answer choice, click on it. To review the passage, click on **VIEW TEXT**.

The end of World War II set the stage for the development of suburbs in the US.

-
-
-

ANSWER CHOICES

A A need for housing led developers to construct suburban homes quickly and cheaply.

B As people continued to flock to the suburbs, the jobs followed them, and their need to visit cities diminished.

C By the 1970s, half the population was commuting by car, and 95% of the workforce had access to public transportation.

D Without the invention of the automobile, suburbs would not have developed in the United States.

E The popularity of the suburbs meant that many cities suffered a decline, a trend that has been reversing in recent years.

F Suburbs have remained very different from the cities, and the movement of people toward cities and away from them looks set to continue.

Youth Culture

Some theorists argue that youth culture has been around since the advent of compulsory schooling. Their logic is that prior to compulsory schooling, the youth were not separated according to age, and they spent a lot of their time interacting with adults. Once kids started school, most of their time was spent interacting with youths of their own age. This is argued by some to be the starting point of youth culture. Others argue that youth culture as we understand it in present-day 2021 has only been around since some time in the mid-1950s, particularly in American society.

The first academic research on the topic can be traced to this time, such as Parsons' *"Age and Sex in the Social Structure of the United States."* It was in the 1950s that youth cultures began to make themselves known on a national level by participating in demonstrations and associating themselves with the Civil Rights Movements. This association with civil unrest and defiance against the establishment led to them being considered delinquent by society at large. Still others argue that youth culture does not exist at all. They maintain that youth culture is no different from 'adult' culture and that separating the two is not necessary.

If youth culture exists, is it a feature of every society in the way that culture is? The answer is not a straightforward one. Some believe that modern, industrialized societies are more inclined towards the development of youth cultures than less developed societies. The reasoning is that societies such as these display a higher level of universalism than perhaps less developed or less industrialized nations do. Universalism is simply the philosophy that certain ideas are held to be universal. They are self-evident truths. Countries with state institutions like schools that tend to be dominated by one or two religions generally adhere to this philosophy. Youth cultures are prone to thriving in such societies because the family is not really the unit within which a young person's identity is formed. Rather, it develops among peer groups where the norms of self-expression and identification are led by the prevailing culture of those same groups. The United States and England are good examples of this kind of society.

Conversely, societies within which the youth do not progress through life in such a predictable manner are less inclined towards forming sub or youth cultures. They are more likely to take their cues from their immediate family or village unit. Predominantly rural, modernizing societies are a good example of this. Their youth are just as likely to identify with family members as they are with their peer group. In societies where universal education is not a reality, many do not attend school beyond a certain age. This means there is less of an opportunity to become involved with youth culture.

Where youth culture exists, it is often marked by its rejection or subversion of the mainstream. Youth culture is not simply an interest in the cultural artifacts that are marketed toward the youth. In fact, youth cultures often resist the commercialization of 'their' movement. Once it becomes infiltrated and mass produced, it can often mean the beginning of the end. This cyclical process has defined youth culture from at least the 1960s onward. A good example of the cyclical nature of youth culture is the punk movement of the 70s and 80s.

Punk was a direct challenge to what its adherents believed was the exploitation and commodification of the hippy movement of the 1960s. There was an emphasis on making your own clothes in to keep the fashion of the culture out of the hands of opportunistic entrepreneurs or retail outlets. Even the music of the era was a response to the often lengthy and theatrical performances of 1960s music. The punk movement was a culture created by the youth as an answer to what they saw as a culture that had become too commercialized and accepted by the mainstream. Just as with the earlier hippy movement, punk fashion and music initially shocked and disgusted parents and the media. Ultimately, it would follow the same trend as the culture it was reacting against. Despite its best efforts, the punk movement would also become a commodity for mass production. In its place would come grunge, and the process began again.

Youth Culture

1 ➡ Some theorists argue that youth culture has been around since the advent of compulsory schooling. Their logic is that prior to compulsory schooling, the youth were not separated according to age, and they spent a lot of their time interacting with adults. Once kids started school, most of their time was spent interacting with youths of their own age. This is argued by some to be the starting point of youth culture. Others argue that youth culture as we understand it in present-day 2021 has only been around since some time in the mid-1950s, particularly in American society.

2 ➡ The first academic research on the topic can be traced to this time, such as Parsons' *"Age and Sex in the Social Structure of the United States"*. It was in the 1950s that youth cultures began to make themselves known on a national level by participating in demonstrations and associating themselves with the Civil Rights Movements. This association with civil unrest and defiance against the establishment led to them being considered delinquent by society at large. Still others argue that youth culture does not exist at all. They maintain that youth culture is no different from 'adult' culture, and that separating the two is not necessary.

1   Which of the following best expresses the essential information in the highlighted sentence in paragraph 1? Incorrect choices change the meaning in important ways or leave out essential information.

   A The youth of today spend most of their time interacting with other students of their own age.

   B Compulsory schooling forced young adults to spend time with adults.

   C Before compulsory schooling, the youth spent more time with adults.

   D Compulsory schooling meant the youth were split up according to their ages.

2   According to paragraph 1, which of the following is true of youth culture?

   A Arguably, it has only existed for about 70 years.

   B Compulsory schooling marked the definitive beginning of youth culture.

   C Youth culture rejects spending a lot of time with adults.

   D There is universal agreement as to when youth culture was established.

3   According to paragraph 2, which of the following is NOT true of youth culture?

   A It reached the national conscience during the 1950s.

   B Its association with academic research led to youth culture being mistrusted by society.

   C Some believe it is part of another culture, not a subculture of its own.

   D Its association with the Civil Rights Movement led to a negative perception of youth culture.

REVIEW

HELP

BACK

NEXT

HIDE TIME 00:54:00

More Available

4　The phrase 'adhere to' in paragraph 3 is closest in meaning to

   (A) maintain

   (B) protect

   (C) bond with

   (D) attach to

5　According to paragraph 3, the United States and England are examples of:

   (A) countries in which schools are dominant religious institutions

   (B) countries that are founded on the idea of universalism

   (C) countries whose society is teens' self-expression and identification are forms by universalism

   (D) countries in which young people's identities are not shaped by the family but by peer groups

6　In paragraph 4, why does the author discuss 'modernizing societies'?

   (A) In order to explain why modernizing societies are less likely to foster youth culture

   (B) To highlight the fact that in these societies, youth are more likely to associate with their family than with peer groups

   (C) To further the argument about where youth culture is not likely to thrive

   (D) To provide examples of nations where youth culture is likely to thrive

3 ➡ If youth culture exists, is it a feature of every society in the way that culture is? The answer is not a straightforward one. Some believe that modern, industrialized societies are more inclined towards the development of youth cultures than less developed societies. The reasoning is that societies such as these display a higher level of universalism than perhaps less developed or less industrialized nations do. Universalism is simply the philosophy that certain ideas are held to be universal. They are self-evident truths. Countries with state institutions like schools that tend to be dominated by one or two religions generally adhere to this philosophy. Youth cultures are prone to thriving in such societies because the family is not really the unit within which a young person's identity is formed. Rather, it develops among peer groups where the norms of self-expression and identification are led by the prevailing culture of those same groups. The United States and England are good examples of this kind of society.

4 ➡ Conversely, societies within which the youth do not progress through life in such a predictable manner are less inclined towards forming sub or youth cultures. They are more likely to take their cues from their immediate family or village unit. Predominantly rural, modernizing societies are a good example of this. Their youth are just as likely to identify with family members as they are with their peer group. In societies where universal education is not a reality, many do not attend school beyond a certain age. This means there is less of an opportunity to become involved with youth culture.

7   Which of the following can be inferred from paragraph 5 about the punk movement?

    Ⓐ It most likely would not survive the interest it garnered from large companies.

    Ⓑ It promoted the attempts to market youth culture to a wider audience.

    Ⓒ Punk was defined by its cyclical nature and would repeat itself each decade.

    Ⓓ The punk movement proved that youth culture could resist a takeover by retail giants.

8   In paragraph 6, there is a missing sentence. Look at the paragraph and indicate (A, B, C and D) where the following sentence could be added to the passage.

In fact, punk bands did not believe that musical talent was a prerequisite for performing live music.

Where would the sentence best fit?

    Ⓐ   Ⓑ   Ⓒ   Ⓓ

9   The word 'commodity' in paragraph 6 is closest in meaning to

    Ⓐ artifact

    Ⓑ mechanism

    Ⓒ export

    Ⓓ product

5 ➡ Where youth culture exists, it is often marked by its rejection or subversion of the mainstream. Youth culture is not simply an interest in the cultural artifacts that are marketed toward the youth. In fact, youth cultures often resist the commercialization of 'their' movement. Once it becomes infiltrated and mass produced, it can often mean the beginning of the end. This cyclical process has defined youth culture from at least the 1960s onward. A good example of the cyclical nature of youth culture is the punk movement of the 70s and 80s.

6 ➡ Punk was a direct challenge to what its adherents believed was the exploitation and commodification of the hippy movement of the 1960s. **(A)** There was an emphasis on making your own clothes, in order to keep the fashion of the culture out of the hands of opportunistic entrepreneurs or retail outlets. **(B)** Even the music of the era was a response to the often lengthy and theatrical performances of 1960s music. **(C)** The punk movement was a culture created by the youth as an answer to what they saw as a culture that had become too commercialized and accepted by the mainstream. **(D)** Just as with the earlier hippy movement, punk fashion and music initially shocked and disgusted parents and the media. Ultimately, it would follow the same trend as the culture it was reacting against. Despite its best efforts, the punk movement would also become a commodity for mass production. In its place would come grunge, and the process began again.

⊟
VIEW TEXT

Q
REVIEW

?
HELP

‹
BACK

›
NEXT

HIDE TIME 00:54:00

10 An introductory sentence for a brief summary of the passage is provided below. Complete the
summary by choosing the THREE answer choices that express the most important ideas in the
passage. Some sentences do not belong in the summary because they express ideas that are
not presented in the passage or are minor ideas in the passage.

Drag your answer choices to the spaces where they belong. To remove an answer choice,
click on it. To review the passage, click on **VIEW TEXT**.

Youth culture is difficult to define, and it is not always easy to describe its evolution.

-
-
-

ANSWER CHOICES

A It is generally agreed that youth culture took off in the 1950s, when compulsory classroom education became prevalent.

B There are those who believe that youth culture emerged as a result of mandatory education, while others argue that youth culture is a relatively new phenomenon.

C Often, youth cultures stand in direct opposition to the status quo and can subsequently be ostracized by society.

D Youth groups and cultures seek to achieve notoriety so that they might gain financially through the commoditization of their movement.

E The lifespan of youth cultures is often cut short once they become compromised by their association with mass production.

F Once a youth or subculture changes, it never reappears in a new form, but is lost for good.

Mass Media

The dissemination of information through a variety of printed and digital formats – known as mass media – has existed since the establishment of the world's first newspaper in the 17th century. Irrespective of the medium from which people receive such information, the goal of mass media is always the same: occupy people's leisure times. Serving primarily as a form of entertainment in the 21st century, it has gone through various adaptations to appeal to a younger and hyper-productive generation, from 'snaps' and 'tweets' for short-attention spans to news 'snippets' for the busy professional. Despite its apparent lighthearted nature, psychologists occupy a contrasting perspective: mass media's role in society is more powerful than simply a pleasant form of distraction.

Some psychologists view mass media's role as an enforcer of social norms by providing information about what is expected of people as part of a society. This is known as the 'functional perspective'. For instance, a TV show about remorseful prisoners or a commercial describing the penalties for avoiding tax can highlight the value of being a law-abiding citizen by reinforcing that criminal behaviors are bad. In this sense, media plays a vital role in socializing and re-socializing viewers to maintain beliefs and sociocultural values within a society. This ideology is largely accepted by psychologists as a positive motivator and accepted by society.

Commercial advertisements are considered an extension of the functionalist approach, making up approximately 35% of airtime on TV and 30% of newspapers and magazines. In fact, studied suggest that the average child sees around 40,000 commercials per year. Psychologists argue that such exposure can be far too persuasive for an underdeveloped mind, adding that mature comprehension of the commercial's subliminal messaging is necessary to decode its function. Their misunderstanding leads to the normalization of unhealthy eating habits, brand-loyalty, and an increased desire to obtain the latest novelties.

The conflict perspective of broadcasting focuses on the portrayal of divisions in society through the media, such as gender, class, ethnicity, and religion. The process in which the information is selected, filtered, and presented to consumers is well-documented and known as *gatekeeping*. Cinematic pictures, radio, newspapers, TV, and the Internet are all subject to gatekeeping, with those making the decisions ranging from media corporations to high-ranking government officials. This filtration often reflects the presiding ideology of that society and is heavily criticized for offering privileges to certain political views, stereotyping minority groups, and portraying women as victims in an objectifying manner. This often causes a negative domino-effect onto society and is reflected in people's everyday actions.

Despite the harmful results of gatekeeping, the conflict perspective also highlights the important role mass media has had as an agent of socialization, outlining its impact on the creation of sub-communities and influential movements, such as LGBTQ and Women's Rights. In an ever computerized 21st century, such groups are instantaneously accessible through the Internet and can help individuals to coalesce and build powerful unions. Convergences like 'Black Lives Matter' have led to necessitous changes across entire nations where once thought impossible. Unfortunately, such open coverage has given a platform for people to spread radical ideologies and glorify violence and hatred.

Mass Media

1 ➡ The dissemination of information through a variety of printed and digital formats - known as *mass media* – has existed since the establishment of the world's first newspaper in the 17th century. Irrespective of the medium from which people receive such information, the goal of mass media is always the same: occupy people's leisure times. Serving primarily as a form of entertainment in the 21st century, it has gone through various adaptations to appeal to a younger and hyper-productive generation, from 'snaps' and 'tweets' for short-attention spans to news 'snippets' for the busy professional. Despite its apparent lighthearted nature, psychologists occupy a contrasting perspective: mass media's role in society is more powerful than simply a pleasant form of distraction.

2 ➡ Some psychologists view mass media's role as an enforcer of social norms by providing information about what is expected of people as part of a society. This is known as the 'functional perspective'. For instance, a TV show about remorseful prisoners or a commercial describing the penalties for avoiding tax can highlight the value of being a law-abiding citizen by reinforcing that criminal behaviors are bad. In this sense, media plays a vital role in socializing and re-socializing viewers to maintain beliefs and sociocultural values within a society. This ideology is largely accepted by psychologists as a positive motivator and accepted by society.

1 Which of the following best expresses the essential information in the highlighted sentence in paragraph 1? Incorrect choices change the meaning in important ways or leave out essential information.

- (A) Psychologists have perspectives about why mass media is so popular as a form of entertainment.
- (B) Psychologists believe that mass media's role in society goes beyond entertainment.
- (C) Although mass media is a pleasant distraction, it is also dangerous for society.
- (D) Psychologists have different theories as to the role of mass media's positive role on society.

2 According to paragraph 2, which of the following is true of the functionalist perspective?

- (A) It only appears to be true for TV shows
- (B) It has led to fewer people being imprisoned because of tax avoidance
- (C) Psychologists are unable to define it reasonably
- (D) It is regarded as a mostly positive viewpoint

3 In context of the passage, what is the purpose of paragraph 3?

(A) To compare the different ideologies supported by psychologists

(B) To demonstrate that commercial advertisements are one of the best ways to deliver ideas

(C) To discuss an idea related to the functionalist perspective and its effects on a particular group in society

(D) To counter the claim that functionalists' ideas are generally accepted by society

4 According to paragraph 3, what is true about commercials' subliminal messages?

(A) They are too convincing to be decoded by young audiences

(B) They have the potential to bring about negative consequences on young viewers.

(C) They are caused by the normalization of unhealthy eating habits, brand-loyalty, and incessant desire for goods.

(D) They are powerful ways in which commercial advertisements impact viewers in general.

3 ➡ Commercial advertisements are considered an extension of the functionalist approach, making up approximately 35% of airtime on TV and 30% of newspapers and magazines. In fact, studied suggest that the average child sees around 40,000 commercials per year. Psychologists argue that such exposure can be far too persuasive for an underdeveloped mind, adding that mature comprehension of the commercials' subliminal messaging is necessary to decode its function. Their misunderstanding leads to the normalization of unhealthy eating habits, brand-loyalty, and an increased desire to obtain the latest and novelties.

More Available

5   According to paragraph 4, which of the following is NOT true of the conflict perspective?

    Ⓐ It is associated with the portrayal of numerous aspects of society.

    Ⓑ Psychologists believe it is the reason people are discriminated against in real-life.

    Ⓒ It considers why media is filtered and its influence on certain groups of people and society as a whole.

    Ⓓ Gatekeeps are often criticized for the realization of this perspective.

6   The word 'presiding' in paragraph 4 is closest in meaning to

    Ⓐ dominant

    Ⓑ xenophobic

    Ⓒ formidable

    Ⓓ established

4 ➡ The conflict perspective of broadcasting focuses on the portrayal of divisions in society through the media, such as gender, class, ethnicity, and religion. The process in which the information is selected, filtered, and presented to consumers is well-documented and known as *gatekeeping*. Cinematic pictures, radio, newspapers, TV and the Internet are all subject to gatekeeping, with those making the decisions ranging from media corporations to high-ranking government officials. This filtration often reflects the presiding ideology of that society and is heavily criticized for offering privileges to certain political views, stereotyping minority groups, and portraying women as victims in an objectifying manner. This often causes a negative domino-effect onto society and is reflected in people's everyday actions.

7   In paragraph 5, why does the author mention 'agent of socialization'?

(A) To suggest that mass media is used as a mediator between people who traditionally have opposing views.

(B) To describe how the Internet has helped people socialize effortlessly.

(C) To identify a positive role of mass media on social groups.

(D) To liken it to gatekeeping and further exemplify the drawbacks of mass media.

8   Which of the following can be inferred from paragraph 5 about mass media's role as an agent of socialization?

(A) Not all things that have resulted from it have been positive.

(B) It has been indispensable for community-building and remains a constructive tool.

(C) It needs to be modified in order to serve its purpose as a means for social change.

(D) Its effectiveness is not yet clear and remains to be seen.

9   In paragraph 5, there is a missing sentence. Look at the paragraph and indicate (A, B, C and D) where the following sentence could be added to the passage.

However controversial, such sub-communities have provided a voice for millions of people.

Where would the sentence best fit?

(A)   (B)   (C)   (D)

5 ➡ Despite the harmful results of gatekeeping, the conflict perspective also highlights the important role mass media has had as an agent of socialization, outlining its impact on the creation of sub-communities and influential movements, such as LGBTQ and Women's Rights. **(A)** In an ever computerized 21ˢᵗ century, such groups are instantaneously accessible through the Internet and can help individuals to coalesce and build powerful unions. **(B)** Convergences like 'Black Lives Matter' have led to necessitous changes across entire nations where once thought impossible. **(C)** Unfortunately, such open coverage has given a platform for people to spread radical ideologies and glorify violence and hatred. **(D)**

10 An introductory sentence for a brief summary of the passage is provided below. Complete the summary by choosing the THREE answer choices that express the most important ideas in the passage. Some sentences do not belong in the summary because they express ideas that are not presented in the passage or are minor ideas in the passage.

> Drag your answer choices to the spaces where they belong. To remove an answer choice, click on it. To review the passage, click on **VIEW TEXT**.

Mass media plays a crucial role in our society, and there are certain, distinct ways to explain its impact on the viewers.

-
-
-

ANSWER CHOICES

A Mass media highlights the portrayal of people based on beliefs and physical characteristics.

B On one hand, mass media can be viewed as serving different functions that play a role in shaping people's beliefs and societal norms and values.

C Mass media is oftentimes criticized for depicting privileges of certain political stances and wrongdoings of prominent figures.

D Mass media's impact can be both harmful and beneficial to society.

E A television program broadcasting about remorseful prisoners or showing the consequences of tax evasion is an example of the functionalist perspective.

F Mass media has been evolving since its introduction to the public, and its impact in society is more powerful than its primary purpose as entertainment.

TOEFL

Reading

Actual Test

TOEFL

Reading
Actual Test

Actual Test
Anthropology

Shamanism

Shamanism is a religious science practiced by the indigenous societies of Central and North Asia, the Americas, Southeastern Asia, Oceania, Tibet, China, and the Far East. It involves a shaman (a type of priest who interacts with the spirit world through altered states of consciousness). Using various practices like initiatory sickness, lucid dreams, dancing and drumming, and trance, the practitioner contacts a spirit world for guidance to fix some personal or community problem. There are two main goals for the shaman. First, he or she directs these spiritual energies into the material world for healing or for some other occult purpose. Second, he or she communes with nature, speaks with ancestors, or reveals a destiny.

Often, the shaman obtains his or her power through an initiatory crisis or divine madness. Medical professionals and anthropologists consider this illness a type of schizophrenia or insanity, but the shamans believe that they speak to the spirit world, and they consider these experiences "real." The difference between the schizophrenic and the shamanic priest is that shamans are trained to work in the spirit world while the schizophrenic drowns in it. Signs of this illness include babbling, strange eating habits, nonstop singing, dancing like a madman, or spirits tormenting them. In tribal cultures, such disasters are interpreted as a sign of a person's fate to become a shaman, rather than a sign of insanity.

Accounts indicate several indicators that define the shamanic experience. Sometimes, shamans report distressing experiences like being beaten repeatedly, going to the peak of a sacred mountain or falling down into its depths, being dismembered, cooked, or possessed by ill spirits. The shamans believe that the spirit world calls to them during this crisis. Once the individual accepts the "calling" to become the "wounded healer," his or her illness usually disappears. This "self-cure" happens so often that anthropologists think anyone without this self-cure should only be known as a "normal healer." The mantle of "wounded healer" is a type of self-sacrifice that the community deems necessary to properly become a priest within the tribe.

After the shaman accepts the calling, he or she uses ecstatic states to learn about the

sickness of his or her patient. Exaltation places the shaman outside himself or herself into a state of transcendence, journeying either high into the heavens or deep into the underworld to attain a possible cure. After he or she "returns" to mundane awareness, the shaman brings back the necessary wisdom to heal. This is accomplished in many ways. First, it's believed that the shaman can affect the physical well-being of the sick. Second, he or she can help the soul of the deceased into the next world. Lastly, he or she can bring back wisdom found within their travels inward.

Trance is one technique shamans use to alter their consciousness. There are many ways to achieve this state. Extreme exhaustion or fasting can also put one under a spell. Drunkenness or the ingestion of sacred plants can also put the shaman into trance. Meditation is another technique. In some cases, it's believed that a spirit can possess them and force them into this trance state. All of these ways aid the shaman in finding the secret knowledge needed to heal the sick, but the experience for the shaman (who is in a trance) and the observer (who watches the shaman) differ wildly because the experience is subjective.

Drumming and dancing are other techniques to enter trance. Shamans worldwide create the rhythmic sounds through drumming, rattling, and chanting. Some beat on reindeer skin drums or tap skulls with a stick, while others shake rattles, clap, stomp, or chant with a beat. Ceremonial dancing often accompanies drumming. Shamans frequently imitate the movements of an animal whose qualities they wish to bring forth. Sometimes, the people from his or her community dance, clap, and chant along with the shaman so that they enter a trance state themselves. Often these community trances are said to heal mass afflictions, to change the weather in the case of a drought, or to guide the destiny of the tribe.

1 According to paragraph 1, what best describes a shaman?

    Ⓐ A person who spreads the gospel

    Ⓑ A person who lives in Asia

    Ⓒ A person who harnesses spiritual powers to heal

    Ⓓ A person who fixes things

2 In paragraph 1, what does the author imply by using the word 'occult'?

    Ⓐ The shaman is a member of a cult.

    Ⓑ The shaman uses his healing energy to only help people in his community.

    Ⓒ The shaman's energy can be used for a supernatural or mystical intention.

    Ⓓ The shaman's ancestors reveal his destiny.

3 According to paragraph 2, an initiatory crisis is important because it

    Ⓐ makes the schizophrenic more mentally ill

    Ⓑ allows the shaman to gain access to the spirit world

    Ⓒ allows the shaman to get lost in the real world

    Ⓓ makes trouble for people in the community

Shamanism

1 ➡ Shamanism is a religious science practiced by the indigenous societies of Central and North Asia, the Americas, Southeastern Asia, Oceania, Tibet, China, and the Far East. It involves a shaman (a type of priest who interacts with the spirit world through altered states of consciousness). Using various practices like initiatory sickness, lucid dreams, dancing and drumming, and trance, the practitioner contacts a spirit world for guidance to fix some personal or community problem. There are two main goals for the shaman. First, he or she directs these spiritual energies into the material world for healing or for some other occult purpose. Second, he or she communes with nature, speaks with ancestors, or reveals a destiny.

2 ➡ Often, the shaman obtains his or her power through an initiatory crisis or divine madness. Medical professionals and anthropologists consider this illness a type of schizophrenia or insanity, but the shamans believe that they speak to the spirit world, and they consider these experiences "real." The difference between the schizophrenic and the shamanic priest is that shamans are trained to work in the spirit world while the schizophrenic drowns in it. Signs of this illness include babbling, strange eating habits, nonstop singing, dancing like a madman, or spirits tormenting them. In tribal cultures, such disasters are interpreted as a sign of a person's fate to become a shaman, rather than a sign of insanity.

Q
REVIEW
?
HELP
‹
BACK
›
NEXT

HIDE TIME 00:54:00

More Available ▲

4 According to paragraph 3, all the following are results of shamanic experience EXCEPT:

(A) Shamans think the spiritual world summons them in times of need

(B) The shaman needs to be wounded somehow to become a healer

(C) The shaman beats others without just reason

(D) Shamans who don't go through a self-sacrificial process are called normal healers

5 Which of the sentences below best expresses the essential information in the highlighted sentence in the passage? Incorrect choices change the meaning in important ways or leave out essential information.

(A) The shaman uses drums to find a trance state so that he or she can cure someone

(B) The shaman uses bliss to move outside the normal perimeters of reality and into a healing state

(C) The shaman moves toward the highest mountain and the lowest depth

(D) In order to obtain a possible cure, the shaman reaches a state of transcendence by moving beyond his or her current state and into ecstasy

6 The word 'mundane' in the passage is closest in meaning to

(A) normal

(B) original

(C) spiritual

(D) conscious

3 ➡ Accounts indicate several indicators that define the shamanic experience. Sometimes, shamans report distressing experiences like being beaten repeatedly, going to the peak of a sacred mountain or falling down into its depths, being dismembered, cooked, or possessed by ill spirits. The shamans believe that the spirit world calls to them during this crisis. Once the individual accepts the "calling" to become the "wounded healer," his or her illness usually disappears. This "self-cure" happens so often that anthropologists think anyone without this self-cure should only be known as a "normal healer." The mantle of "wounded healer" is a type of self-sacrifice that the community deems necessary to properly become a priest within the tribe.

4 ➡ After the shaman accepts the calling, he or she uses ecstatic states to learn about the sickness of his or her patient. Exaltation places the shaman outside himself or herself into a state of transcendence, journeying either high into the heavens or deep into the underworld to attain a possible cure. After he or she "returns" to mundane awareness, the shaman brings back the necessary wisdom to heal. This is accomplished in many ways. First, it's believed that the shaman can affect the physical well-being of the sick. Second, he or she can help the soul of the deceased into the next world. Lastly, he or she can bring back wisdom found within their travels inward.

7   Which of the following is NOT true according to paragraph 5?

Ⓐ One of the ways a shaman can enter trance is through fasting.

Ⓑ There are several ways shamans can find the secret knowledge to cure the sick.

Ⓒ What a shaman and an observer experience differ very little.

Ⓓ It is possible to reach a trance state by consuming plants.

8   Look at paragraph 5 and indicate (A, B, C and D) where the following sentence could be added to the passage.

This state of intoxication should be monitored by a trustworthy figure.

Where would the sentence best fit?

Ⓐ   Ⓑ   Ⓒ   Ⓓ

9   Why does the author mention 'community trances' in the passage?

Ⓐ To demonstrate the dangers of mass afflictions

Ⓑ To show that the shaman is not the only one who can enter a trance state

Ⓒ To emphasize how entertaining dancing can be

Ⓓ To compare the community trance with the shamanic trance

5 ➜ Trance is one technique shamans use to alter their consciousness. There are many ways to achieve this state. **(A)** Extreme exhaustion or fasting can also put one under a spell. Drunkenness or the ingestion of sacred plants can also put the shaman into trance. **(B)** Meditation is another technique. **(C)** In some cases, it's believed that a spirit can possess them and force them into this trance state. All of these ways aid the shaman in finding the secret knowledge needed to heal the sick, but the experience for the shaman (who is in a trance) and the observer (who watches the shaman) differ wildly because the experience is subjective. **(D)**

6 ➜ Drumming and dancing are other techniques to enter trance. Shamans worldwide create the rhythmic sounds through drumming, rattling, and chanting. Some beat on reindeer skin drums or tap skulls with a stick, while others shake rattles, clap, stomp, or chant with a beat. Ceremonial dancing often accompanies drumming. Shamans frequently imitate the movements of an animal whose qualities they wish to bring forth. Sometimes, the people from his or her community dance, clap, and chant along with the shaman so that they enter a trance state themselves. Often these community trances are said to heal mass afflictions, to change the weather in the case of a drought, or to guide the destiny of the tribe.

10 **Directions**: An introductory sentence for a brief summary of the passage is provided below. Complete the summary by choosing the THREE answer choices that express the most important ideas in the passage. Some sentences do not belong in the summary because they express ideas that are not presented in the passage or are minor ideas in the passage.

Drag your answer choices to the spaces where they belong. To remove an answer choice, click on it. To review the passage, click on **VIEW TEXT**.

Shamans play an important role in their tribe, and there are various techniques they use to alter their consciousness to fulfill their duties.

-
-
-

ANSWER CHOICES

A A shaman's role is to travel to various parts of Asia and the Americas in hopes to contact the spirit world.

B Shamans can employ diverse methods, including dancing and meditation, to enter into trance, which is used to heal the sick.

C Shamans experience different forms of illness, and once they accept their fate, the illness disappears and they obtain their power to heal.

D Community trances involve the use of rhythmic beats and chants, as well as extreme exhaustion or fasting.

E Shamans inspire the community to heal themselves by entering their own trances, although the experience can be subjective.

F Typically, shamans can transcend the physical world and experience ecstatic states that provide them with knowledge about curing the sick.

The Roman Empire

   The Roman Empire was one of the largest and most powerful empires of the ancient world. At its height, it covered nearly two million square miles and boasted a population of around 70 million people. From the founding of Rome – the city which became the capital – sometime around 800 B.C.E. to the fall of the Western Roman Empire in 476 C.E., the Romans were responsible for some of the most important technological innovations in history, and their influence on art, architecture, laws, language, and politics has been far-reaching and long-lasting. Building on the legacy of those civilizations that had come before them – the Ancient Greeks, Egyptians, Persians, and others – the Romans developed a unique cultural identity. This monumental legacy survived the collapse of the empire and remains resilient even today.

   Perhaps the Roman's greatest legacy is their influence on politics and government. When the founding fathers of the United States gathered to draw up plans for the government of their new nation, they borrowed heavily from the traditions of the Romans. Just as there were three branches of government in Rome, so too are there three branches of government in the United States today. The founding fathers liked and adopted the idea that each of the three branches of government served as a check and balance to the others, which meant that one branch could not have absolute power. Like the Romans did thousands of years ago, many people in different countries around the world elect their leaders. The Romans were not the first to invent or to implement democracy, but the value that they placed on civic participation and civic responsibility was hugely influential to future societies.

   The Romans are also remembered today for their lasting achievements in the fields of architecture and engineering. The Romans were excellent builders, and many of their innovations enabled the construction of larger, stronger structures. The staggering number of Roman ruins scattered around Europe, North Africa, Asia Minor, and the Levant are a testament to Roman ingenuity. The delicate balance between science and art that the Romans managed to find with many of their building projects continues to inspire modern architects. The Romans experimented with different kinds of building materials.

These experiments led to the invention of concrete, which is one of the most widely used materials in construction today; however, the materials they used were perhaps not as important as the designs they devised. Roman roads were built using layers, one stacked on top another, so that they were more durable and less prone to wearing down over time. The Romans would often build using arches, which, because of their curved or rounded shapes, were able to support much more weight than other shapes could. The Romans were experts at merging form and function so that their structures were not only sturdy but also aesthetically appealing. They would often incorporate large open areas within larger structures so that their buildings managed to blend the man-made with the natural world that surrounded them.

Along with their rich traditions in art, architecture, and politics, the Romans contributed greatly to language and literature. Rome was home to some of the greatest writers of the ancient world. The works of Virgil and Ovid are still standard reading in schools all around the world today. Roman historians have provided us with some of the finest depictions of life during the eras in which they lived, and many poems and plays and even speeches are still being studied and enjoyed today. The language of ancient Rome was Latin, and while it was the language of poets and politicians, it was also the language of the people.

The span of time from the founding of Rome to the end of the Western Roman Empire is roughly the same span of time that separates us from the Song Dynasty. Life in ancient Rome was strikingly different from what it was at the tail end of the Roman period. The Romans were instrumental in the spread of Christianity across Europe and adjacent parts of the world starting in the third and fourth centuries. The Catholic Church remains headquartered in the Holy See, completely surrounded by the city of Rome. Roman influence can be felt all over the world. From the buildings we erect to the laws we enact, from the languages we speak to the calendar we use to measure time, we have the Romans to thank for all of it.

The Roman Empire

1 ➡ The Roman Empire was one of the largest and most powerful empires of the ancient world. At its height, it covered nearly two million square miles and boasted a population of around 70 million people. From the founding of Rome - the city which became the capital - sometime around 800 B.C.E. to the fall of the Western Roman Empire in 476 C.E., the Romans were responsible for some of the most important technological innovations in history, and their influence on art, architecture, laws, language, and politics has been far-reaching and long-lasting. Building on the legacy of those civilizations that had come before them – the Ancient Greeks, Egyptians, Persians, and others – the Romans developed a unique cultural identity. This monumental legacy survived the collapse of the empire and remains resilient even today.

1 In paragraph 1, what is the author's purpose in mentioning pre-Roman civilizations?

(A) Those civilizations have also had a profound impact on modern society.

(B) The author wants to establish that the Romans did not create a culture entirely on their own.

(C) It is the author's belief that if it were not for the influence of older civilizations, Rome would never have become so powerful.

(D) The author is establishing a link between their technological innovations and those of Rome itself.

2 Which of the following best expresses the essential information in the highlighted sentence in paragraph 1? Incorrect choices change the meaning in important ways or leave out essential information.

(A) The Roman Empire was in existence for approximately 1300 years, and their culture has remained relevant to the present day.

(B) Rome was founded around 800 B.C.E., and it split into East and West sometime around 476 C.E.

(C) Many of the technologies we use today have their foundations in Roman discoveries.

(D) Rome has had a bigger influence on Western culture than any other civilization before or since.

3   According to paragraph 2, why did the founding fathers follow the Roman structure of Government?

  Ⓐ They believed in democracy, and ancient Rome shared their faith in a democratic government.

  Ⓑ The founding fathers understood that the most stable governmental structure is one containing three separate branches.

  Ⓒ They realized that the Roman model meant that each branch of government could ensure that the others were not abusing their power.

  Ⓓ They believed, just as the Romans did, that people should have the right to elect their own leaders.

4   According to paragraph 3, which of the following is NOT true of Roman architecture?

  Ⓐ There are examples of it still standing throughout their former territories.

  Ⓑ Modern architects are inspired by Roman buildings and their adherence to scientific form.

  Ⓒ The Romans did not use any one material exclusively in their constructions.

  Ⓓ The Romans preferred to strike a balance between science and art when they were designing a building.

2 ➡ Perhaps the Roman's greatest legacy is their influence on politics and government. When the founding fathers of the United States gathered to draw up plans for the government of their new nation, they borrowed heavily from the traditions of the Romans. Just as there were three branches of government in Rome, so too are there three branches of government in the United States today. The founding fathers liked and adopted the idea that each of the three branches of government served as a check and balance to the others, which meant that one branch could not have absolute power. Like the Romans did thousands of years ago, many people in different countries around the world elect their leaders. The Romans were not the first to invent or to implement democracy, but the value that they placed on civic participation and civic responsibility was hugely influential to future societies.

3 ➡ The Romans are also remembered today for their lasting achievements in the fields of architecture and engineering. The Romans were excellent builders, and many of their innovations enabled the construction of larger, stronger structures. The staggering number of Roman ruins scattered around Europe, North Africa, Asia Minor, and the Levant are a testament to Roman ingenuity. The delicate balance between science and art that the Romans managed to find with many of their building projects continues to inspire modern architects. The Romans experimented with different kinds of building materials.

5   In context of the passage, what is the function of paragraph 4?

Ⓐ To illustrate one outcome of the process mentioned in the previous paragraph

Ⓑ To counter the claim made earlier in the passage

Ⓒ To foreshadow a claim that will be made in the following paragraph

Ⓓ To highlight the impact of the information depicted in the preceding paragraph

6   Which of the following is true according to paragraph 4?

Ⓐ Romans were the first to utilize arches in architecture.

Ⓑ It was more important for Romans to invent concrete than for them to design buildings.

Ⓒ Romans placed great importance in maintaining balance between the artificial and natural world.

Ⓓ Layering structures allowed Romans to easily wear down the building materials.

4 ➡ These experiments led to the invention of concrete, which is one of the most widely used materials in construction today; however, the materials they used were perhaps not as important as the designs they devised. Roman roads were built using layers, one stacked on top another, so that they were more durable and less prone to wearing down over time. The Romans would often build using arches, which, because of their curved or rounded shapes, were able to support much more weight than other shapes could. The Romans were experts at merging form and function so that their structures were not only sturdy but also aesthetically appealing. They would often incorporate large open areas within larger structures so that their buildings managed to blend the man-made with the natural world that surrounded them.

Q
REVIEW

?
HELP

<
BACK

>
NEXT

HIDE TIME 00:54:00

More Available ▲

7 In paragraph 5, there is a missing sentence. Look at the paragraph and indicate (A, B, C and D) where the following sentence could be added to the passage.

As are those of Cicero, the great statesman and speaker, 800 of whose personal letters still exist.

Where would the sentence best fit?

(A)   (B)   (C)   (D)

8 Why does the author mention the 'works of Virgil and Ovid'?

(A) To highlight the importance of literature in understanding Roman history

(B) To suggest that many greater writers were influenced by the Romans

(C) To emphasize the fact that many ancient works are still read today

(D) To illustrate the long-lasting impact of Roman literature in contemporary society.

5 ➡ Along with their rich traditions in art, architecture, and politics, the Romans contributed greatly to language and literature. **(A)** Rome was home to some of the greatest writers of the ancient world. The works of Virgil and Ovid are still standard reading in schools all around the world today. **(B)** Roman historians have provided us with some of the finest depictions of life during the eras in which they lived, and many poems and plays and even speeches are still being studied and enjoyed today. **(C)** The language of ancient Rome was Latin, and while it was the language of poets and politicians, it was also the language of the people. **(D)**

End ▲

9 Which of the following can be inferred about the Romans from paragraph 7?

Ⓐ The early Roman Empire was vastly different from the later Roman Empire.

Ⓑ The Romans were zealous Christians to such a degree that Christianity's most holy site is still located in Rome.

Ⓒ The Roman Empire and the Song Dynasty were instrumental in bringing Christianity to Europe and its neighbors.

Ⓓ If it were not for the Romans, modern society would not have developed things like calendars and courts of law.

6 ➡ The span of time from the founding of Rome to the end of the Western Roman Empire is roughly the same span of time that separates us from the Song Dynasty. Life in ancient Rome was strikingly different from what it was at the tail end of the Roman period. The Romans were instrumental in the spread of Christianity across Europe and adjacent parts of the world starting in the third and fourth centuries. The Catholic Church remains headquartered in the Holy See, completely surrounded by the city of Rome. Roman influence can be felt all over the world. From the buildings we erect to the laws we enact, from the languages we speak to the calendar we use to measure time, we have the Romans to thank for all of it.

10 **Directions**: An introductory sentence for a brief summary of the passage is provided below. Complete the summary by choosing the THREE answer choices that express the most important ideas in the passage. Some sentences do not belong in the summary because they express ideas that are not presented in the passage or are minor ideas in the passage.

Drag your answer choices to the spaces where they belong. To remove an answer choice, click on it. To review the passage, click on **VIEW TEXT**.

Rome was one of the most long-lived civilizations in history, and it has arguably had a bigger impact on the modern world than any other civilization.

-
-
-

ANSWER CHOICES

A There are definite parallels to be drawn between the system of government in ancient Rome and that in many modern countries, in particular the United States.

B Rome's democratic philosophy can be said to have directly been responsible for the implementation of democracy in modern societies.

C Concrete, one of the most widely used building materials even today, was invented by the Romans.

D Roman architects were not only interested in the functionality of a building, they were also concerned with its visual appeal.

E A large swathe of modern Europe speaks some derivatives of the language of Rome, Latin.

F The length of time between the founding of Rome and the collapse of the Eastern Roman Empire is the same as that between modernity and the Chinese Song Dynasty.

Halloween

Most countries in the world have a holiday dedicated to the dead. There is Obon in Japan, Boon Para Wate in Thailand, Día de los Muertos in Mexico, and, in predominantly Western Christian countries, Halloween. The word Halloween comes from 'All Hallows Eve'. Traditionally, this was the night before All Hallows Day, also known as All Saints Day. The term 'Halloween' was first seen in Scotland in the 18th century. In the Scots language, the word eve is pronounced even, which is why All Hallows Eve was shortened to Halloween over time. The holiday is celebrated annually on 31st October.

The roots of Halloween are thought to go back to the Gaelic festival known as Samhain. Samhain was a Celtic tradition dating back some 2,000 years. This pagan festival marked the beginning of winter and the dark half of the year. It was thought to be a liminal time, when the veil between the worlds of the living and the dead became permeable. The first mention of Samhain in the written record comes from the 10th century Gaelic tale Tochmarc Empire. It is from this and similar mythological stories that some of the practices we still observe today were inherited.

Bonfires are believed to have been a central feature of Samhain, and they have remained an integral part of Halloween tradition up to the present day. During Samhain, the fires were believed to have a cleansing effect on the community, and sacrifices of animals and food were often cast into them. They were also seen as a symbol of the sun and as a final bright light before the onset of the long dark winter. Bonfires are still lit on 31st October in many countries including Scotland, Ireland, and Canada.

Another favored activity of revelers during Halloween is to dress up in costumes and go from door to door 'trick or treating'. Many of the costumes on display will invariably be supernatural in theme. This tradition closely resembles that of 'guising' and 'mumming'. Both of these practices have a long history in the British Isles and are first mentioned in the 16th century. Mumming involved troupes of actors or 'guisers' dressing up and re-enacting scenes from popular folk tales. Guising describes the tradition of dressing up and visiting neighbors in the hope of getting money or food after reciting a story or poem. Guising had many local variations in both costume and performance.

Halloween and its associated practices are now widespread throughout North America. However, the holiday only reached the New World in the nineteenth century. Most sources agree that it came over with Irish and Scottish immigrants and was initially confined to the neighborhoods they settled. By the first decade of the twentieth century, it had spread throughout North America, regardless of the ethnicity or religion of those celebrating it. Today, Americans spend between 2.5 and 3 billion dollars on candy and chocolate for Halloween

Halloween

1 ➡ Most countries in the world have a holiday dedicated to the dead. There is Obon in Japan, Boon Para Wate in Thailand, Día de los Muertos in Mexico, and, in predominantly Western Christian countries, Halloween. The word Halloween comes from 'All Hallows Eve'. Traditionally, this was the night before All Hallows Day, also known as All Saints Day. The term 'Halloween' was first seen in Scotland in the 18th century. In the Scots language, the word eve is pronounced even, which is why All Hallows Eve was shortened to Halloween over time. The holiday is celebrated annually on 31st October.

2 ➡ The roots of Halloween are thought to go back to the Gaelic festival known as Samhain. Samhain was a Celtic tradition dating back some 2,000 years. This pagan festival marked the beginning of winter and the dark half of the year. It was thought to be a liminal time, when the veil between the worlds of the living and the dead became permeable. The first mention of Samhain in the written record comes from the 10th century Gaelic tale Tochmarc Empire. It is from this and similar mythological stories that some of the practices we still observe today were inherited.

1 Which of the following best expresses the essential information in the highlighted sentence in paragraph 1? Incorrect choices change the meaning in important ways or leave out essential information.

   Ⓐ In the Scots language, the word 'eve' is pronounced as 'even'.

   Ⓑ Halloween comes from Scotland, where the tradition is believed to have developed over time.

   Ⓒ The Scots's pronunciation of 'All Hallows Eve' ultimately changed the name of the day to 'Halloween'.

   Ⓓ All Hallows Eve and Halloween are in fact the same day.

2 According to paragraph 1, which of the following is true of Halloween?

   Ⓐ It is celebrated throughout the world.

   Ⓑ Every country in the world has a version of Halloween.

   Ⓒ Its pronunciation affected when the holiday was celebrated.

   Ⓓ Countries celebrating Halloween are mainly Christian.

3 The word 'permeable' in paragraph 2 is closest in meaning to

   Ⓐ penetrable

   Ⓑ absorbent

   Ⓒ spongy

   Ⓓ accessible

4 According to paragraph 2, which of the following is NOT true of Halloween?

   Ⓐ It is, in part, derived from an older pagan celebration known as Samhain.

   Ⓑ Halloween influenced a particular Gaelic festival centuries ago.

   Ⓒ Some of its practices were taken from written text.

   Ⓓ Samhain and Halloween are not the same celebration but may be related.

Q
REVIEW
? HELP
< BACK
> NEXT

HIDE TIME 00:54:00

More Available ▲

5   Which of the following is true according to paragraph 3?

Ⓐ Bonfires continue to play an important role in the Halloween custom.

Ⓑ Maintaining integrity in Halloween tradition has been very important.

Ⓒ Scotland, Ireland, and Canada use bonfires the most.

Ⓓ Bonfires serve as a symbol of darkness that precede bright light.

6   In paragraph 4, why does the author mention the probable roots of 'trick or treating'?

Ⓐ In order to connect it with the ancient festival of Samhain.

Ⓑ To mention all of the activities associated with Halloween.

Ⓒ As a way of exploring how the modern celebration of Halloween developed.

Ⓓ To prove that the roots of Halloween are pagan in origin.

7   Which of the following is true about 'guising'?

Ⓐ Its costumes exhibit supernatural themes.

Ⓑ It is a more popular tradition than mumming.

Ⓒ It involves a custom in which payment is received in turn for dressing up.

Ⓓ Its tradition is uniform throughout societies.

3 ➡ Bonfires are believed to have been a central feature of Samhain, and they have remained an integral part of Halloween tradition up to the present day. During Samhain, the fires were believed to have a cleansing effect on the community, and sacrifices of animals and food were often cast into them. They were also seen as a symbol of the sun and as a final bright light before the onset of the long dark winter. Bonfires are still lit on 31ˢᵗ October in many countries including Scotland, Ireland, and Canada.

4 ➡ Another favored activity of revelers during Halloween is to dress up in costumes and go from door to door 'trick or treating'. Many of the costumes on display will invariably be supernatural in theme. This tradition closely resembles that of 'guising' and 'mumming'. Both of these practices have a long history in the British Isles and are first mentioned in the 16ᵗʰ century. Mumming involved troupes of actors or 'guisers' dressing up and re-enacting scenes from popular folk tales. Guising describes the tradition of dressing up and visiting neighbors in the hope of getting money or food after reciting a story or poem. Guising had many local variations in both costume and performance.

8   Which of the following is NOT true according to paragraph 5?

Ⓐ One's religion and ethnicity have little to do with celebrating Halloween.

Ⓑ Many countries that practice Halloween are concentrated in the New World.

Ⓒ Many Americans purchase treats needed for Halloween.

Ⓓ It has been confirmed that people in North America spend the most money on Halloween candy and chocolate.

9   In the paragraph 6, there is a missing sentence. Look at the paragraph and indicate (A, B, C and D) where the following sentence could be added to the passage.

This was probably due to the tendency of immigrants of the time to speak their native language and exist within their own cultural sphere.

Where would the sentence best fit?

Ⓐ   Ⓑ   Ⓒ   Ⓓ

5 ➡ Halloween and its associated practices are now widespread throughout North America. **(A)** However, the holiday only reached the New World in the nineteenth century. Most sources agree that it came over with Irish and Scottish immigrants and was initially confined to the neighborhoods they settled. **(B)** By the first decade of the twentieth century, it had spread throughout North America, regardless of the ethnicity or religion of those celebrating it. **(C)** Today, Americans spend between 2.5 and 3 billion dollars on candy and chocolate for Halloween. **(D)**

10 Directions: An introductory sentence for a brief summary of the passage is provided below. Complete the summary by choosing the THREE answer choices that express the most important ideas in the passage. Some sentences do not belong in the summary because they express ideas that are not presented in the passage or are minor ideas in the passage.

Drag your answer choices to the spaces where they belong. To remove an answer choice, click on it. To review the passage, click on **VIEW TEXT**.

The modern celebration of Halloween has borrowed from various times and traditions to arrive at its current iteration.

-
-
-

ANSWER CHOICES

A The earliest influence on the current form of the holiday is believed to date back to the Celtic festival of Samhain.

B All of the activities we now associate with Halloween can be traced back to the Gaelic festival, Samhain.

C Many of the activities enjoyed today during Halloween such as bonfires and trick or treating were adopted from much earlier traditions.

D The date of Halloween was selected by Christian missionaries for its importance to their religion.

E Although Halloween is recognized throughout America as an annual celebration, it is a relatively new holiday.

F Halloween spread to North America with the Christian missionaries who traveled there in the 19th century.

TOEFL

Reading

Actual Test

Actual Test
Architecture

Machu Picchu

The archaeological site of Machu Picchu is one of the most recognizable and well-preserved discoveries around the world to-date. Its name, Machu Picchu, derives from the Quechua language spoken by the native Incas of that time and is roughly translated as 'old peak', for reasons unbeknown to historians. The site is set in the heights of the Peruvian Andes at more than 2,400 meters above sea level and covers roughly 33,000 hectares of mountains and valleys, bigger than that of any other civilization pre-1000 B.C. How did the Incas complete this incredible accomplishment in such a challenging terrain? Researchers have estimated that Machu Picchu was built during the 15th century and consider it an incredible engineering and archaeological feat, given the lack of tools available and the sophistication of the structures.

The Incas built hundreds of structures in the form of residences, storage, churches, and stone-gated terraces. To gather the materials, the Incas would forage smaller stones from the mud following earthquakes, or from neighboring riverbanks. These smaller pellets were carried in sacks on the backs of llamas. However, few could bare a hefty load. Therefore, larger stones which had been extracted from the granite cliffs had to be hauled up steep hills by men and women using ropes. Archaeologists have since unearthed skeletal remains at the foot of the valley, buried under enormous stones.

Erecting the buildings was less arduous, though it required the fine skills of stonemasons to pound and shape each rock and then lower them into place. This process was intricate, combining a sophisticated understanding of geometry and architecture. The rocks were split perfectly and slotted together like a jigsaw puzzle. Some of the bricks are so snugly packed together that a coin cannot be placed between the cracks. Archaeologists believe that the Incas drilled into the rocks to generate fissures which would allow a wooden wedge to be placed inside to fragment the stone. Nevertheless, they concede that nowadays this achievement would be difficult to replicate, despite our current technology.

A pioneering drainage system built below Machu Picchu allowed the Incas to maintain the condition of their stone buildings despite the harsh climate. Geo-archaeologicals have determined that Machu Picchu was constructed intentionally on a network of tectonic faults, making use of the fracture lines in the rock which allowed rainwater to be collected once fallen. Consequently, the corrosion of the stone walls was avoided, as was the risk of them sliding down the hills. The completion of such an irrigation system is regarded by historians as a symbol of engineering ingenuity on behalf of the Incas.

The geographical location of Machu Picchu was as equally important as the physical ground on which it was constructed. Surrounded by luscious green forests, high mountain peaks, and streams, the remote position of Machu Picchu provided secrecy from adversaries and a permanent supply of sustenance. The entire complex featured only one entrance, to the south, meaning it could remain unguarded yet still protected. The elevated walls of each structure had been sized meticulously, to ensure a clear onlook down the sloping hill towards the Urubamba Valley and thus provide some form of defense. The site is as fortified as it is picturesque.

Given the isolated location of the site, Inca farmers had to be skilled in maximizing agricultural production with minimal landmass. Within the flat terraces they had created, they planted soil, vegetables and plants. The heavy stone walls provided insulation from the harsh winters while allowing water to trickle into the compounds. Besides plants, the hunting of animals, such as 'cuy' (guinea pig), was fundamental for the Inca's nourishment. The Incas built trapdoors into the floors of the enclosure which led to a vertical drop – imprisoning any cuy which managed to fall through it. Machu Picchu was evidently an architectural masterpiece given the period of development and the lack of technology.

Machu Picchu

1 ➡ The archaeological site of Machu Picchu is one of the most recognizable and well-preserved discoveries around the world to-date. Its name, Machu Picchu, derives from the Quechua language spoken by the native Incas of that time and is roughly translated as 'old peak', for reasons unbeknown to historians. The site is set in the heights of the Peruvian Andes at more than 2,400 meters above sea level and covers roughly 33,000 hectares of mountains and valleys, bigger than that of any other civilization pre-1000 B.C. How did the Incas complete this incredible accomplishment in such a challenging terrain? Researchers have estimated that Machu Picchu was built during the 15th century and consider it an incredible engineering and archaeological feat, given the lack of tools available and the sophistication of the structures.

2 ➡ The Incas built hundreds of structures in the form of residences, storage, churches, and stone-gated terraces. To gather the materials, the Incas would forage smaller stones from the mud following earthquakes, or from neighboring riverbanks. These smaller pellets were carried in sacks on the backs of llamas. However, few could bare a hefty load. Therefore, larger stones which had been extracted from the granite cliffs had to be hauled up steep hills by men and women using ropes. Archaeologists have since unearthed skeletal remains at the foot of the valley, buried under enormous stones.

1 According to paragraph 1, why do researchers find Machu Picchu so impressive?

(A) It has withstood half a millennium and still remains in good condition

(B) It was constructed on terrain that seems almost impossible to build on because of its high altitude

(C) The site extends over a much larger area of land that was thought possible for civilizations of that time

(D) The absence of machinery means the construction was far ahead of its time

2 In paragraph 2, what does the author imply about the rocks?

(A) Moving the smaller rocks was not a priority for the Incas

(B) Finding them was difficult due to the altitude in which they were living

(C) Transporting them was hazardous and laborious work for those involved

(D) The use of granite was a mistake, as it was too heavy for the Incas to haul up the hill

More Available ▲

3   The word 'arduous' in the passage is closest in meaning to

(A) physical

(B) demanding

(C) substantial

(D) time-consuming

4   According to paragraph 3, stonemasons were important because they

(A) could form stones delicately and effectively

(B) had the necessary skills to build precise structures

(C) created techniques to help the Incas drill holes in the stone

(D) were the best architects available at that time

3 ➡ Erecting the buildings was less arduous, though it required the fine skills of stonemasons to pound and shape each rock and then lower them into place. This process was intricate, combining a sophisticated understanding of geometry and architecture. The rocks were split perfectly and slotted together like a jigsaw puzzle. Some of the bricks are so snugly packed together that a coin cannot be placed between the cracks. Archaeologists believe that the Incas drilled into the rocks to generate fissures which would allow a wooden wedge to be placed inside to fragment the stone. Nevertheless, they concede that nowadays this achievement would be difficult to replicate, despite our current technology.

▼

5   According to paragraph 4, all of the following about the drainage system are true EXCEPT:

   Ⓐ it was purposely built on top of naturally occurring cracks

   Ⓑ it acted as a long-term storage system for water

   Ⓒ it helped to protect the buildings from rough weather

   Ⓓ archaeologists praise its construction

6   Which of the sentences below best expresses the essential information in the highlighted sentence in the passage? Incorrect choices change the meaning in important ways or leave out essential information.

   Ⓐ The irrigation system was an achievement that has not been replicated since the Incas completed it.

   Ⓑ The accomplishment of building an irrigation system was regarded as ingenious by the Incas, according to historians.

   Ⓒ The Incas built an irrigation system which historians consider to be resourceful and creative.

   Ⓓ Historians consider the Incas to be experts when it comes to building this kind of system.

4 ➡ A pioneering drainage system built below Machu Picchu allowed the Incas to maintain the condition of their stone buildings despite the harsh climate. Geo-archaeologicals have determined that Machu Picchu was constructed intentionally on a network of tectonic faults, making use of the fracture lines in the rock which allowed rainwater to be collected once fallen. Consequently, the corrosion of the stone walls was avoided, as was the risk of them sliding down the hills. The completion of such an irrigation system is regarded by historians as a symbol of engineering ingenuity on behalf of the Incas.

7 Which of the following is NOT a reason
Machu Picchu was constructed in a
particular region?

  Ⓐ Food was easily accessible

  Ⓑ The area was suitable for hunting

  Ⓒ Adversaries were observable

  Ⓓ The region's remote location made it a
     safe location from enemies

8 The word 'adversaries' in the passage is
closest in meaning to

  Ⓐ peers

  Ⓑ enemies

  Ⓒ neighbors

  Ⓓ strangers

9 In the paragraph 6, there is a missing
sentence. Look at the paragraph and
indicate (A, B, C and D) where the
following sentence could be added to the
paragraph.

**This acted like a slow-running faucet
that upheld dampness and increased
cultivation in the compounds.**

Where would the sentence best fit?

  Ⓐ   Ⓑ   Ⓒ   Ⓓ

5 ➡ The geographical location of Machu
Picchu was as equally important as the
physical ground on which it was constructed.
Surrounded by luscious green forests, high
mountain peaks, and streams, the remote
position of Machu Picchu provided secrecy
from adversaries and a permanent supply
of sustenance. The entire complex featured
only one entrance, to the south, meaning it
could remain unguarded yet still protected.
The elevated walls of each structure had been
sized meticulously, to ensure a clear onlook
down the sloping hill towards the Urubamba
Valley and thus provide some form of defense.
The site is as fortified as it is picturesque.

6 ➡ Given the isolated location of the site,
Inca farmers had to be skilled in maximizing
agricultural production with minimal landmass.
(A). Within the flat terraces they had created,
they planted soil, vegetables, and plants. **(B)**.
The heavy stone walls provided insulation
from the harsh winters while allowing water
to trickle into the compounds. **(C)**. Besides
plants, the hunting of animals, such as 'cuy'
(guinea pig), was fundamental for the Inca's
nourishment. **(D)**. The Incas built trapdoors
into the floors of the enclosure which led to
a vertical drop – imprisoning any cuy which
managed to fall through it. Machu Picchu was
evidently an architectural masterpiece given
the period of development and the lack of
technology.

10 **Directions**: An introductory sentence for a brief summary of the passage is provided below. Complete the summary by choosing the THREE answer choices that express the most important ideas in the passage. Some sentences do not belong in the summary because they express ideas that are not presented in the passage or are minor ideas in the passage.

Drag your answer choices to the spaces where they belong. To remove an answer choice, click on it. To review the passage, click on **VIEW TEXT**.

High in the Andes mountains, Machu Picchu stands as an incredible accomplishment in terms of architecture and engineering.

-
-
-

ANSWER CHOICES

A The Incas overcame many tribulations and still managed to build the complex with a great deal of intricacy.

B The harshness of the climate meant that agriculture could not develop until the completion of the stone walls around Machu Picchu.

C Machu Picchu's location was vital for the survival of the Incas, providing defensibility and nourishment.

D Stonemasons were incredibly skillful in carving and putting together the rocks in order to build the structures around the site.

E The complex design and construction of Machu Picchu was time-consuming and cost lives, but it allowed the Incas to survive at high altitudes.

F Today, Machu Picchu remains in a fantastic condition, thanks to the irrigation the Incas built to preserve the stone walls.

Hagia Sophia

The Hagia Sophia has existed in various capacities for almost 1500 years, and its name translates to 'Wisdom of God'. It is located in the Turkish capital, Istanbul (formerly Constantinople), and today its worshipers visit to offer prayers to Allah. It was previously an Eastern Orthodox (Christian) church from its construction in 537 through to the capture of Constantinople by the Ottoman Empire in 1453, when it subsequently became a designated mosque. However, between 1935 and 2019 this UNESCO World Heritage Site was used as a repository for significant cultural artifacts from the Christian and Muslim worlds, as the Istanbul Museum.

The cathedral was the largest in the world until that accolade was passed to The Cathedral of Saint Mary of the See in Seville, Spain in the early 16th century. It is an outstanding specimen of Byzantine Architecture, which had as some of its features domed roofs, columns and interior mosaics. The Hagia Sophia displays classical examples of all of these features. Its dome rests on four pendentives and has a diameter of one hundred and seven feet, with a thickness of two feet. Forty windows were built into the dome structure, which had the purposes of creating a light, airy interior space, and lessening the use of heavy brick and mortar walls. The weight of the dome has been a problem for the building throughout its long history. It is believed that those in charge of constructing the colossal dome may have used the theories of Hero of Alexandria, a Greek mathematician from 1st century Roman Egypt, in its construction.

The numerous mosaics in the structure have caused a certain amount of controversy. When the church changed hands after 1453, Islamic aniconism dictated that any material representations of the natural or supernatural worlds would have to be covered up. There were also some periods of Byzantine Iconoclasm, when the use of religious images was banned. In contrast, many of the mosaics were restored, as a result of the building being declared secular. Those working on the project strived to strike a fair balance between Christian and Islamic art.

Another notable feature of the building are the four minarets which enclose the building.

These were not part of the original design but were added when the church was converted to a mosque. Minarets are very typical features of Islamic architecture and mosques in particular. The Muezzin, responsible for calling out the adhan, or call to prayer, would use an external gallery built on the minaret to be heard by as many worshipers as possible. Although this still takes place, many mosques now rely on a loudspeaker to call the faithful to pray. Over the years, twenty-four flying buttresses have been added to support the structure. A flying buttress forms an arc with the wall it supports and works by channeling the force created by the wall into the ground instead.

The upper gallery of the Hagia Sophia is laid out in the shape of a horseshoe. This gallery is also known as a matroneum. The auditorium in Hagia Sophia would have been kept for the Empress and her court. Interestingly, some runic graffiti has been found on this level. There is no consensus as to what it reads, but there is evidence to suggest that it follows the quintessential style used through that period in history. Some have speculated that it may have been a member of the Varangian Guard who were responsible for the graffiti, due to their number being made up of men from Scandinavia, where at that time a runic alphabet was in use.

REVIEW

HELP

BACK

NEXT

HIDE TIME 00:54:00

Beginning

Hagia Sophia

1 ➡ The Hagia Sophia has existed in various capacities for almost 1500 years, and its name translates to 'Wisdom of God'. It is located in the Turkish capital, Istanbul (formerly Constantinople), and today its worshipers visit to offer prayers to Allah. It was previously an Eastern Orthodox (Christian) church from its construction in 537 through to the capture of Constantinople by the Ottoman Empire in 1453, when it subsequently became a designated mosque. However, between 1935 and 2019 this UNESCO World Heritage Site was used as a repository for significant cultural artifacts from the Christian and Muslim worlds, as the Istanbul Museum.

2 ➡ The cathedral was the largest in the world until that accolade was passed to The Cathedral of Saint Mary of the See in Seville, Spain in the early 16th century. It is an outstanding specimen of Byzantine Architecture, which had as some of its features domed roofs, columns and interior mosaics. The Hagia Sophia displays classical examples of all of these features. Its dome rests on four pendentives and has a diameter of one hundred and seven feet, with a thickness of two feet. Forty windows were built into the dome structure, which had the purposes of creating a light, airy interior space, and lessening the use of heavy brick and mortar walls. The weight of the dome has been a problem for the building throughout its long history. It is believed that those in charge of constructing the colossal dome may have used the theories of Hero of Alexandria, a Greek mathematician from 1st century Roman Egypt, in its construction.

1 According to the first paragraph, when did the Hagia Sophia become a designated mosque?
- (A) In 537 and 2020
- (B) Between 537 and 1453
- (C) Between 1453 and 1935
- (D) Between 1935 and 2019

2 According to paragraph 2, what reduced the need for brick and mortar walls?
- (A) The light and airy interior made the structure lighter.
- (B) The theories of Hero of Alexandria led to a reduction in the overall weight.
- (C) The construction of 40 windows.
- (D) Its domed roof, a classic example of Byzantine Architecture.

3 Paragraph 2 states that the Hagia Sophia is an example of
- (A) a Christian cathedral
- (B) an Islamic mosque
- (C) a Byzantine architecture
- (D) the theories of Hero of Alexandria

PASSAGE 2

Q
REVIEW

?
HELP

<
BACK

>
NEXT

HIDE TIME 00:54:00

More Available

4   Which of the following is true according to paragraph 3?

   Ⓐ The mosaics used in the structure were not immune from debates.

   Ⓑ in 1453, the church decided that any supernatural or natural manifestations needed to be covered.

   Ⓒ Fortunately, all mosaics were restored after secular declarations.

   Ⓓ Byzantine Iconoclasm suggests extensive use of religious images.

5   In the context of the sentence, what does the word 'secular' mean in paragraph 3?

   Ⓐ artistic

   Ⓑ educational

   Ⓒ spiritual

   Ⓓ non-religious

3 ➡ The numerous mosaics in the structure have caused a certain amount of controversy. When the church changed hands after 1453, Islamic aniconism dictated that any material representations of the natural or supernatural worlds would have to be covered up. There were also some periods of Byzantine Iconoclasm, when the use of religious images was banned. In contrast, many of the mosaics were restored, as a result of the building being declared secular. Those working on the project strived to strike a fair balance between Christian and Islamic art.

6   Which of the following best expresses the essential information in the highlighted sentence in paragraph 4? Incorrect choices change the meaning in important ways or leaver out essential information.

  (A) The muezzin was the one responsible for announcing the call to prayer.

  (B) Generally, an external gallery was built on the minaret.

  (C) The Muezzin used an outside gallery in order to be heard by more worshippers.

  (D) In Arabic, the term 'adhan' means a call to prayer.

7   What is the purpose of paragraph 4 as a whole?

  (A) To defines what minarets are and its significance in architecture

  (B) To exemplify minarets in context of Islamic architecture

  (C) To explain the significance of minarets implemented in Hagia Sofia

  (D) To compare and contrast each minaret constructed in Hagia Sofia

4 ➡ Another notable feature of the building are the four minarets which enclose the building. These were not part of the original design but were added when the church was converted to a mosque. Minarets are very typical features of Islamic architecture and mosques in particular. The Muezzin, responsible for calling out the adhan, or call to prayer, would use an external gallery built on the minaret to be heard by as many worshipers as possible. Although this still takes place, many mosques now rely on a loudspeaker to call the faithful to pray. Over the years, twenty-four flying buttresses have been added to support the structure. A flying buttress forms an arc with the wall it supports and works by channeling the force created by the wall into the ground instead.

8. Which of the following is NOT true about the runic graffiti?

Ⓐ It was discovered on the auditorium level in Hagia Sophia.

Ⓑ There is general agreement about what the graffiti depicts.

Ⓒ There are speculations as to who the graffiti artist could be, based on the origin of the alphabets used in it.

Ⓓ What makes the graffiti interesting is the location where it is found.

9. Taken as a whole, which of the following best captures the structure of the passage?

Ⓐ The origin of Hagia Sophia is explained, followed by the history of the Cathedral of Saint Mary of the See in Spain and then the meanings behind mosaics.

Ⓑ A significance of Hagia Sophia is described, followed by detailed historical background to it.

Ⓒ The name of Hagia Sophia is analyzed in detail, followed by its significance as world-famous architect and history behind it.

Ⓓ A general overview about Hagia Sophia is given, followed by detailed depiction of both exterior and interior of it.

5 ➡ The upper gallery of the Hagia Sophia is laid out in the shape of a horseshoe. This gallery is also known as a matroneum. The auditorium in Hagia Sophia would have been kept for the Empress and her court. Interestingly, some runic graffiti has been found on this level. There is no consensus as to what it reads, but there is evidence to suggest that it follows the quintessential style used through that period in history. Some have speculated that it may have been a member of the Varangian Guard who were responsible for the graffiti, due to their number being made up of men from Scandinavia, where at that time a runic alphabet was in use.

10 **Directions**: An introductory sentence for a brief summary of the passage is provided below. Complete the summary by choosing the THREE answer choices that express the most important ideas in the passage. Some sentences do not belong in the summary because they express ideas that are not presented in the passage or are minor ideas in the passage.

Drag your answer choices to the spaces where they belong. To remove an answer choice, click on it. To review the passage, click on **VIEW TEXT**.

With its unique architectural aspects, Hagia Sophia remains as one of the important cultural artifacts of both Christian and Muslim worlds.

-
-
-

ANSWER CHOICES

A Hagia Sophia has been designated as a UNESCO World Heritage Site, storing different religious artifacts.

B Hagia Sophia is representative of Byzantine architecture, with mosaics, domed roofs and minarets.

C Minarets are structures that enclose the building and is very typical of Islamic architecture and mosques.

D The presence of intriguing graffiti in Hagia Sophia serves as point of heated debate.

E Some of the famous mosaics on Hagia Sophia include religious figures.

F For a long time, it was very challenging for architects of Hagia Sophia to resolve the issue of heavyweight dome

Sagrada Familia

Designed by Catalan architect Antoni Gaudi (1852–1926), La Sagrada Familia is an immense unfinished minor basilica located in Barcelona, Spain. Architect Francisco de Paula del Villar started construction on the Sagrada Familia in 1882, but Gaudi took over as chief architect in 1883. Gaudi transformed the project with his innovative architectural and engineering style that shirked straight structures in favor of forms that resembled nature. At the time of his death in 1926, he completed about a quarter of the project. UNESCO now considers the nearly finished basilica a World Heritage Site.

The Sagrada Familia was started as a Roman Catholic church, before being designated as a cathedral (considered the seat of a bishop) and finally a minor basilica in 2010. When the Sagrada Familia is finally completed, it will stand as the tallest religious building in Europe. The basilica's central tower stands one meter less than the city's highest point, the 180-meter tall mountain called Montjuic. Gaudi thought nothing artificial should ever be higher than the work of God. Astonishingly, the construction of the basilica has taken longer than that of the Great Pyramids. According to scholars, the pyramids took 20 years to build while the Sagrada Familia will have taken between 144 and 146 years by the time of completion.

When the Sagrada Familia is finally completed, 18 towers will reach the sky. 12 towers will represent the apostles: John, Peter, Mark, and Paul. Four will represent the evangelists: Matthew, Mark, Luke, and John. One will be designated for the Virgin Mary. The final one, the highest in the middle, will represent Jesus Christ. The Sagrada Familia has three facades. Gaudi built the Nativity Facade himself, but the Passion Facade and the Glory Facade came later. A sculpture of Christ on the crucifix was added to the Passion Facade by Josep Maria Subirachs, but many people thought the figure was too abstract and strayed too far from Gaudi's vision as an architect.

The Sagrada Familia contains many forms of symbolism. Besides all the religious symbols stated above, there are more mysterious representations. First, Gaudi wanted each generation of architects to incorporate their own style into each facade. Second, the pillars inside the basilica resemble trees. When a viewer looks up at the pillar's shapes, they change

like real trees sometimes do. A turtle holds up the pillars, which embody the earth and the sea. Finally, Gaudi installed a 4x4 magic square of 15 numbers on a wall of the basilica; the magic constant—the sum of all numbers horizontally or vertically—is 33, Christ's age when he was crucified.

During the first days of the Sagrada Familia's construction, Gaudi built a school on the site for the children of construction workers. The children could attend while their fathers worked day and night. Its construction was finalized in 1909 and named 'the Sagrada Familia Schools building'. Its current role is that of an exhibition area for the entire Sagrada Familia complex. When construction first started on the basilica, it was funded mainly by private patrons. Over the years, it has received funds from donations or alms, but nowadays, it is funded mostly from the money collected from entrance tickets.

Gaudi dedicated his final days entirely to the Sagrada Familia, so much so that he was usually unkept and was mistaken for a beggar. On June 7, 1926, at the age of 73, Gaudi was hit by a tram. Because he looked like a beggar and he had no identification papers, help came slowly. A policeman finally called a taxi to get him to the hospital. By the time he was seen to, he had already died from his wounds and was later laid to rest in the basement of the Sagrada Familia. His tomb is on display to this day. It contains four chapels, each dedicated to a different religious figure with his designated to the El Carmen Virgin

PASSAGE 3

Q
REVIEW   ?
HELP   <
BACK   >
NEXT

HIDE TIME 00:54:00

Beginning ▲

La Sagrada Familia

1 ➡ Designed by Catalan architect Antoni Gaudi (1852–1926), La Sagrada Familia is an immense unfinished minor basilica located in Barcelona, Spain. Architect Francisco de Paula del Villar started construction on the Sagrada Familia in 1882, but Gaudi took over as chief architect in 1883. Gaudi transformed the project with his innovative architectural and engineering style that shirked straight structures in favor of forms that resembled nature. At the time of his death in 1926, he completed about a quarter of the project. UNESCO now considers the nearly finished basilica a World Heritage Site.

2 ➡ The Sagrada Familia was started as a Roman Catholic church, before being designated as a cathedral (considered the seat of a bishop) and finally a minor basilica in 2010. When the Sagrada Familia is finally completed, it will stand as the tallest religious building in Europe. The basilica's central tower stands one meter less than the city's highest point, the 180-meter tall mountain called Montjuic. Gaudi thought nothing artificial should ever be higher than the work of God. Astonishingly, the construction of the basilica has taken longer than that of the Great Pyramids. According to scholars, the pyramids took 20 years to build while the Sagrada Familia will have taken between 144 and 146 years by the time of completion.

---

1 According to paragraph 1, what does the author imply about the Sagrada Familia?

   (A) It will be completed in the near future.

   (B) It is revered as a masterpiece.

   (C) It embodies more than one architectural style.

   (D) It looks like it is carved out of natural materials.

2 According to paragraph 2, which of the following is NOT true of the Sagrada Familia?

   (A) It started as a church and then became a basilica.

   (B) It is the tallest religious building in all of Europe.

   (C) It has taken longer to complete than the Great Pyramids.

   (D) It was declared a minor basilica in 2010.

3 The word 'artificial' in the passage is closest in meaning to

   (A) replicated

   (B) ordinary

   (C) manufactured

   (D) superficial

4   According to paragraph 3, which of the following is not true of the Sagrada Familia's towers?

ⓐ The basilica will have 18 towers when it is finally completed.

ⓑ The basilica highlights Roman Catholic religious figures.

ⓒ The basilica has three facades designed by Gaudi.

ⓓ The basilica's highest spire dedicated to Jesus Christ.

3 ➡ When the Sagrada Familia is finally completed, 18 towers will reach the sky. 12 towers will represent the apostles: John, Peter, Mark, and Paul. Four will represent the evangelists: Matthew, Mark, Luke, and John. One will be designated for the Virgin Mary. The final one, the highest in the middle, will represent Jesus Christ. The Sagrada Familia has three facades. Gaudi built the Nativity Facade himself, but the Passion Facade and the Glory Facade came later. A sculpture of Christ on the crucifix was added to the Passion Facade by Josep Maria Subirachs, but many people thought the figure was too abstract and strayed too far from Gaudi's vision as an architect.

5   Which of the sentences below best expresses the essential information in the highlighted sentence in the passage? Incorrect choices change the meaning in important ways or leave out essential information.

(A) Gaudi installed a magic square of 33 numbers on a wall of the basilica with Christ's age

(B) Gaudi included a magic square with the sum of all the numbers horizontally or vertically, adding up to Christ's age when the religious figure died

(C) Gaudi installed a magic four-sided puzzle of 15 numbers on Christ's wall

(D) Gaudi made a 4x4 magic square and put it on a wall of the basilica; it contained the magic constant

6   According to paragraphs 3 and 4, which of the following is true about the Sagrada Familia?

(A) The depictions of apostles, evangelists, the Virgin Mary and Jesus Christ are the 12 symbols.

(B) The symbols found in the Sagrada Familia are both explicit and implicit.

(C) The most important symbolic representation of the age when Jesus was crucified.

(D) All three facades deeply reflect Gaudi's architectural passion in designing the Sagrada Familia.

4 ➡ The Sagrada Familia contains many forms of symbolism. Besides all the religious symbols stated above, there are more mysterious representations. First, Gaudi wanted each generation of architects to incorporate their own style into each facade. Second, the pillars inside the basilica resemble trees. When a viewer looks up at the pillar's shapes, they change like real trees sometimes do. A turtle holds up the pillars, which embody the earth and the sea. Finally, Gaudi installed a 4x4 magic square of 15 numbers on a wall of the basilica; the magic constant—the sum of all numbers horizontally or vertically—is 33, Christ's age when he was crucified.

7   The author mentions 'school' in the passage as an example of which of the following?

    Ⓐ An example of a method of earning money for the basilica

    Ⓑ An example of Gaudi's construction focus

    Ⓒ An example of Gaudi's thoughtfulness and innovation

    Ⓓ An example of alms or donations

8   In the paragraph below, there is a missing sentence. Look at the paragraph and indicate (A, B, C and D) where the following sentence could be added to the passage.

This made the work more productive.

Where would the sentence best fit?

    Ⓐ   Ⓑ   Ⓒ   Ⓓ

5 ➡ During the first days of the Sagrada Familia's construction, Gaudi built a school on the site for the children of construction workers. **(A)** The children could attend while their fathers worked day and night. **(B)** Its construction was finalized in 1909 and named 'the Sagrada Familia Schools building'. Its current role is that of an exhibition area for the entire Sagrada Familia complex. **(C)** When construction first started on the basilica, it was funded mainly by private patrons. **(D)** Over the years, it has received funds from donations or alms, but nowadays, it is funded mostly from the money collected from entrance tickets.

9   What can be inferred about Gaudi according to paragraph 6?

  (A) His physical appearance did play a role in his unfortunate death.

  (B) It has been suggested that he wanted to be buried in the Sagrada Familia.

  (C) It was easy to undermine his reputation because he was often mistaken as a beggar.

  (D) One of the reasons that make the Sagrada Familia famous is the location of Gaudi's tomb. .

6 ➡ Gaudi dedicated his final days entirely to the Sagrada Familia, so much so that he was usually unkept and was mistaken for a beggar. On June 7, 1926, at the age of 73, Gaudi was hit by a tram. Because he looked like a beggar and he had no identification papers, help came slowly. A policeman finally called a taxi to get him to the hospital. By the time he was seen to, he had already died from his wounds and was later laid to rest in the basement of the Sagrada Familia. His tomb is on display to this day. It contains four chapels, each dedicated to a different religious figure with his designated to the El Carmen Virgin.

VIEW TEXT

REVIEW

HELP

BACK

NEXT

HIDE TIME 00:54:00

10 **Directions**: An introductory sentence for a brief summary of the passage is provided below. Complete the summary by choosing the THREE answer choices that express the most important ideas in the passage. Some sentences do not belong in the summary because they express ideas that are not presented in the passage or are minor ideas in the passage.

Drag your answer choices to the spaces where they belong. To remove an answer choice, click on it. To review the passage, click on **VIEW TEXT**.

In summary, the Sagrada Familia is a wonder of architecture and commitment of Gaudi.

-
-
-

ANSWER CHOICES

A The Sagrada Familia is considered an UNESCO World Heritage Site and is visited by many tourists from all around the world.

B Gaudi was dedicated to constructing the basilica and school for the workers' children is a manifestation of his ingenious style.

C The wonder of the Sagrada Familia is clear to see, with its countless features and the sheer number years it took to complete.

D Gaudi was dedicated to constructing many religious symbols and stylistic architectural designs into the Sagrada Familia.

E Gaudi suffered an unfortunate death as a result of an accident with public transportation.

F The Sagrada Familia has experienced a few instances of defecation over the years but remains a well-preserved edifice.

TOEFL

Reading
Actual Test

Actual Test
Physics

The Manhattan Project

The Manhattan Project was a program undertaken by the United States Army in 1942. It was initiated partially in response to the accidental discovery of nuclear fission by German scientists Otto Hahn and Fritz Strassman in 1938. This discovery prompted a warning from two eminent Hungarian-American scientists to President Franklin D. Roosevelt that the discovery could lead to the development of a devastating new kind of weapon in Nazi Germany. This warning was signed by none other than Albert Einstein. It also recommended that the United States should accelerate their own research into developing nuclear capabilities.

The aim of the project was to create a bomb capable of detonating using nuclear fission before Nazi Germany. Although the Manhattan Project marked an escalation in United States nuclear research, it did not mark the beginning of it. Nuclear research was already being conducted at several universities around the United States. It is also notable that, around this time, the British program for nuclear research was at a more advanced stage than that of the United States. It was known as the MAUD Committee and would eventually assist the Manhattan Project by sharing its research with its U.S. allies.

Nuclear material was essential in the development of the 'Little Boy' and 'Fat Man' bombs which were the results of the Manhattan Project. Nuclear material can only come from three source metals: plutonium, uranium, and thorium. The Manhattan Project developed weapons grade materials from two of these elements – plutonium and uranium. Uranium does not occur naturally in a pure enough form to make it suitable for use in a nuclear fission bomb. Therefore, it must be enriched. Uranium is enriched through isotopic enrichment, becoming uranium-235. Plutonium can occur naturally, but not in quantities vast enough for the project. Plutonium can be created when uranium atoms absorb neutrons. It is then enriched in a nuclear reactor.

The production of uranium-235 and plutonium-239 would prove to be the biggest undertakings of the whole Manhattan Project. It is estimated that 80-90% of the project's budget was spent on this pursuit. Aside from the research and development involved in

producing weapons grade material from the natural form of the metal, uranium had to be sourced and mined before being transported back to the United States. Most of the uranium used in the Manhattan Project was taken from the Shinkolobwe mine in the Congo.

During the lifetime of the Manhattan Project, the United States produced two different types of bombs capable of delivering a nuclear warhead. The first type was known as a gun type weapon and it had a uranium-235 core. A gun type nuclear weapon works by shooting a hollow uranium 'bullet' at the solid core. The core is made of the same material. This releases the energy necessary to begin a nuclear chain reaction. The second type of bomb produced by the program was an implosion type device with a plutonium core. The key difference between a gun type device and an implosion type device is that the implosion type device detonates on the exterior. There are 'lenses' placed around the outside of the bomb to ensure that the explosion is focused inward. This inward force increases the density of the material, in this case solid plutonium, until it becomes supercritical and begins a nuclear chain reaction. This type of bomb was detonated twice. The first time was as part of a trial run known as the Trinity nuclear test. The second time was when it fell on Nagasaki, a city in Japan.

The Manhattan Project

1 ➡ The Manhattan Project was a program undertaken by the United States Army in 1942. It was initiated partially in response to the accidental discovery of nuclear fission by German scientists Otto Hahn and Fritz Strassman in 1938. This discovery prompted a warning from two eminent Hungarian-American scientists to President Franklin D. Roosevelt that the discovery could lead to the development of a devastating new kind of weapon in Nazi Germany. This warning was signed by none other than Albert Einstein. It also recommended that the United States should accelerate their own research into developing nuclear capabilities.

1   Which of the following best expresses the essential information in the highlighted sentence in paragraph 1? Incorrect choices change the meaning in important ways or leave out essential information.

   (A) Two Hungarian-American scientists sent a warning to Franklin D. Roosevelt.

   (B) An important discovery was made by two scientists.

   (C) Franklin D. Roosevelt received a warning from two scientists who alerted him of the development of a new weapon.

   (D) The development of a new kind of weapon might lead to the life of Franklin D. Roosevelt being threatened.

2   According to paragraph 1, which of the following is true of the Manhattan Project?

   (A) It prompted the discovery of nuclear fission.

   (B) It led to a warning being issued by two leading scientists to the United States president.

   (C) German scientists were instrumental in its discovery and development.

   (D) It was undertaken for fear of how Nazi Germany might use nuclear fission.

3   The word 'escalation' in paragraph 2 is
    closest in meaning to
    (A) intensification
    (B) leap
    (C) rise
    (D) aggravation

4   According to paragraph 2, which of the
    following is NOT true of the Manhattan
    Project?
    (A) Nuclear research in the United States
        began with The Manhattan Project.
    (B) British research was ahead of the
        United States at the outset of the
        program.
    (C) Its aim was to beat Nazi Germany to
        the creation of a nuclear weapon.
    (D) It was not based at one location but
        spread across the United States.

2 ➡ The aim of the project was to create a
bomb capable of detonating using nuclear
fission before Nazi Germany. Although the
Manhattan Project marked an escalation in
United States nuclear research, it did not
mark the beginning of it. Nuclear research
was already being conducted at several
universities around the United States. It is
also notable that, around this time, the British
program for nuclear research was at a more
advanced stage than that of the United States.
It was known as the MAUD Committee and
would eventually assist the Manhattan Project
by sharing its research with its U.S. allies.

More Available ▲

5   What is the primary function of paragraph 3?

(A) It discusses the two important materials needed to develop nuclear weapons.

(B) It compares the ways in which uranium and plutonium are developed.

(C) It describes what the 'Little Boy' and 'Fat Man' are during the given historical context.

(D) It elaborates on the success of the Manhattan Project in terms of weapon development.

6   In paragraph 4, why does the author discuss the production and acquisition of uranium?

(A) In order to show how expensive it was and how much of the budget was used on acquiring it.

(B) To convey how important uranium production was to the success of the Manhattan Project.

(C) To show that the Congo was exploited for its mineral resources by the United States.

(D) To indicate the location of most of the uranium that was mined.

7   Which of the following can be inferred from paragraph 4 about the 'Shinkolobwe mine' in the Congo?

(A) It was prohibitively expensive to mine uranium from there.

(B) If it was not for the Shinkolobwe mine, it would have been impossible to procure enough uranium for the project to continue.

(C) It took a long time to ship uranium from the Congo to where it was needed in the United States.

(D) The Shinkolobwe mine was not the only place where uranium was procured.

3 ➡ Nuclear material was essential in the development of the 'Little Boy' and 'Fat Man' bombs which were the results of the Manhattan Project. Nuclear material can only come from three source metals: plutonium, uranium, and thorium. The Manhattan Project developed weapons grade materials from two of these elements – plutonium and uranium. Uranium does not occur naturally in a pure enough form to make it suitable for use in a nuclear fission bomb. Therefore, it must be enriched. Uranium is enriched through isotopic enrichment, becoming uranium-235. Plutonium can occur naturally, but not in quantities vast enough for the project. Plutonium can be created when uranium atoms absorb neutrons. It is then enriched in a nuclear reactor.

4 ➡ The production of uranium-235 and plutonium-239 would prove to be the biggest undertakings of the whole Manhattan Project. It is estimated that 80-90% of the project's budget was spent on this pursuit. Aside from the research and development involved in producing weapons grade material from the natural form of the metal, uranium had to be sourced and mined before being transported back to the United States. Most of the uranium used in the Manhattan Project was taken from the Shinkolobwe mine in Congo.

8 According to paragraph 5, which of the following is true about the bombs made during the Manhattan Project days?

   (A) There were two main types of nuclear bomb, both of which use uranium-235 core as its primary power source.

   (B) An implosion type of bomb was more powerful than the gun type.

   (C) A gun type nuclear weapon was detonated twice in history.

   (D) An implosion type of bomb uses an exterior explosion to detonate the interior materials.

9 In paragraph 5, there is a missing sentence. Look at the paragraph and indicate (A, B, C and D) where the following sentence could be added to the passage.

   This test occurred about a month before the bomb was dropped 'live', as scientists were unsure if it would detonate correctly.

   Where would the sentence best fit?

   (A)   (B)   (C)   (D)

5 ➡ During the lifetime of the Manhattan Project, the United States produced two different types of bombs capable of delivering a nuclear warhead. The first type was known as a gun type weapon and it had a uranium-235 core. A gun type nuclear weapon works by shooting a hollow uranium 'bullet' at the solid core. The core is made of the same material. This releases the energy necessary to begin a nuclear chain reaction. The second type of bomb produced by the program was an implosion type device with a plutonium core. **(A)** The key difference between a gun type device and an implosion type device is that the implosion type device detonates on the exterior. **(B)** There are 'lenses' placed around the outside of the bomb to ensure that the explosion is focused inward. This inward force increases the density of the material, in this case solid plutonium, until it becomes supercritical and begins a nuclear chain reaction. **(C)** This type of bomb was detonated twice. The first time was as part of a trial run known as the Trinity nuclear test. **(D)** The second time was when it fell on Nagasaki, a city in Japan.

HIDE TIME 00:54:00

10 **Directions**: An introductory sentence for a brief summary of the passage is provided below. Complete the summary by choosing the THREE answer choices that express the most important ideas in the passage. Some sentences do not belong in the summary because they express ideas that are not.

Drag your answer choices to the spaces where they belong. To remove an answer choice, click on it. To review the passage, click on **VIEW TEXT**.

The Manhattan Project was a wartime endeavor that would be instrumental in the development of nuclear power.

-
-
-

ANSWER CHOICES

A There are critics who blame the project for the nuclear arms race between the United States and Russia that would bring the world to the brink of destruction during the Cold War.

B The primary purpose of the project was to develop a nuclear bomb that could outpace that of Nazi Germany.

C Plutonium and uranium were two most important elements used in developing weapons during the project.

D The project is responsible for creating both implosion and gun type of weapons, with plutonium and uranium at their core.

E The most important accomplishment of the project is the bombing of the 'Little Boy,' which was dropped on Hiroshima, Japan.

F The project involved many prominent figures, including Albert Einstein, President F.D Roosevelt, Otto Hahn, and Fritz Strassman.

Magnetic Fields

In physics, a magnetic field acts as a vector field. It illustrates the magnetic influence on an electric charge of other charges or magnetized materials. A charge that moves in a magnetic field has a force perpendicular to its own velocity and to the magnetic field. Permanent magnets illustrate the effects of magnetic fields. These pullon magnetic materials like iron. A magnetic field that has different locations exerts force on non-magnetic materials; it affects the action of outer atomic electrons. Magnetic fields always surround magnetized materials. They are created by electric currents such as those used in electromagnets and by electric fields varying in time.

A magnet exerts a force on certain materials, including other magnets. This is called magnetic force. The force covers a distance and includes attractive and repulsive forces. The north and south ends of two magnets attract, while two north ends or two south ends repel. Two subsets of magnets exist: permanent and electromagnetic. Permanent magnets have continuous magnetism while electromagnets require electricity to retain their magnetism. Four categories of perpetual-motion magnets occur: alnico, neodymium iron boron, samarium cobalt, and ceramic or ferrite magnets. Three basic types of electromagnets exist: robust ones, superconductors, and hybrids.

The Earth's magnetic field acts as a magnetic dipole (a quantity involving polarity). The magnetic field's south pole is near the Earth's geographic north pole, and the north pole is near the geographic south pole. This makes compass use possible for navigation. Dynamo theory explains the cause of the field by showing that a rotating, electrically conducting fluid maintains a magnetic field over astronomical time periods. The Earth's magnetic field, also known as the geomagnetic field, forms the magnetosphere. It reaches a staggering several tens of thousands of kilometers into space and is estimated to be around 3.5 billion years old.

The magnetic fields of the magnetosphere shield the Earth's surface from charged solar wind particles. Electric currents from many areas of the Earth contribute to the magnetosphere. The Earth's day side has a compressed field due to the force of the arriving particles. The Earth's night side has an extended field largely protected from solar wind.

The Van Allen radiation belt also traps charged particles from the solar wind. Some particles manage to travel to the Earth's upper atmosphere and ionosphere into the auroral zones, so astronomers can only observe the solar wind on the Earth during the aurora or geomagnetic storms.

The Earth's magnetic field is approximated by the magnetic dipole positioned near the Earth's center. A central axis defines the dipole's orientation. The two places where the dipole's axis best fit the geomagnetic field intersecting the Earth are named the North and South geomagnetic poles. The dipole rests about 500 km off the Earth's center. This offset field causes the South Atlantic Anomaly, a place in the Southern Atlantic Ocean where the field is weakest. Therefore, if the Earth's magnetic field was exactly dipolar, the geomagnetic and magnetic poles would overlap. Nevertheless, the position of the two pole types is in different places.

The magnetic pole position is defined in two ways. The magnetic dipole is a point on the Earth's surface where the magnetic field stands vertical, or the inclination of the Earth's field is 90° at the North Magnetic Pole and -90° at the South Magnetic Pole. As far as the compass is concerned, at a magnetic pole, the horizontal plane points erratically. With that said, local deviations happen. These are called blackout zones—areas where one cannot trust the compass. The dipole can migrate up to 40 km per year for the North Magnetic Pole.

Three variables affect the magnitude and the direction of the Earth's magnetic field. First, the magnetic declination acts as the angle between true north and the magnetic north pole. True north is never at a constant position on the horizontal plane and it varies depending upon the position on the Earth's surface and time. Second is the magnetic inclination, also known as the angle of dip. It is the angle made against the horizontal plane on the Earth's surface. Finally, the Earth's magnetic field has two factors to explain the strength of the Earth's magnetic field: the horizontal component, and the vertical component.

Magnetic Fields

1 ➡ In physics, a magnetic field acts as a vector field. It illustrates the magnetic influence on an electric charge of other charges or magnetized materials. A charge that moves in a magnetic field has a force perpendicular to its own velocity and to the magnetic field. Permanent magnets illustrate the effects of magnetic fields. These pullon magnetic materials like iron. A magnetic field that has different locations exerts force on non-magnetic materials; it affects the action of outer atomic electrons. Magnetic fields always surround magnetized materials. They are created by electric currents such as those used in electromagnets and by electric fields varying in time.

2 ➡ A magnet exerts a force on certain materials, including other magnets. This is called magnetic force. The force covers a distance and includes attractive and repulsive forces. The north and south ends of two magnets attract, while two north ends or two south ends repel. Two subsets of magnets exist: permanent and electromagnetic. Permanent magnets have continuous magnetism while electromagnets require electricity to retain their magnetism. Four categories of perpetual-motion magnets occur: alnico, neodymium iron boron, samarium cobalt, and ceramic or ferrite magnets. Three basic types of electromagnets exist: robust ones, superconductors, and hybrids.

1   According to paragraph 1, what best describes 'magnetic influence'?

   Ⓐ a force that creates vector fields

   Ⓑ the impact a charge has on other charges

   Ⓒ a permanent magnet that creates electric currents

   Ⓓ a force that produces a magnetic field

2   The word 'exerts' in the paragraph 2 is closest in meaning to

   Ⓐ attempts

   Ⓑ applies

   Ⓒ pulls

   Ⓓ pushes

3   According to paragraph 2, which of the following is NOT true of magnets?

   Ⓐ They contain attractive and repulsive forces

   Ⓑ There are two different magnet types

   Ⓒ Some magnets are permanent, while others need an electrical source

   Ⓓ The force doesn't extend over a distance

4 According to paragraph 3, all the following are results of the magnetic field EXCEPT:

(A) The magnetic fields near the Earth's poles allow for the use of compasses.

(B) The magnetic field makes possible navigation.

(C) It forms the magnetosphere.

(D) It is over 3 billion years old.

5 Which of the sentences below best expresses the essential information in the highlighted sentence in the passage? Incorrect choices change the meaning in important ways or leave out essential information.

(A) Astronomers witness the solar wind during the aurora or geomagnetic storms because some particles travel to the Earth

(B) Astronomers witness some particles travel into the Earth's upper atmosphere and ionosphere

(C) Astronomers see the aurora or geomagnetic storms because of the upper atmosphere and ionosphere

(D) Astronomers can see the solar wind during the aurora or geomagnetic storms because some particles travel into the Earth's upper atmosphere and ionosphere

3 ➡ The Earth's magnetic field acts as a magnetic dipole (a quantity involving polarity). The magnetic field's south pole is near the Earth's geographic north pole, and the north pole is near the geographic south pole. This makes compass use possible for navigation. Dynamo theory explains the cause of the field by showing that a rotating, electrically conducting fluid maintains a magnetic field over astronomical time periods. The Earth's magnetic field, also known as the geomagnetic field, forms the magnetosphere. It reaches a staggering several tens of thousands of kilometers into space and is estimated to be around 3.5 billion years old.

4 ➡ The magnetic fields of the magnetosphere shield the Earth's surface from charged solar wind particles. Electric currents from many areas of the Earth contribute to the magnetosphere. The Earth's day side has a compressed field due to the force of the arriving particles. The Earth's night side has an extended field largely protected from solar wind. The Van Allen radiation belt also traps charged particles from the solar wind. Some particles manage to travel to the Earth's upper atmosphere and ionosphere into the auroral zones, so astronomers can only observe the solar wind on the Earth during the aurora or geomagnetic storms.

6 The author mentions "dipole" in the passage as an example of which of the following?

(A) A central axis with two magnetic ends

(B) An offset field

(C) A magnetic field

(D) A geomagnetic anomaly

7 Look at paragraph 5 and indicate (A, B, C and D) where the following sentence could be added to the passage.

In other words, the dipole goes straight through the planet.

Where would the sentence best fit?

(A)   (B)   (C)   (D)

8 Why does the author mention 'blackout zones' in the passage?

(A) To demonstrate that the magnetic fields have instability

(B) To show the migration of the dipole

(C) To emphasize that the compass is untrustworthy

(D) To compare the North and South poles

5 ➡ The Earth's magnetic field is approximated by the magnetic dipole positioned near the Earth's center. **(A)** A central axis defines the dipole's orientation. **(B)** The two places where the dipole's axis best fit the geomagnetic field intersecting the Earth are named the North and South geomagnetic poles. The dipole rests about 500 km off the Earth's center. **(C)** This offset field causes the South Atlantic Anomaly, a place in the Southern Atlantic Ocean where the field is weakest. Therefore, if the Earth's magnetic field was exactly dipolar, the geomagnetic and magnetic poles would overlap. **(D)** Nevertheless, the position of the two pole types is in different places.

6 ➡ The magnetic pole position is defined in two ways. The magnetic dipole is a point on the Earth's surface where the magnetic field stands vertical, or the inclination of the Earth's field is 90° at the North Magnetic Pole and -90° at the South Magnetic Pole. As far as the compass is concerned, at a magnetic pole, the horizontal plane points erratically. With that said, local deviations happen. These are called blackout zones—areas where one cannot trust the compass. The dipole can migrate up to 40 km per year for the North Magnetic Pole.

9 According to paragraph 7, which of the following about the variables that affect the Earth's magnetic field is true?

(A) The magnetic declination is different depending on the Earth's true constant.

(B) There are three variables that explain the magnetic field of the Earth.

(C) The angle formed against the horizontal plane of the Earth's surface is one of the variables.

(D) Both the horizontal and vertical components are used to describe the direction of the Earth's magnetic field.

7 ➡ Three variables affect the magnitude and the direction of the Earth's magnetic field. First, the magnetic declination acts as the angle between true north and the magnetic north pole. True north is never at a constant position on the horizontal plane and it varies depending upon the position on the Earth's surface and time. Second is the magnetic inclination, also known as the angle of dip. It is the angle made against the horizontal plane on the Earth's surface. Finally, the Earth's magnetic field has two factors to explain the strength of the Earth's magnetic field: the horizontal component, and the vertical component.

VIEW TEXT

REVIEW

HELP

BACK

NEXT

HIDE TIME 00:54:00

10 **Directions**: An introductory sentence for a brief summary of the passage is provided below. Complete the summary by choosing the THREE answer choices that express the most important ideas in the passage. Some sentences do not belong in the summary because they express ideas that are not presented in the passage or are minor ideas in the passage.

Drag your answer choices to the spaces where they belong. To remove an answer choice, click on it. To review the passage, click on **VIEW TEXT**.

In summary, magnetic fields are incredibly important to the earth in many ways.

-
-
-

ANSWER CHOICES

A The magnetic inclination, magnetic declination, and both axis components are variables that help explain the direction and magnitude of the Earth's magnetic fields.

B The Earth's magnetic fields have magnetic influences on an electric charge of other charges or magnetized materials.

C A magnetic force covers a large distance and includes attractive and repulsive forces.

D The Earth's magnetic field acts as a magnetic dipole – the Earth's north and south poles – which forms the magnetosphere, protecting the Earth's surface.

E It is important to understand how the magnetic pole positions are defined, for they are helpful in understanding anomalies, such as blackout zones.

F There are two subsets of magnets, four categories of perpetual-motion magnets, and three fundamental types of electromagnets.

Gamma-Rays and Radiation

Gamma rays, otherwise known as *symbol γ.* are the highest radiation-emitting protons on the electromagnetic spectrum. Discovered shortly after x-rays in 1900 because of their shared properties, they were considered too hazardous for the better part of a century, when investigations laid bare their health benefits. This consideration was due to their high penetrability when exposed to the human body. Released from atom nuclei, gamma rays are produced as consequence of excessive energy in a radioactive atom, resulting in the expulsion of high-speed electron beta particles in the form of *γ*. These wavelengths travel at such extreme frequencies and velocities that they are able to completely penetrate all but thick layers of concrete and lead.

Ionizing gamma radiation disrupts our biometric machinery and high levels of it can wreak havoc on the body, which is why protection from it is so important. Fortunately, the strongest gamma rays are emitted by matters some millions of lightyears away, deep in outer space - such as black holes, supernova explosions, and the collision of neutron stars - meaning most humans are largely safe from such a lethal exposure. These occurrences are referred to as Gamma-Ray Bursts (GRB), where gamma rays are fired along narrow beams following an impact with two or more atomic nuclei. At their most intense levels, a cosmological distribution of GRB can harness more energy in a few seconds than the absolute 10-million-year lifetime of the sun. Gamma rays that do come into the vicinity of our planet are less concentrated and are blocked by the ozone layer.

On the earth's surface, humans are safe from radiation, besides mostly benign quantities of gamma radiation, which is released from radioisotopes in soil and food, as well as the natural, radioactive decay of uranium. All the rocks and plates which form the crust and the decaying material that lays upon it are radioactive in nature. Unsurprisingly, some minerals such as Pitchblende and Chalcoli, which contain thorium and uranium can emit levels of radiation that are harmful if absorbed over many years. Scientific studies in India and France found correlations between birth defects and DNA alterations in populations living in granite-rich areas where they were exposed to higher doses of natural radiation from rocks and beaches.

Around three decades ago, gamma radiation began to be used in the medical sector, particularly in the field of oncology. It was found, through trial-and-error, that high levels of radiation could be used to stop the growth and division of cancerous cells by blasting malignment tumors with gamma rays through an accelerator machine. Despite being experts in knowledge of the use of radiation in a medical setting, scientists used the trial stage to test the machines on themselves using sizably lower doses – a process known as 'photo-testing'. The consequences with this approach would result in their death, as many of them died from leukemia due to such high-frequent low-grade radiation exposure.

Moderate levels of gamma radiation have the potential to kill microorganisms without causing any other undesirable effects. Gamma irradiation is a means of sterilization in which gamma rays are passed through medical equipment to inhibit bacterial division by destroying microbe DNA. The same process can be used in the microbial reduction of food to stop it from spoiling. In larger quantities, gamma rays can be used in the disinfestation of livestock and other agricultural products by destroying live insects and bacteria.

However, the release of gamma rays from artificial sources such as the fallout from reactor meltdowns and thermonuclear bombs, are fatal. In the immediate seconds following a nuclear-isomer explosion, the fission products in the fireball disperse a tremendous number of gamma-rays. These penetrate the body at unfathomable rates, causing the breakdown of tissues, organs, and destruction of cells. The immediate consequences range from thermal burns to blindness and for those in the immediate area: incineration. If the initial blast is survived, the damage to the cells is usually beyond repair and the body begins to breakdown, most commonly from cancer as a result of the damage.

Beginning

Gamma-Rays and Radiation

1 ➡ Gamma rays, otherwise known as *symbol γ*, are the highest radiation-emitting protons on the electromagnetic spectrum. Discovered shortly after x-rays in 1900 because of their shared properties, they were considered too hazardous for the better part of a century, when investigations laid bare their health benefits. This consideration was due to their high penetrability when exposed to the human body. Released from atom nuclei, gamma rays are produced as consequence of excessive energy in a radioactive atom, resulting in the expulsion of high-speed electron beta particles in the form of γ. These wavelengths travel at such extreme frequencies and velocities that they are able to completely penetrate all but thick layers of concrete and lead.

2 ➡ Ionizing gamma radiation disrupts our biometric machinery and high levels of it can wreak havoc on the body, which is why protection from it is so important. Fortunately, the strongest gamma rays are emitted by matters some millions of lightyears away, deep in outer space - such as black holes, supernova explosions, and the collision of neutron stars - meaning most humans are largely safe from such a lethal exposure. These occurrences are referred to as Gamma-Ray Bursts (GRB), where gamma rays are fired along narrow beams following an impact with two or more atomic nuclei. At their most intense levels, a cosmological distribution of GRB can harness more energy in a few seconds than the absolute 10-million-year lifetime of the sun. Gamma rays that do come into the vicinity of our planet are less concentrated and are blocked by the ozone layer.

1 According to paragraph 1, which of the following is true about gamma rays?

- (A) They share similarities to x-rays
- (B) At the time of writing, they do not outweigh the dangers of gamma rays.
- (C) They are considered more dangerous than x-rays.
- (D) They produce an excessive amount of radioactive energy

2 Which of the sentences below best expresses the essential information in the highlighted sentence in the passage? Incorrect choices change the meaning in important ways or leave out essential information.

- (A) Emitted by matter deep in space, the most lethal gamma rays are too distant to significantly affect humankind.
- (B) The strongest gamma rays occur outside the earth in neutron stars, black holes, and supernovas.
- (C) Black holes and supernovas give off the strongest gamma rays.
- (D) Lethal levels of gamma rays occur only outside the earth, meaning humans are safe.

3   The word 'benign' in the passage is closest in meaning to…

   Ⓐ insignificant
   Ⓑ nonthreatening
   Ⓒ substantial
   Ⓓ kind

4   According to paragraph 3, which of the following is NOT true of gamma radiation?

   Ⓐ It is the result of a naturally occurring event.
   Ⓑ Some elements release radiation.
   Ⓒ It damagingly affects the earth's surface.
   Ⓓ It may cause unwelcomed changes in humans' biology.

5   The phrase 'through trial-and-error' in the passage is closest in meaning to…

   Ⓐ Using new techniques to overcome mistakes
   Ⓑ Experimenting until a successful outcome is found
   Ⓒ Investigating results to find inaccuracies
   Ⓓ Testing ways to reduce the number of errors

6   The author mentions "photo-testing" in the passage to

   Ⓐ dispute the claim that scientists were fully aware of the negative consequences of using gamma radiation.
   Ⓑ give an example of how the use of radiation in a medical setting was verified.
   Ⓒ highlight the cause behind the death of the aforementioned scientists.
   Ⓓ identify a scientific method that was used to investigate the effects of gamma radiation.

3 ➡ On the earth's surface, humans are safe from radiation, besides mostly benign quantities of gamma radiation, which is released from radioisotopes in soil and food, as well as the natural, radioactive decay of uranium. All the rocks and plates which form the crust and the decaying material that lays upon it are radioactive in nature. Unsurprisingly, some minerals such as Pitchblende and Chalcoli, which contain thorium and uranium can emit levels of radiation that are harmful if absorbed over many years. Scientific studies in India and France found correlations between birth defects and DNA alterations in populations living in granite-rich areas where they were exposed to higher doses of natural radiation from rocks and beaches.

4 ➡ Around three decades ago, gamma radiation began to be used in the medical sector, particularly in the field of oncology. It was found, through trial-and-error, that high levels of radiation could be used to stop the growth and division of cancerous cells by blasting malignment tumors with gamma rays through an accelerator machine. Despite being experts in knowledge of the use of radiation in a medical setting, scientists used the trial stage to test the machines on themselves using sizably lower doses – a process known as 'photo-testing'. The consequences with this approach would result in their death, as many of them died from leukemia due to such high-frequent low-grade radiation exposure.

7 Which of the following best captures the purpose of paragraph 5 in relation to the previous paragraph?

Ⓐ The paragraph supports a claim made in paragraph 4.

Ⓑ The paragraph contradicts a claim made about 'photo-testing' in the previous passage.

Ⓒ The paragraph discusses a safer way of implementing gamma radiation.

Ⓓ The paragraph introduces a solution to a problem made in paragraph 4.

8 In paragraph 6, the word 'unfathomable' is closest in meaning to

Ⓐ implausible

Ⓑ uninhibited

Ⓒ immediate

Ⓓ unimaginable

9 In the paragraph below, there is a missing sentence. Look at the paragraph and indicate (A, B, C and D) where the following sentence could be added to the passage.

The aftereffects of this blast lasts not just for weeks and months, but often decades.

Where would the sentence best fit?

Ⓐ   Ⓑ   Ⓒ   Ⓓ

5 ➡ Moderate levels of gamma radiation have the potential to kill microorganisms without causing any other undesirable effects. Gamma irradiation is a means of sterilization in which gamma rays are passed through medical equipment to inhibit bacterial division by destroying microbe DNA. The same process can be used in the microbial reduction of food to stop it from spoiling. In larger quantities, gamma rays can be used in the disinfestation of livestock and other agricultural products by destroying live insects and bacteria.

6 ➡ However, the release of gamma rays from artificial sources such as the fallout from reactor meltdowns and thermonuclear bombs, are fatal. **(A)** In the immediate seconds following a nuclear-isomer explosion, the fission products in the fireball disperse a tremendous number of gamma-rays. These penetrate the body at unfathomable rates, causing the breakdown of tissues, organs, and destruction of cells. **(B)** The immediate consequences range from thermal burns to blindness and for those in the immediate area: incineration. **(C)** If the initial blast is survived, the damage to the cells is usually beyond repair and the body begins to breakdown, most commonly from cancer as a result of the damage. **(D)**

10 Directions: An introductory sentence for a brief summary of the passage is provided below. Complete the summary by choosing the THREE answer choices that express the most important ideas in the passage. Some sentences do not belong in the summary because they express ideas that are not presented in the passage or are minor ideas in the passage.

Drag your answer choices to the spaces where they belong. To remove an answer choice, click on it. To review the passage, click on **VIEW TEXT**.

Gamma radiation is one of the most useful, yet destructive findings in recent human history.

-
-
-

ANSWER CHOICES

A Although protected from the most harmful gamma rays, humans have developed the ability to trigger fatal levels of gamma radiation.

B Some gamma radiation has been contained and used for medical purposes to treat life-threatening diseases and sterilize medical equipment.

C Despite occurring naturally in minerals, most uses of gamma radiation are from artificial sources and are both useful and non-threatening.

D The use of gamma rays in destroying harmful microbes means that food can be kept fresh for longer and safer for consumption

E The fissions in the fireball of a nuclear explosion send gamma rays firing out, causing devastation to humans nearby.

F The application of radiation-use in the agricultural sector has meant that food can be kept fresh in its transportation and distribution.

TOEFL

Reading
Actual Test

Actual Test
Astronomy

Wildfires

Wildfires are classified as uncontrolled conflagrations that begin in rural areas. The flammable material in such fires consists of combustible plant species and organic matter. Wildfires are often named for the type of matter which fuels them. Some examples of this include peat fires, grass fires and forest fires. The weather is often a factor in the creation of a wildfire, such as with lightning, or in its ability to sustain itself, such as with high winds. Archaeologists have been able to use charcoal samples to date the earliest wildfires to approximately 420 million years ago.

Wildfires either start naturally, or they are started through human activity. Some of the natural causes of wildfires include lightning, as already mentioned, volcanic eruptions, and very dry climates. Evidently, regions with drier climates are more prone to experiencing naturally occurring wildfires than cooler regions. There is a plethora of ways in which fires can start through the activities of people. Carelessly discarded cigarette butts, open campfires and heated fragments from rifle bullets have all been demonstrated to have been the cause of some severe fires. Industry can sometimes cause fires to start accidentally too, when sparks from equipment ignite the vegetation or a hot engine is left unattended. Unfortunately, arson is also a major cause of wildfires in many regions of the world.

One of the things that makes wildfires so difficult to control is the rapidity with which they spread. This spread is determined by the material being consumed by the fire as well as the local weather conditions. Ground fires are characterized by smoldering and smoke. These fires burn organic material under the surface such as roots or peat and can last for days. Surface fires are found in heavily forested areas and are fueled by the thick shrubbery that is often a feature in forests. Ladder fires burn fuel that exists between the surface level and the tree canopy, while crown fires are those which burn material at the level of the treetops.

It is thought that wildfires have been in existence since shortly after surface vegetation first appeared. This means that wildfires have been a feature of many ecosystems since they first started to develop, leading scientists to believe that they might have been instrumental in the development of the plants and animals they came into contact with. Many plants rely on fires to spread or have developed resistances to high temperatures in order to survive the annual wildfire season.

Wildfires can also have a real and long-lasting effect on the planet's atmosphere. Smoke and debris from wildfires have been shown to reach at least to the troposphere, the lowest layer of the atmosphere. It is here that most of earth's pollution can be found. More locally, the emissions given off by wildfires can affect the levels of fine particles in the air, in turn leading to cardio-vascular problems for the local population. Wildfires release unheard of amounts of CO_2 into the atmosphere, which could be playing a role in heating up the Earth.

As much as we want to keep people safe from wildfires and prevent unnecessary damage to property, it doesn't look like there is any simple solution to the issue. Indeed, wildfires are a part of some cultures, to the extent that it might be less radical to begin to explore avenues in which people can learn how to live with them instead of trying to eradicate them. Local governments can enforce laws and restrictions to control how forests are cultivated and prosecute those who abuse such controls or cause excessive damage without reason.

Wildfires

1 ➡ Wildfires are classified as uncontrolled conflagrations that begin in rural areas. The flammable material in such fires consists of combustible plant species and organic matter. Wildfires are often named for the type of matter which fuels them. Some examples of this include peat fires, grass fires and forest fires. The weather is often a factor in the creation of a wildfire, such as with lightning, or in its ability to sustain itself, such as with high winds. Archaeologists have been able to use charcoal samples to date the earliest wildfires to approximately 420 million years ago.

2 ➡ Wildfires either start naturally, or they are started through human activity. Some of the natural causes of wildfires include lightning, as already mentioned, volcanic eruptions, and very dry climates. Evidently, regions with drier climates are more prone to experiencing naturally occurring wildfires than cooler regions. There is a plethora of ways in which fires can start through the activities of people. Carelessly discarded cigarette butts, open campfires and heated fragments from rifle bullets have all been demonstrated to have been the cause of some severe fires. Industry can sometimes cause fires to start accidentally too, when sparks from equipment ignite the vegetation or a hot engine is left unattended. Unfortunately, arson is also a major cause of wildfires in many regions of the world.

1. According to paragraph 1, which of the following is NOT true of wildfires?
   - (A) They are blazes which are not controlled by people.
   - (B) The type of blaze often depends on what the fire is fueled by.
   - (C) For 420 million years, archeologists have been estimating the start of wildfires.
   - (D) Wildfires are generally confined to rural areas.

2. Which of the following is true about the causes of wildfires, according to paragraph 2?
   - (A) Most of wildfires are caused by natural means.
   - (B) Wildfires can start in industrial areas due to people's intentional carelessness.
   - (C) Deliberately igniting fire is one culprit behind wildfires around the globe,
   - (D) Causes of man-made wildfires include volcanic eruption and lightning.

3. Which of the following best expresses the essential information in the highlighted sentence in paragraph 2? Incorrect choices change the meaning in important ways or leave out essential information.
   - (A) Natural wildfires start in areas with dry climates more often than in areas with cold climates.
   - (B) Cooler regions are more fertile than drier ones, meaning more fuel for wildfires to burn.
   - (C) Man-made fires tend to happen more readily in drier climates where there is a higher human population.
   - (D) Natural wildfires occur more often than man made ones.

4 What is the author's purpose in discussing the types of wildfires in paragraph 3?

(A) He wants to say that humanity is responsible for wildfires and should be more cautious.

(B) The author is elaborating on one characteristic of wildfires mentioned earlier.

(C) The author is condemning those who start wildfires purposely.

(D) His purpose is to demonstrate how easily a wildfire can be started.

5 In paragraph 4, why does the author mention the first appearance of "surface vegetation"?

(A) To emphasize the fact that wildfires have long been a feature of ecosystem

(B) To provide readers with familiar idea in order to highlight the long history of wildfires

(C) To facilitate readers' understanding of different types of vegetations

(D) To demonstrate the fact that wildfires have been important in the development of animals and vegetation.

6 In paragraph 4, there is a missing sentence. Look at the paragraph and indicate (A, B, C and D) where the following sentence could be added to the passage.

Wildfires also have the effect of burning away competing plant life that have not developed the same resistances.

Where would the sentence best fit?

(A)   (B)   (C)   (D)

3 ➡ One of the things that makes wildfires so difficult to control is the rapidity with which they spread. This spread is determined by the material being consumed by the fire as well as the local weather conditions. Ground fires are characterized by smoldering and smoke. These fires burn organic material under the surface such as roots or peat and can last for days. Surface fires are found in heavily forested areas and are fueled by the thick shrubbery that is often a feature in forests. Ladder fires burn fuel that exists between the surface level and the tree canopy, while crown fires are those which burn material at the level of the treetops.

4 ➡ **(A)** It is thought that wildfires have been in existence since shortly after surface vegetation first appeared. **(B)** This means that wildfires have been a feature of many ecosystems since they first started to develop, leading scientists to believe that they might have been instrumental in the development of the plants and animals they came into contact with. **(C)** Many plants rely on fires to spread or have developed resistances to high temperatures in order to survive the annual wildfire season. **(D)**

PASSAGE 1

REVIEW

? HELP

< BACK

> NEXT

HIDE TIME 00:54:00

More Available

7   What can be inferred from paragraph 4 about plants?

   Ⓐ Not all plants develop the traits which allow them to thrive in areas where wildfires occur.

   Ⓑ It would be impossible for some plants to survive without regular exposure to wildfires.

   Ⓒ Plants resistant to heat were vital for the development of forests.

   Ⓓ Some plants spontaneously combust and cause natural wildfires to start.

8   According to paragraph 5, which of the following is true of wildfires?

   Ⓐ Wildfires cause most of the pollution in the troposphere.

   Ⓑ Wildfires can cause serious health problems for the populations who live nearby.

   Ⓒ The particles and smoke from wildfires have been known to reach the outer layer of the atmosphere.

   Ⓓ It has been proven that wildfires are responsible for the warming up of planet earth.

9   The word 'eradicate' in paragraph 7 is closest in meaning to

   Ⓐ kill

   Ⓑ erase

   Ⓒ eliminate

   Ⓓ abolish

5 ➡ Wildfires can also have a real and long-lasting effect on the planet's atmosphere. Smoke and debris from wildfires have been shown to reach at least to the troposphere, the lowest layer of the atmosphere. It is here that most of earth's pollution can be found. More locally, the emissions given off by wildfires can affect the levels of fine particles in the air, in turn leading to cardio-vascular problems for the local population. Wildfires release unheard of amounts of CO_2 into the atmosphere, which could be playing a role in heating up the Earth.

6 ➡ As much as we want to keep people safe from wildfires and prevent unnecessary damage to property, it doesn't look like there is any simple solution to the issue. Indeed, wildfires are a part of some cultures, to the extent that it might be less radical to begin to explore avenues in which people can learn how to live with them instead of trying to eradicate them. Local governments can enforce laws and restrictions to control how forests are cultivated and prosecute those who abuse such controls or cause excessive damage without reason.

10 **Directions**: An introductory sentence for a brief summary of the passage is provided below. Complete the summary by choosing the THREE answer choices that express the most important ideas in the passage. Some sentences do not belong in the summary because they express ideas that are not presented in the passage or are minor ideas in the passage.

> Drag your answer choices to the spaces where they belong. To remove an answer choice, click on it. To review the passage, click on **VIEW TEXT**.

Wildfires have been with us for almost as long as the plants that fuel them and play an important role in the rejuvenation of the areas they occur, but not all of them are naturally occurring.

-
-
-

ANSWER CHOICES

A When it occurs naturally, wildfire can be a benefit to the ecosystem, but very often wildfires are started through negligence or malicious intent by humans.

B Whether occurring naturally or as the result of human error, wildfires have a positive effect on the environment.

C Fires caused by mother nature are a common result of volcanic activity and dry climates, but human error is the most common cause of these disasters.

D Wildfires can bring about long-term effect both on the Earth's atmosphere and human health.

E The only way to overcome wildfires is to make sure they never happen again.

F Wildfires are a relatively recent phenomenon, coinciding with the increased industrial activity close to combustible vegetation.

The Telescope

Man has always been fascinated by the night sky. In time immemorial, the setting of the sun and the onset of dusk brought a sense of trepidation to our ancestors. All over the world, people would gather around small fires and stare up into the heavens. The moon, the stars, and other heavenly bodies have inspired myth and mystery for countless generations. Some of the earliest stories in existence today trace their origins back to man's quest to understand the universe and his place in it. But while humankind would unlock the secrets to a great many terrestrial mysteries, those of the heavens continued to elude us until fairly modern times. They remained hidden from us prior to the invention of the telescope.

The study of the heavens is called astronomy. Early astronomers were limited by a lack of instruments, so in ancient times, astronomy consisted solely of observing celestial objects with the naked eye. Despite being limited by the scarcity of tools, ancient astronomers were able to make some important discoveries and record some valuable information. Over time, astronomers were able to develop methods to be able to see greater portions of the night sky and to record their findings more accurately, but the science of astronomy was changed forever with the invention of the telescope.

What is a telescope? There are many different types. Some are so simple and lightweight that a child could operate without assistance. Others are incredibly powerful and so large that they occupy an entire building and can only be operated by teams of scientists. But whether a telescope is uncomplicated and portable or state of the art and massive, the principles on which it operates will remain very much the same, and the internal components will be unvaried: they all use lenses and mirrors to make distant objects visible.

As it is with practically every groundbreaking invention, there are several different theories about the origin of the telescope. While it's a widely held misconception that Galileo Galilei invented the first telescope, many historians agree that the earliest verifiable proof we can point to support the theory that the man behind the design for the first telescope was a Dutchman by the name of Hans Lippershey who attempted to patent his idea in 1608. Subsequent improvements to the initial design were made by some of the men whose names would become synonymous with the discipline to which they devoted themselves - Galileo, Kepler, Huygens.

The invention of the telescope completely changed the procedures and conventions of astronomy. Mankind's knowledge of the world beyond the Earth progressed at an astonishingly rapid pace. New developments to the basic design of the telescope have enabled us to penetrate farther and farther into the heavens, and it can only be predicted that future improvements to existing telescopes will grant us access to new wonders in years to come. The telescope affords us the opportunity to discover the secrets that eluded our ancestors for millennia and to answer some of the questions that we have posed to ourselves since before the dawn of recorded history.

Who are we? Where did we come from? Are we alone? What's out there beyond the edge of what's visible to us? It's likely that we as a species were asking ourselves these very same questions before we acquired the language to be able to put them into words. Has the invention of the telescope brought us any closer to actually answering any of these questions? Well, in a sense, yes it has. And it can only be expected that as we move forward, we will continue to unravel the mysteries of the universe one by one.

The Telescope

1 ➡ Man has always been fascinated by the night sky. In time immemorial, the setting of the sun and the onset of dusk brought a sense of trepidation to our ancestors. All over the world, people would gather around small fires and stare up into the heavens. The moon, the stars, and other heavenly bodies have inspired myth and mystery for countless generations. Some of the earliest stories in existence today trace their origins back to man's quest to understand the universe and his place in it. But while humankind would unlock the secrets to a great many terrestrial mysteries, those of the heavens continued to elude us until fairly modern times. They remained hidden from us prior to the invention of the telescope.

1 According to paragraph 1, which of the following is true of our ancestors?

(A) Darkness brought with it fear, because they were scared of what they did not understand.

(B) They told stories around small fires to try and understand the night sky.

(C) The oldest stories we have ever uncovered explain the formation of the universe.

(D) The moon and the stars have caused fear in people for a long time.

2 The word elude in the passage is closest in meaning to

(A) flee

(B) lose

(C) dodge

(D) evade

REVIEW

HELP

BACK

NEXT

HIDE TIME 00:54:00

More Available

3   Which of the following best expresses the essential information in the highlighted sentence in paragraph 2? Incorrect choices change the meaning in important ways or leave out essential information.

   (A) In pre-modern times, astronomers were incapable of inventing instruments to observe the heavens.

   (B) When people first started observing the sky, they had to do so without tools, and used their eyes.

   (C) In ancient times, it was impossible to observe objects in the night sky with only your eyes.

   (D) At first, astronomers had no instruments to observe the sky.

4   In context of the passage, what is the primary purpose of paragraph 2?

   (A) It gives an overview of the development of telescopes.

   (B) It provides a general idea about the times before the advent of telescopes.

   (C) It foreshadows the developmental pattern of the passage as a whole.

   (D) It defines the key terminology needed in understanding the passage.

2 ⇒ The study of the heavens is called astronomy. Early astronomers were limited by a lack of instruments, so in ancient times, astronomy consisted solely of observing celestial objects with the naked eye. Despite being limited by the scarcity of tools, ancient astronomers were able to make some important discoveries and record some valuable information. Over time, astronomers were able to develop methods to be able to see greater portions of the night sky and to record their findings more accurately, but the science of astronomy was changed forever with the invention of the telescope.

PASSAGE 2

REVIEW

HELP

BACK

NEXT

HIDE TIME 00:54:00

More Available ▲

5 According to paragraph 3, which of the following is NOT true of telescopes.

Ⓐ They all operate using the same idea.

Ⓑ Most telescopes are uncomplicated and portable, and a child could use them.

Ⓒ The parts inside the various telescopes don't vary greatly from model to model.

Ⓓ Certain telescopes require a whole building to operate effectively.

6 Which of the following is true about the origin of the telescope, according to paragraph 4?

Ⓐ There is a general consensus that Galileo Galilei invented the first telescope.

Ⓑ There is valid evidence suggesting that a Dutch scientist could have been the first to design the first telescope.

Ⓒ Galileo, Kepler, and Huygens patented the first design of the telescope.

Ⓓ Many scientists agree with one overarching theory about the origin of the telescope.

7 In paragraph 4, there is a missing sentence. Look at the paragraph and indicate (A, B, C and D) where the following sentence could be added to the passage.

Another individual who lived in the same town and was also involved in making optical instruments was Zacharias Janssen.

Where would the sentence best fit?

Ⓐ   Ⓑ   Ⓒ   Ⓓ

3 ➡ What is a telescope? There are many different types. Some are so simple and lightweight that a child could operate without assistance. Others are incredibly powerful and so large that they occupy an entire building and can only be operated by teams of scientists. But whether a telescope is uncomplicated and portable or state of the art and massive, the principles on which it operates will remain very much the same, and the internal components will be unvaried: they all use lenses and mirrors to make distant objects visible.

4 ➡ **(A)** As it is with practically every groundbreaking invention, there are several different theories about the origin of the telescope. **(B)** While it's a widely held misconception that Galileo Galilei invented the first telescope, many historians agree that the earliest verifiable proof we can point to support the theory that the man behind the design for the first telescope was a Dutchman by the name of Hans Lippershey who attempted to patent his idea in 1608. **(C)** Subsequent improvements to the initial design were made by some of the men whose names would become synonymous with the discipline to which they devoted themselves - Galileo, Kepler, Huygens. **(D)**

REVIEW

HELP

BACK

NEXT

HIDE TIME 00:54:00

End ▲

8   What can be inferred from paragraph 5
    about the author's attitude toward the
    telescope?

    (A) He believes it is the greatest invention
        in the history of mankind.

    (B) He dismisses it as having changed
        our lives at too rapid pace.

    (C) He is optimistic about the future
        development of telescopes.

    (D) He praises for inducing developments
        and new knowledge about the
        heavens.

9   What is the author's purpose in asking so
    many questions in the final paragraph?

    (A) To review the questions that were
        answered by the invention and
        development of the telescope.

    (B) To recall the mysteries that were
        mentioned in the first paragraph, and
        the telescope's part in answering
        them.

    (C) To list the questions that humanity will
        continue to ask, and which only further
        development of the telescope can
        answer.

    (D) To highlight how far the telescope has
        come amongst humanity's greatest
        inventions.

5 ➡   The invention of the telescope completely
changed the procedures and conventions
of astronomy. Mankind's knowledge of the
world beyond the Earth progressed at an
astonishingly rapid pace. New developments
to the basic design of the telescope have
enabled us to penetrate farther and farther into
the heavens, and it can only be predicted that
future improvements to existing telescopes
will grant us access to new wonders in
years to come. The telescope affords us the
opportunity to discover the secrets that eluded
our ancestors for millennia and to answer
some of the questions that we have posed to
ourselves since before the dawn of recorded
history.

6 ➡   Who are we? Where did we come from?
Are we alone? What's out there beyond the
edge of what's visible to us? It's likely that
we as a species were asking ourselves these
very same questions before we acquired the
language to be able to put them into words.
Has the invention of the telescope brought
us any closer to actually answering any of
these questions? Well, in a sense, yes it
has. And it can only be expected that as we
move forward, we will continue to unravel the
mysteries of the universe one by one.

10 **Directions**: An introductory sentence for a brief summary of the passage is provided below. Complete the summary by choosing the THREE answer choices that express the most important ideas in the passage. Some sentences do not belong in the summary because they express ideas that are not presented in the passage or are minor ideas in the passage.

Drag your answer choices to the spaces where they belong. To remove an answer choice, click on it. To review the passage, click on **VIEW TEXT**.

Humankind has always wondered what lies beyond the clouds, but it is only recently that we have been able to get some answers to this age-old question – thanks to telescopes.

-

-

-

ANSWER CHOICES

A Early astronomers were unable to discover as much as more modern scholars as they lacked the scientific knowledge and methods we possess today.

B Although there are numerous different kinds of telescope, they are fundamentally constructed in a similar way.

C The invention of the telescope has to rate as one of humanity's greatest achievements, it has let us look further than ever before, and might help us answer questions about our own existence.

D It is universally acknowledged that the inventor of the telescope was a Dutchman, Hans Lippershey.

E The telescope has answered many profound questions for the human race, such as where do we come from, and are we alone in the universe?

F Many people contributed to the development of the telescope, but the one who first patented the design was unquestionably Hans Lippershey

Pluto

In the outer limits of our galaxy, on the cusp of the Kuiper Belt, orbits an object which has experienced the fame and starlight of a modern-day celebrity. Pluto was discovered in 1930 by astronomer Clyde Tombaugh and was celebrated as the solitary 'planet' to ever be discovered by an American. The discovery brought to scientists a sense of excitement and curiosity about the number of planetary objects yet to be discovered in our solar system, albeit with a tinge of pessimism about ever being to examine it closely. Despite almost a century fleeting by since its first sighting, Pluto remains shrouded in celestial obscurity because of our technological incapability to explore such far-reaching locations.

Pluto is unforgiving, comprising predominantly of nitrogen ice and rock, with the former accounting for 98%. This means temperatures of around -240 degrees Celsius and low-atmospheric pressure, making it near-impossible for the planet to harbor living organisms. Scientists observing part of Pluto's 248-year orbital period around the sun have suggested that at aphelion, its gassy atmosphere freezes solid, with ices sublimating only at perihelion - its closest position on its solar-orbit. Though uninhabitable, images sent back to earth via the Long-Range Reconnaissance Imager (LRRI) aboard the New Horizon rover show glaciers and valleys, as well as jagged mountains which bear some resemblance to those on Earth.

Despite its harsh environment, many attempts to study Pluto through scrupulous Hubble observations have revealed unexpected substances on Pluto's surface that may contain the building blocks for life: carbon. Observing the absorption of UV light in its crust, astrobiologists speculate that complex hydrocarbon compounds may be at fault. Will these organic molecules be enough to give rise to life on Pluto? Scientists found the discovery rousing given the initial skepticism about the prospect of living organisms there, contending that the finding was an indicator of possible pre-biotic chemistry happening for life on Pluto. Researchers argue that the presence of molecules like amino acids and nucleobases may point towards abiotic processes in subsurface regions of Pluto.

Much in the way lakes freeze over in the winter, New Horizons has photographed signs of water-filled cracks below Pluto's icy surface, pointing towards signs that the planet hosts

oceans closer to its core. Some planetary scientists hypothesize that Pluto may have begun as an ocean planet, before going through multiple ice ages and 're-freezing' repeatedly. The water some hundred kilometers below the surface could have interacted with the warm radioactive core and had enough minerals to be habitable, before expanding and re-freezing, locking organisms in the cracks. When Pluto reaches aphelion again, they may, hypothetically, be released long enough to multiply.

Analyzing Pluto's surface more carefully using the LRRI, evidence of ammonia-rich ice near its jagged fissures were unearthed. Combined with Pluto's mountainous characteristics, incrusted ice sheets, and indication of a fiery interior core, these could collectively point towards the existence of cryovolcanoes. This idea would suggest volcanic activity, spilling liquid water onto the surface below and incessantly re-freezing to form the aforementioned sheets. Speaking speculatively, astrobiologists play with the idea that if the water were to remain liquified for some period, organisms could have emerged. Likewise, if the water remained deep in cryovolcanic chambers, and close enough to radiation, microorganisms may be present.

There is no doubt that the quality of research into life on Pluto has drastically improved since its discovery a century ago, and even since its reclassification two decades ago. The use of more sensitive telescopes, space probes, and perhaps rovers, will all contribute to an improved understanding of this dwarf planet. Astronomers and planetary geologists are moving in the right direction and are becoming increasingly educated about the once utterly mysterious. Nevertheless, as Pluto begins its voyage away from the sun, the shadows of the circumstellar disc cast darkness over it and make it more challenging to collect fresh data.

Pluto

1 ➡ In the outer limits of our galaxy, on the cusp of the Kuiper Belt, orbits an object which has experienced the fame and starlight of a modern-day celebrity. Pluto was discovered in 1930 by astronomer Clyde Tombaugh and was celebrated as the solitary 'planet' to ever be discovered by an American. The discovery brought to scientists a sense of excitement and curiosity about the number of planetary objects yet to be discovered in our solar system, albeit with a tinge of pessimism about ever being to examine it closely. Despite almost a century fleeting by since its first sighting, Pluto remains shrouded in celestial obscurity because of our technological incapability to explore such far-reaching locations.

2 ➡ Pluto is unforgiving, comprising predominantly of nitrogen ice and rock, with the former accounting for 98%. This means temperatures of around -240 degrees Celsius and low-atmospheric pressure, making it near-impossible for the planet to harbor living organisms. Scientists observing part of Pluto's 248-year orbital period around the sun have suggested that at aphelion, its gassy atmosphere freezes solid, with ices sublimating only at perihelion - its closest position on its solar-orbit. Though uninhabitable, images sent back to earth via the Long-Range Reconnaissance Imager (LRRI) aboard the New Horizon rover show glaciers and valleys, as well as jagged mountains which bear some resemblance to those on Earth.

1 According to paragraph 1, which of the following is true of Pluto's discovery?

Ⓐ It was the most famous discovery by an astronomer.

Ⓑ It was discovered by the first American astronomer.

Ⓒ Scientists have mixed feelings about the news.

Ⓓ It began a project to discovery other planets in the solar system.

2 Which of the following is NOT true according to paragraph 2?

Ⓐ It is hardly likely for a life to exist in Pluto.

Ⓑ Some evidence suggests a similarity between Pluto and Earth.

Ⓒ An overwhelming composition of Pluto is nitrogen ice.

Ⓓ Images were taken with LRRI primarily due to the planet's habitability.

3 Which of the sentences below best expresses the essential information in the highlighted sentence in the passage? Incorrect choices change the meaning in important ways or leave out essential information.

Ⓐ Scientists observing Pluto's orbit and made distinctions between the perihelion and aphelion positions.

Ⓑ Pluto's atmosphere freezes when far from the sun, with the ice vaporizing as it gets close to the sun.

Ⓒ Pluto's orbit is so long that it takes time for the ice to vaporize, meaning the atmosphere stays frozen for many years.

Ⓓ At perihelion, Pluto's atmosphere is frozen solid for 248 years, meaning life on the planet is impossible.

More Available

4   The word 'scrupulous' in the passage is closest in meaning to…

  (A) thorough

  (B) continuing

  (C) prolonged

  (D) multiple

5   What is the main idea of paragraph 3?

  (A) There is a possibility for life to exist in Pluto.

  (B) There have been numerous attempts to examine Pluto.

  (C) It is now confirmed that life exists in Pluto.

  (D) The debate regarding existence of life in Pluto is near completion.

3 ➡ Despite its harsh environment, many attempts to study Pluto through scrupulous Hubble observations have revealed unexpected substances on Pluto's surface that may contain the building blocks for life: carbon. Observing the absorption of UV light in its crust, astrobiologists speculate that complex hydrocarbon compounds may be at fault. Will these organic molecules be enough to give rise to life on Pluto? Scientists found the discovery rousing given the initial skepticism about the prospect of living organisms there, contending that the finding was an indicator of possible pre-biotic chemistry happening for life on Pluto. Researchers argue that the presence of molecules like amino acids and nucleobases may point towards abiotic processes in subsurface regions of Pluto.

6 According to paragraph 4, which of the following did Hubble observations NOT true of the scientific observations?

Ⓐ Organisms are released from the ice when Pluto nears the sun on its orbit.

Ⓑ Pluto may have experienced multiple, extreme events which changed its conditions drastically.

Ⓒ Cracks along Pluto's surface show the contents of trapped liquified water.

Ⓓ Some suggest that Pluto may have not always been an ice planet.

7 The author mentions a "radioactive core" in the passage in order to

Ⓐ To indicate where microorganisms may have existed deep below the planet's surface.

Ⓑ To give an example of how some water may have remained liquidized despite the intense sub-zero temperatures.

Ⓒ To suggest that it may have had an impact on the biological contents of the water which it was in contact with.

Ⓓ To give evidence of the various complex characteristics of Pluto's composition.

8 In the paragraph below, there is a missing sentence. Look at the paragraph and indicate (A, B, C and D) where the following sentence could be added to the passage.

Volcanic activity is a strong indicator of inhabitable planetary conditions.

Where would the sentence best fit?

Ⓐ   Ⓑ   Ⓒ   Ⓓ

4 ⇒ Much in the way lakes freeze over in the winter, New Horizons has photographed signs of water-filled cracks below Pluto's icy surface, pointing towards signs that the planet hosts oceans closer to its core. Some planetary scientists hypothesize that Pluto may have begun as an ocean planet, before going through multiple ice ages and 're-freezing' repeatedly. The water some hundred kilometers below the surface could have interacted with the warm radioactive core and had enough minerals to be habitable, before expanding and re-freezing, locking organisms in the cracks. When Pluto reaches perihelion again, they may, hypothetically, be released long enough to multiply.

5 ⇒ (A) Analyzing Pluto's surface more carefully using the LRRI, evidence of ammonia-rich ice near its jagged fissures were unearthed. (B) Combined with Pluto's mountainous characteristics, incrusted ice sheets, and indication of a fiery interior core, these could collectively point towards the existence of cryovolcanoes. (C) This idea would suggest volcanic activity, spilling liquid water onto the surface below and incessantly re-freezing to form the aforementioned sheets. Speaking speculatively, astrobiologists play with the idea that if the water were to remain liquified for some period, organisms could have emerged. Likewise, if the water remained deep in cryovolcanic chambers, and close enough to radiation, microorganisms may be present. (D)

9 In paragraph 6, what can be inferred about the evidence scientists have presented?

Ⓐ It has been concluded and there is not much left to explore in the future.

Ⓑ It is not yet tangible enough to prove that organisms can exist and last on Pluto.

Ⓒ It has not advanced too much in recent years, despite their best efforts.

Ⓓ There is no way to know if it will be beneficial to us in the future.

6 ➡ There is no doubt that the quality of research into life on Pluto has drastically improved since its discovery a century ago, and even since its reclassification two decades ago. The use of more sensitive telescopes, space probes, and perhaps rovers, will all contribute to an improved understanding of this dwarf planet. Astronomers and planetary geologists are moving in the right direction and are becoming increasingly educated about the once utterly mysterious. Nevertheless, as Pluto begins its voyage away from the sun, the shadows of the circumstellar disc cast darkness over it and make it more challenging to collect fresh data.

VIEW TEXT

REVIEW

HELP

BACK

NEXT

HIDE TIME 00:54:00

10 **Directions**: An introductory sentence for a brief summary of the passage is provided below. Complete the summary by choosing the THREE answer choices that express the most important ideas in the passage. Some sentences do not belong in the summary because they express ideas that are not presented in the passage or are minor ideas in the passage.

> Drag your answer choices to the spaces where they belong. To remove an answer choice, click on it. To review the passage, click on **VIEW TEXT**.

Although previously considered inhabitable by scientists, evidence of potential life on dwarf planet Pluto has developed of late.

- •
- •
- •

ANSWER CHOICES

A The finding of molecules like amino acids and nucleobases are significant in identifying whether life can persevere on Pluto.

B Pluto has known as a planet for many years, until its declassification, which left scientists feeling negative and irritated.

C Pluto's surface went through periods of freezing and melting, which allowed cracks to form and water to both escape from and be trapped inside.

D At its closest point from the sun, Pluto's icy interior closest to its core may temporarily vaporize, long enough for organisms to escape and multiply.

E Cryovolcanoes deep below Pluto's surface could have had the necessary conditions and homed enough nutrients and liquified water to suggest life, in some form.

F Pluto's crust shows signs of absorbing enough UV light that hydrocarbon compounds could be present, pertaining to the idea that abiotic processes are occurring.

TOEFL

Reading

Actual Test

Actual Test
Chemistry

Chemical Warfare Ethics

Chemical warfare includes using chemical substances and their toxic properties as weapons of mass destruction. This is not to be confused with nuclear warfare, biological warfare, or radiological warfare. None of these are considered conventional weapons, and they all have strong ethical arguments against using them. Some experts advocate that with proper protective equipment, training, and decontamination methods, the effects of chemical weapons can be managed. The problem is that most victims of chemical warfare are unprepared and defenseless. Therefore, they have caused much misery throughout the world. Nevertheless, many nations continue to possess vast stockpiles in preparation for wartime, despite the fact that chemical weapons are prohibited under international humanitarian law.

The use of chemical weapons reaches back to the distant past. However, in the Industrial age, the modern conception of chemical warfare became prevalent. Many nations have backed scientists who have proposed the implementation of asphyxiating poisonous gasses. The remainder of nations have become so alarmed that multiple international treaties have passed banning chemical weapons. Unfortunately, many of these treaties appeared after the two world wars. In World War I in particular, many nations used chlorine gas, among other chemical weapons, to try to break the trench warfare deadlock. The gases rarely killed people, but they did mutilate or injure them. Experts say 1.3 million gas casualties included up to 260,000 civilian casualties.

Chemical weapons were used very little during World War II, but both sides were prepared to use them. The Axis powers used them sparingly, and the Allies never brought them out. The Nazis developed them, but they may have feared that the Allies would retaliate with their own chemical weapons because the Allies made wide-ranging plans for defensive, including stockpiling large quantities of chemical warfare agents. In Asia, Japanese forces used them more extensively against their Asian enemies because they also feared Western retaliation. Nevertheless, the Nazis did use Zyklon B and carbon monoxide gas against noncombatants in the Holocaust, resulting in a reported three million deaths. This incident remains the deadliest poison gas use in history.

Between 1962 and 1971 during the Vietnam War, the United States military applied nearly 20,000,000 U.S. gallons of "rainbow herbicides" and defoliants in Vietnam, eastern Laos, and parts of Cambodia. During the Iran–Iraq War, 100,000 Iranian troops were subjects of Iraqi chemical weapons. During the 1988 Halabja chemical attack, Iran used mustard gas and nerve agents on its own people. Organophosphates were used in Angola during the Cuban Intervention. Sarin, chlorine, and mustard gas were used in the Syrian civil war. Terrorists have used chemical weapons in many cases, but most notably in the Tokyo subway sarin attack and the Matsumoto incident.

They injure and kill combatants and civilians alike in a silent manner. The use of weaponized chemicals requires chemistry knowledge. Chemists have created explosives, defoliants, incendiaries, and chemicals that assault the skin and lungs. They have helped to invent technologies to deploy these chemicals. They have also created the industries that produce these chemicals. Therefore, chemists, people funding the chemical profession, and the chemical industry are responsible. If they vowed not to participate in such activities perhaps the international community could outlaw these heinous weapons of war permanently.

Sadly, many scientists and chemists become entangled in political pressures, economic interests, and professional ambition, but are they free of responsibility from their inventions? Awareness of this problem has grown amongst professional chemistry communities, and many organizations have issued codes of ethics and conduct. With transparency, the professionals active in chemistry and the associated sciences must build trust within the international community. Illustrating responsible scientific practices and safeguarding ethical norms and humane tenets must be the foundation on which chemists and scientists can show their responsibility. Human rights should be the focus of this quest to eradicate the way of thinking that led to the first two world wars, and the atrocities associated with them. An international discussion should be maintained and encouraged, so that chemists and scientists are held responsible for their creations.

Chemical Warfare Ethics

1 ➡ Chemical warfare includes using chemical substances and their toxic properties as weapons of mass destruction. This is not to be confused with nuclear warfare, biological warfare, or radiological warfare. None of these are considered conventional weapons, and they all have strong ethical arguments against using them. Some experts advocate that with proper protective equipment, training, and decontamination methods, the effects of chemical weapons can be managed. The problem is that most victims of chemical warfare are unprepared and defenseless. Therefore, they have caused much misery throughout the world. Nevertheless, many nations continue to possess vast stockpiles in preparation for wartime, despite the fact that chemical weapons are prohibited under international humanitarian law.

2 ➡ The use of chemical weapons reaches back to the distant past. However, in the Industrial age, the modern conception of chemical warfare became prevalent. Many nations have backed scientists who have proposed the implementation of asphyxiating poisonous gasses. The remainder of nations have become so alarmed that multiple international treaties have passed banning chemical weapons. Unfortunately, many of these treaties appeared after the two world wars. In World War I in particular, many nations used chlorine gas, among other chemical weapons, to try to break the trench warfare deadlock. The gases rarely killed people, but they did mutilate or injure them. Experts say 1.3 million gas casualties included up to 260,000 civilian casualties.

1 According to paragraph 1, what best describes chemical warfare?

Ⓐ Weapons of mass destruction that have strong ethical arguments against using them

Ⓑ Weapons of mass destruction that have vast stockpiles

Ⓒ Weapons of mass destruction like nuclear, biological, and radiological

Ⓓ Weapons of mass destruction that have chemical properties

2 The word 'misery' in the passage is closest in meaning to

Ⓐ mistrust

Ⓑ depression

Ⓒ heartache

Ⓓ torment

3 According to paragraph 2, which of the following is NOT true of chemical weapons?

Ⓐ They have been used since ancient times

Ⓑ They rarely kill, but they do wound indiscriminately

Ⓒ They are only chlorine gas

Ⓓ They were used in both world wars

4   According to paragraph 3, all the following are results of World War II chemical warfare EXCEPT:

  Ⓐ The Allies never used them, but the Axis powers did

  Ⓑ World War II wasn't the deadliest use in history

  Ⓒ The Japanese army used them, but only on Asian enemies

  Ⓓ The Nazis used them in their concentration camps

5   Which of the sentences below best expresses the essential information in the highlighted sentence in the passage? Incorrect choices change the meaning in important ways or leave out essential information.

  Ⓐ The United States army used 20,000,000 U.S. gallons of "rainbow herbicides" in Vietnam and the surrounding areas.

  Ⓑ Between 1962 and 1971, the United States army used an insignificant number of chemical agents in Vietnam, eastern Laos, and parts of Cambodia.

  Ⓒ Throughout the Vietnam War, the US military used almost 20,000,000 U.S. gallons of chemical agents in Southeast Asia.

  Ⓓ The United States military used an excess of 20,000,000 U.S. gallons of defoliants in Vietnam, eastern Laos, and parts of Cambodia.

3 ➡ Chemical weapons were used very little during World War II, but both sides were prepared to use them. The Axis powers used them sparingly, and the Allies never brought them out. The Nazis developed them, but they may have feared that the Allies would retaliate with their own chemical weapons because the Allies made wide-ranging plans for defensive, including stockpiling large quantities of chemical warfare agents. In Asia, Japanese forces used them more extensively against their Asian enemies because they also feared Western retaliation. Nevertheless, the Nazis did use Zyklon B and carbon monoxide gas against noncombatants in the Holocaust, resulting in a reported three million deaths. This incident remains the deadliest poison gas use in history.

4 ➡ Between 1962 and 1971 during the Vietnam War, the United States military applied nearly 20,000,000 U.S. gallons of "rainbow herbicides" and defoliants in Vietnam, eastern Laos, and parts of Cambodia. During the Iran–Iraq War, 100,000 Iranian troops were subjects of Iraqi chemical weapons. During the 1988 Halabja chemical attack, Iran used mustard gas and nerve agents on its own people. Organophosphates were used in Angola during the Cuban Intervention. Sarin, chlorine, and mustard gas were used in the Syrian civil war. Terrorists have used chemical weapons in many cases, but most notably in the Tokyo subway sarin attack and the Matsumoto incident.

6   The author mentions "incendiaries" in the passage as an example of which of the following?

  (A) Weapons that don't utilize chemistry

  (B) Weapons that rarely kill people

  (C) Weapons that harm specific targets

  (D) Weapons that catch things aflame

7   In the paragraph below, there is a missing sentence. Look at the paragraph and indicate (A, B, C and D) where the following sentence could be added to the passage.

Chemical weapons cause terrible harm indiscriminately.

Where would the sentence best fit?

  (A)   (B)   (C)   (D)

5 ➡ **(A)** They injure and kill combatants and civilians alike in a silent manner. The use of weaponized chemicals requires chemistry knowledge. Chemists have created explosives, defoliants, incendiaries, and chemicals that assault the skin and lungs. **(B)** They have helped to invent technologies to deploy these chemicals. They have also created the industries that produce these chemicals. **(C)** Therefore, chemists, people funding the chemical profession, and the chemical industry are responsible. **(D)** If they vowed not to participate in such activities perhaps the international community could outlaw these heinous weapons of war permanently.

8   Why does the author mention 'political pressures' in the passage?

    Ⓐ To demonstrate that chemists and scientists have demands placed on them by society

    Ⓑ To show the codes of ethics and conduct

    Ⓒ To emphasize the heinous nature of chemical warfare

    Ⓓ To compare chemical warfare with traditional warfare

9   According to paragraph 6, what can be inferred about chemists' and scientists' responsibilities?

    Ⓐ Chemists and scientists have little moral obligation for the current technology and development of weapons.

    Ⓑ Chemists and scientists must be legally responsible for the damages caused by the invention of chemical weapons.

    Ⓒ More responsibility regarding codes of conduct is now being placed on international community and organizations.

    Ⓓ Chemists and scientists are not alone in being responsible for resolving ethical issues behind chemical weapons.

6 ➡ Sadly, many scientists and chemists become entangled in political pressures, economic interests, and professional ambition, but are they free of responsibility from their inventions? Awareness of this problem has grown amongst professional chemistry communities, and many organizations have issued codes of ethics and conduct. With transparency, the professionals active in chemistry and the associated sciences must build trust within the international community. Illustrating responsible scientific practices and safeguarding ethical norms and humane tenets must be the foundation on which chemists and scientists can show their responsibility. Human rights should be the focus of this quest to eradicate the way of thinking that led to the first two world wars, and the atrocities associated with them. An international discussion should be maintained and encouraged, so that chemists and scientists are held responsible for their creations.

10 **Directions**: An introductory sentence for a brief summary of the passage is provided below. Complete the summary by choosing the THREE answer choices that express the most important ideas in the passage. Some sentences do not belong in the summary because they express ideas that are not presented in the passage or are minor ideas in the passage.

Drag your answer choices to the spaces where they belong. To remove an answer choice, click on it. To review the passage, click on **VIEW TEXT**.

Since their creation, chemical weapons have been regarded as highly contentious and extremely unethical.

-
-
-

ANSWER CHOICES

A Chemical warfare uses the toxic properties of chemical substances as weapons of mass destruction to inflict controversial mayhem on societies.

B Chemical weapons were divisively used in both World War I and World War II to maim, injure, or disfigure soldiers.

C In order to make transparent ethical standards, chemists and scientists need to be more responsible when inventing new weapons.

D The Nazis used chemical weapons during the Holocaust, and its impact was soon spread to Asia, including Vietnam, eastern Laos and Cambodia.

E Chemists are not only solely responsible for inventing chemical weapons, but also for spreading knowledge about the weapons and industries associated with them.

F The Organization for the Prohibition of Chemical Weapons (OPCW) has helped create ethical standards.

Alchemy

Alchemy is the precursor of chemistry. It is also considered a branch of natural philosophy and a proto-scientific tradition. Alchemy has been practiced throughout Europe, Africa, China and throughout Asia with mysterious origins. In the East, first mentions of alchemy originate from 73 to 49 BC China. In the West, its origins indicate Greco-Roman Egypt in the first few centuries CE, but evidence exists that the art goes further back into ancient Egypt. In fact, the Greek word for "the Black Land" is Khemia, which refers to the flood plains around the fertile Nile. The Egyptians believed in an immortal afterlife, and their mummification procedures have said to give rise to rudimentary chemical knowledge. The Arabs occupied Egypt in the 7th Century, and they added "al" which resulted in the word "alchemy."

In 332 BC, Alexander the Great conquered Egypt. As a result, Greek philosophers became interested in Egyptian knowledge. According to Aristotelian philosophy, alchemists played an important role in early chemistry and medicine. Islamic and European alchemical practitioners invented the basic laboratory methods, theory, vocabulary, and experimental methods which many scientists still use today. The alchemists guarded their knowledge in ciphers and perplexing symbolism because they posed a threat to the control of precious metals, and so nobody could decipher the information. Besides the scientific discoveries, they also focused on magic, mythology, and religion with the intention to purify, mature, and perfect certain materials.

The most important goal of alchemy was transmutation. In most cases this included the changing of "base metals" (typically lead) into "noble metals" (usually gold), sometimes referred to as chrysopoeia. Secondary aims included the formulation of the elixir of immortality, the invention of medicines that can cure any disease, and the development of a universal solvent (the alkahest). The final ambition was the perfection of the human body and soul through the achievement of gnosis. All these ambitions were connected to a venture they called the "philosopher's stone" or "magnum opus," and it was the primary aim of transmutation.

All these aims were achieved through the understanding of an elemental system which sometimes translated into chemical properties. The Arabic world used eight elements that originated with the court alchemist Jabir ibn Hayyan. These included the five classical elements (aether, air, earth, fire, and water) plus three other chemical elements: sulphur, mercury, and salt. Western alchemists—including the father of modern medicine Paracelsus—used this understanding for advances in medicine, metallurgy, and even astronomy, and Asian alchemists even invented gunpowder and fireworks based off this system.

Alchemical philosophy proved important to the formulation of theory of gravity by Sir Isaac Newton. But by the 18th century, modern chemistry pushed alchemy to the fringes by separating religion and spirituality from the empirical framework based on the scientific method. In the past, alchemy meant "gold making", which led to the alchemists being labeled as charlatans who dealt with superstitious methods of "magic." Despite this, some alchemists still practice today with techniques in traditional medicine, using a combination of pharmacological and spiritual techniques. Alchemical symbolism is even used in modern psychology to represent Carl Jung's collective unconscious of the West. Even secret societies like the Freemasons and Rosicrucians use alchemical symbolism.

The important contributions made by the alchemists are innumerable. Advances in metalworking, refining, gunpowder production, ceramic and glass making, inks, dyes, paints, cosmetics, extracts, and liquors were due to alchemists and their ideas. They were the first to invent periodic tables, introduce the distillation process, and extricate metals from ores - which led to the invention of high carbon steel and many alloys. They created many inorganic acids and bases and are also responsible for the preparations of hydrochloric acid, tin tetrachloride, ammonium sulfate, and aqua regia (royal water).

The prolongation of life and the transmutation of base metals into gold were the goals of alchemy, but neither has been accomplished in the modern world, unless one considers the consequences of modern chemotherapy or the cyclotron (a particle accelerator invented by Ernest O. Lawrence). Modern scholars still like to divide alchemy between its practical scientific applications and its esoteric spiritual characteristics, but many scholars think they should be understood as complementary. Still, some consider alchemy the precursor of the physical sciences and chemistry devoid of the philosophical and religious contexts attributed to the art.

REVIEW

HELP

BACK

NEXT

HIDE TIME 00:54:00

Beginning

1   According to paragraph 1, what does the author imply about alchemy?

    (A) Alchemy is believed to originate in the West

    (B) Alchemy is an ancient practice

    (C) Alchemy started in ancient Egypt

    (D) Alchemy is the same as chemistry

2   The word 'rudimentary' in the passage is closest in meaning to

    (A) rude

    (B) raw

    (C) basic

    (D) uncomplicated

3   According to paragraph 2, which of the following is NOT true of the alchemists?

    (A) They used complicated encryptions to keep their discoveries secret

    (B) They were integral to the advancement of chemistry and medicine

    (C) They wanted to forbid kings and queens from practicing it

    (D) They devised basic laboratories and created the methods associated with them

Alchemy

1 ➡ Alchemy is the precursor of chemistry. It is also considered a branch of natural philosophy and a proto-scientific tradition. Alchemy has been practiced throughout Europe, Africa, China and throughout Asia with mysterious origins. In the East, first mentions of alchemy originate from 73 to 49 BC China. In the West, its origins indicate Greco-Roman Egypt in the first few centuries CE, but evidence exists that the art goes further back into ancient Egypt. In fact, the Greek word for "the Black Land" is *Khemia*, which refers to the flood plains around the fertile Nile. The Egyptians believed in an immortal afterlife, and their mummification procedures have said to give rise to rudimentary chemical knowledge. The Arabs occupied Egypt in the 7th Century, and they added "al" which resulted in the word "alchemy."

2 ➡ In 332 BC, Alexander the Great conquered Egypt. As a result, Greek philosophers became interested in Egyptian knowledge. According to Aristotelian philosophy, alchemists played an important role in early chemistry and medicine. Islamic and European alchemical practitioners invented the basic laboratory methods, theory, vocabulary, and experimental methods which many scientists still use today. The alchemists guarded their knowledge in ciphers and perplexing symbolism because they posed a threat to the control of precious metals, and so nobody could decipher the information. Besides the scientific discoveries, they also focused on magic, mythology, and religion with the intention to purify, mature, and perfect certain materials.

More Available

4   According to paragraph 3, which of the following is true?

    Ⓐ Metals can be turned into medicines

    Ⓑ Transmutation involved transforming basic metals to valuable ones

    Ⓒ The elixir of immortality would change into the universal solvent

    Ⓓ The philosopher's stone turned into the magnum opus

3 ➡ The most important goal of alchemy was transmutation. In most cases this included the changing of "base metals" (typically lead) into "noble metals" (usually gold), sometimes referred to as chrysopoeia. Secondary aims included the formulation of the elixir of immortality, the invention of medicines that can cure any disease, and the development of a universal solvent (the alkahest). The final ambition was the perfection of the human body and soul through the achievement of gnosis. All these ambitions were connected to a venture they called the "philosopher's stone" or "magnum opus," and it was the primary aim of transmutation.

5 According to paragraph 4, what impact did Arab's understanding of elemental system have on other parts of the world?

   Ⓐ It facilitated a better understanding of medicinal knowledge for Western alchemists.

   Ⓑ It was sometimes dismissed by Asian alchemists who preferred different elemental systems.

   Ⓒ It was spread over different parts of the world thanks to chemist Jabir ibn Hayyan.

   Ⓓ It was highly celebrated in Asia for generating gunpowder and fireworks.

6 Which of the sentences below best expresses the essential information in the highlighted sentence in the passage? Incorrect choices change the meaning in important ways or leave out essential information.

   Ⓐ Western and Asian alchemists invented gunpowder and fireworks based on the alchemical system of medicine, metallurgy, and astronomy.

   Ⓑ The father of modern medicine Paracelsus created gunpowder based on his understanding of medicine, metallurgy, and astronomy.

   Ⓒ Western alchemists advanced medicine, metallurgy, and astronomy as Asian alchemists invented gunpowder.

   Ⓓ Alchemists like Paracelsus used their knowledge for advances in science, and inventions like gunpowder and fireworks were created because of their system.

4 ➡ All these aims were achieved through the understanding of an elemental system which sometimes translated into chemical properties. The Arabic world used eight elements that originated with the court alchemist Jabir ibn Hayyan. These included the five classical elements (aether, air, earth, fire, and water) plus three other chemical elements: sulphur, mercury, and salt. Western alchemists— including the father of modern medicine Paracelsus—used this understanding for advances in medicine, metallurgy, and even astronomy, and Asian alchemists even invented gunpowder and fireworks based off this system.

REVIEW HELP BACK NEXT

HIDE TIME 00:54:00

More Available ▲

7 In the paragraph below, there is a missing sentence. Look at the paragraph and indicate (A, B, C and D) where the following sentence could be added to the passage.

Some alchemists were put to death for their research.

Where would the sentence best fit?

Ⓐ   Ⓑ   Ⓒ   Ⓓ

8 Why does the author mention 'innumerable' in the passage?

Ⓐ To demonstrate that the alchemists were busy

Ⓑ To show that the alchemists were important

Ⓒ To emphasize that the alchemists made countless beneficial discoveries

Ⓓ To compare the different alchemical inventions

5 ➡ Alchemical philosophy proved important to the formulation of theory of gravity by Sir Isaac Newton. **(A)** But by the 18th century, modern chemistry pushed alchemy to the fringes by separating religion and spirituality from the empirical framework based on the scientific method. **(B)** In the past, alchemy meant "gold making", which led to the alchemists being labeled as charlatans who dealt with superstitious methods of "magic." **(C)** Despite this, some alchemists still practice today with techniques in traditional medicine, using a combination of pharmacological and spiritual techniques. **(D)** Alchemical symbolism is even used in modern psychology to represent Carl Jung's collective unconscious of the West. Even secret societies like the Freemasons and Rosicrucians use alchemical symbolism.

6 ➡ The important contributions made by the alchemists are innumerable. Advances in metalworking, refining, gunpowder production, ceramic and glass making, inks, dyes, paints, cosmetics, extracts, and liquors were due to alchemists and their ideas. They were the first to invent periodic tables, introduce the distillation process, and extricate metals from ores - which led to the invention of high carbon steel and many alloys. They created many inorganic acids and bases and are also responsible for the preparations of hydrochloric acid, tin tetrachloride, ammonium sulfate, and aqua regia (royal water).

9 In context of the passage, what function does paragraph 7 serve as a whole?

(A) Paragraph 7 summarizes the main points made in earlier paragraphs.

(B) Paragraph 7 portrays the different evaluations scholars have about alchemy.

(C) Paragraph 7 criticizes alchemists for failing to achieve their goal of transmutation.

(D) Paragraph 7 counters the claim that alchemy has been a successful scientific aspiration for a long time.

7 ➡ The prolongation of life and the transmutation of base metals into gold were the goals of alchemy, but neither has been accomplished in the modern world, unless one considers the consequences of modern chemotherapy or the cyclotron (a particle accelerator invented by Ernest O. Lawrence). Modern scholars still like to divide alchemy between its practical scientific applications and its esoteric spiritual characteristics, but many scholars think they should be understood as complementary. Still, some consider alchemy the precursor of the physical sciences and chemistry devoid of the philosophical and religious contexts attributed to the art.

10 **Directions**: An introductory sentence for a brief summary of the passage is provided below. Complete the summary by choosing the THREE answer choices that express the most important ideas in the passage. Some sentences do not belong in the summary because they express ideas that are not presented in the passage or are minor ideas in the passage.

Drag your answer choices to the spaces where they belong. To remove an answer choice, click on it. To review the passage, click on **VIEW TEXT**.

In summary, alchemy has a rich history with many interesting discoveries associated with it.

-
-
-

ANSWER CHOICES

A   Alchemy is the predecessor to chemistry with roots in Ancient Egypt, and it played an important role in early chemistry and medicine by introducing basic laboratory methods, theory, and vocabulary still used in the present day.

B   Alchemists took on various roles important to chemistry and medicine, but since they knew the risks to the control of precious metals, alchemists encrypted their knowledge.

C   Sir Isaac Newton was an alchemist who invented the theory of gravity and went on to become one of the most coveted scientists in modern history.

D   Alchemy is used in modern psychology but also has practical applications in science and spirituality.

E   There were eight elements in the Arabic elemental system, including sulphur, mercury, and salt

F   Many scientific discoveries in metalworking, refining, and distilling have been attributed to the alchemists, despite modern science often dismissing their contributions.

The Periodic Table

Some would say it is in the nature of scientists to seek to organize and structure the world around them. In a sense, this is what the Periodic Table represents. It is an attempt to categorize the known chemical elements according to a logical system and according to how they relate to each other. Antoine Lavoisier is credited with having produced the first chemistry textbook, Traité élémentaire de chimie, in 1789. In it, he explained how elements could not be broken down any further by any known process and how chemical compounds are formed from elements. Crucially to the development of the Periodic Table, Lavoisier grouped the known elements into four categories; gases, metals, nonmetals, and earths.

The next important step in the development of the table was The Law of Triads, as observed by Johann Wolfgang Döbereiner in 1829. This was not truly a law, because it did not apply universally to all of the chemical elements. Döbereiner discovered that many of the chemicals could be put into groups of three according to their chemical make-up. He also noticed that the atomic weight of the second element was generally equal to the average of the first and third. Döbereiner's work formed the foundation for the organization of the Periodic Table.

Atomic weight, or atomic mass, is the mass of an atom, which is made up of protons, neutrons, electrons, and binding energy. Valency is the term used to describe how an element can bind with another element when forming a chemical compound. Both of these measurements were critical in helping scientists understand how different chemical elements relate to each other. They also helped scientists to predict whether there was a missing element on the Periodic Table, or to confirm an element's position once placed.

In 1862, French geologist Alexandre-Émile Béguyer de Chancourtois was the first to organize the elements according to their atomic weight. This would eventually lead to the Law of Octaves. Just as with an octave in a piece of music, John Newlands discovered that every eighth element was similar to the first when they were plotted from lightest atomic weight to heaviest. These advances in understanding, along with all of those that came before, would lead to the publication of two periodic tables by the two men most associated with its development, Dimitri Mendeleev and Julius Lothar Meyer.

The two men published their versions of the Periodic Table just a year apart: Mendeleev in 1869 and Meyer in 1870. Both tables used atomic weight to structure the position of the elements, and both started a new row or column according to when characteristics started to repeat themselves, as per the Law of Octaves. Posterity has tended to credit Mendeleev with publishing the first comprehensive Periodic Table and there are several factors which might explain why. Firstly, his was published first. Secondly, Mendeleev's table left spaces for elements which had not yet been discovered but must exist, according to the atomic weight and valency of the chemical elements around them. Finally, Mendeleev did not order his table exclusively according to atomic weight but would sometimes reorder elements to group them more elegantly.

The Periodic Table that most people are familiar with and that has become the standard was devised by Horace Groves Deming in 1923. His version of the Periodic Table was printed and widely distributed throughout the United States and the rest of the world. There are inevitably variations on this standard form, including a spiral Periodic Table created by Theodor Benfey. It is important to remember too that Mendeleev's table approaches the elements from the point of view of a chemist, but other tables exist which place elements as they interact according to a more physics-based approach. Either way, new chemical elements have been discovered as recently as 2016, so it is unlikely that the Periodic Table has reached its final form

1 Which of the following best expresses the essential information in the highlighted sentence in paragraph 1? Incorrect choices change the meaning in important ways or leave out essential information.

  Ⓐ The Periodic Table is used for recording all the known elements in the universe.

  Ⓑ Chemical elements change depending on how they are placed on the Periodic Table.

  Ⓒ Each element on the Periodic Table is divided into several categories.

  Ⓓ The Periodic Table is organized logically, and each element has its place based on the position of those around it.

2 According to paragraph 1, which of the following is true of Antoine Lavoisier?

  Ⓐ He discovered how elements are created from chemical compounds.

  Ⓑ His research was very important in the creation of the Periodic Table.

  Ⓒ Lavoisier observed how the world was structured by using the Periodic Table.

  Ⓓ In his book, he discovered four metals, gases, earths, and nonmetals.

3 According to paragraph 2, which of the following is NOT true of The Law of Triads?

  Ⓐ Elements can always be put in groups of three according to their chemical structure.

  Ⓑ It states that the average weight of the 1st and 3rd elements is equal to the 2nd.

  Ⓒ It could not be applied universally to all elements.

  Ⓓ The Law of Triads helped later scientists to construct the Periodic Table.

The Periodic Table

1 ➡ Some would say it is in the nature of scientists to seek to organize and structure the world around them. In a sense, this is what the Periodic Table represents. It is an attempt to categorize the known chemical elements according to a logical system and according to how they relate to each other. Antoine Lavoisier is credited with having produced the first chemistry textbook, Traité élémentaire de chimie, in 1789. In it, he explained how elements could not be broken down any further by any known process and how chemical compounds are formed from elements. Crucially to the development of the Periodic Table, Lavoisier grouped the known elements into four categories: gases, metals, nonmetals, and earths.

2 ➡ The next important step in the development of the table was The Law of Triads, as observed by Johann Wolfgang Döbereiner in 1829. This was not truly a law, because it did not apply universally to all of the chemical elements. Döbereiner discovered that many of the chemicals could be put into groups of three according to their chemical make-up. He also noticed that the atomic weight of the second element was generally equal to the average of the first and third. Döbereiner's work formed the foundation for the organization of the Periodic Table.

4   According to paragraph 3, why does the author mention valency?

   Ⓐ To accurately define what atomic weight is

   Ⓑ To provide context for when energy binding occurs

   Ⓒ To introduce another important factor in understanding the relationship between elements

   Ⓓ To highlight the fact that it played an important role in proving the incomplete nature of the Periodic Table.

5   In paragraph 4, why does the author mention 'the Law of Octaves'?

   Ⓐ To make a connection between Alexandre-Émile Béguyer de Chancourtois and John Newlands.

   Ⓑ To explain how it would impact the formation of future versions of the Periodic Table.

   Ⓒ To highlight the similarities between musical composition and chemical elements.

   Ⓓ To stress the reason Dimitri Mendeleev came to be so well respected.

3 ➡ Atomic weight, or atomic mass, is the mass of an atom, which is made up of protons, neutrons, electrons, and binding energy. Valency is the term used to describe how an element can bind with another element when forming a chemical compound. Both of these measurements were critical in helping scientists understand how different chemical elements relate to each other. They also helped scientists to predict whether there was a missing element on the Periodic Table, or to confirm an element's position once placed.

4 ➡ In 1862, French geologist Alexandre-Émile Béguyer de Chancourtois was the first to organize the elements according to their atomic weight. This would eventually lead to the Law of Octaves. Just as with an octave in a piece of music, John Newlands discovered that every eighth element was similar to the first when they were plotted from lightest atomic weight to heaviest. These advances in understanding, along with all of those that came before, would lead to the publication of two periodic tables by the two men most associated with its development, Dimitri Mendeleev and Julius Lothar Meyer.

6 Which of the following can be inferred from paragraph 5 about Lothar Meyer?

(A) Meyer's Periodic table was inferior to Mendeleev's in many ways.

(B) Lothar Meyer disliked Mendeleev intensely because of the success of his Periodic Table.

(C) Meyer's Periodic Table did not leave gaps for elements that had not been discovered yet.

(D) Meyer preferred to use valency to position elements on his table.

7 In paragraph 6, there is a missing sentence. Look at the paragraph and indicate (A, B, C and D) where the following sentence could be added to the passage.

He was an American chemist, and although he did not directly alter the Periodic Table, he was responsible for the format used widely today.

Where would the sentence best fit?

(A)   (B)   (C)   (D)

8 The word 'inevitably' in paragraph 6 is closest in meaning to

(A) exactly

(B) uncertainly

(C) unfortunately

(D) undoubtedly

5 ➡ The two men published their versions of the Periodic Table just a year apart: Mendeleev in 1869 and Meyer in 1870. Both tables used atomic weight to structure the position of the elements, and both started a new row or column according to when characteristics started to repeat themselves, as per the Law of Octaves. Posterity has tended to credit Mendeleev with publishing the first comprehensive Periodic Table and there are several factors which might explain why. Firstly, his was published first. Secondly, Mendeleev's table left spaces for elements which had not yet been discovered but must exist, according to the atomic weight and valency of the chemical elements around them. Finally, Mendeleev did not order his table exclusively according to atomic weight but would sometimes reorder elements to group them more elegantly.

6 ➡ **(A)** The Periodic Table that most people are familiar with and that has become the standard was devised by Horace Groves Deming in 1923. **(B)** His version of the Periodic Table was printed and widely distributed throughout the United States and the rest of the world. **(C)** There are inevitably variations on this standard form, including a spiral Periodic Table created by Theodor Benfey. **(D)** It is important to remember too that Mendeleev's table approaches the elements from the point of view of a chemist, but other tables exist which place elements as they interact according to a more physics-based approach. Either way, new chemical elements have been discovered as recently as 2016, so it is unlikely that the Periodic Table has reached its final form.

PASSAGE 3

Q
REVIEW

?
HELP

<
BACK

>
NEXT

HIDE TIME 00:54:00

End

9   Which of the following best captures the
     structure of the passage?

     Ⓐ It chronologically illustrates how
        the period table we know today has
        developed.

     Ⓑ It gives a detailed summary of the
        scientific achievement involved in the
        development of the periodic table.

     Ⓒ It highlights the biographies of the
        scientists decided in the development
        of the periodic table.

     Ⓓ It chronologically develops how the
        limitations in the period table began to
        be mended.

VIEW TEXT

REVIEW

HELP

BACK

NEXT

HIDE TIME 00:54:00

10 Directions: An introductory sentence for a brief summary of the passage is provided below. Complete the summary by choosing the THREE answer choices that express the most important ideas in the passage. Some sentences do not belong in the summary because they express ideas that are not presented in the passage or are minor ideas in the passage.

Drag your answer choices to the spaces where they belong. To remove an answer choice, click on it. To review the passage, click on **VIEW TEXT**.

The modern Periodic Table is a standard sight in most schools, but its creation took at least two centuries and was part of the evolution of chemistry itself.

- •
- •
- •

ANSWER CHOICES

A The Law of Octaves enabled scientists to advance the publication of the Periodic Table.

B The Periodic Table is important to science because it sets out the elements in an organized way.

C With the publication of Mendeleev's table in 1869, the Periodic Table had finished its evolution.

D The nature of the Periodic Table is such that it can predict new elements by the valency and atomic weight of existing chemical elements.

E The development of the Periodic Table owes a lot to the genius and vision of Horace Groves Deming.

F The Law of Triads played an important role in further understanding the nature of elements, such as their grouping of three and weight.

TOEFL

Reading

Actual Test

Actual Test
Biology

The Founder Effect

Genes are ribbons of DNA that determine our traits. They are not fixed. Genes often mutate and can take several different forms, known as alleles. An often-cited example of this variation is that of eye color. Humans have a particular gene that determines eye color, but it is the variant of the gene, the allele, that determines what color the eye will be. This expression of a particular trait is known as a phenotype - an outwardly expressed, physical characteristic. Phenotypes visible to the average human come in the form of hair styles and eye color. The genetic code which determines these physical traits is known as the genotype.

Each individual gene consists of two alleles, one inherited from the mother, and one inherited from the father. These alleles can either be dominant or recessive. There will not necessarily be one dominant and one recessive allele for each gene. Recessive alleles only reveal themselves when two are present simultaneously. The Founder Effect refers to the decrease in genetic variance that takes place when a new colony is established by a very small population from a larger, parent population. This decrease in genetic variation can lead to the new population appearing distinctively different from the parent population. These differences are manifested both phenotypically and genotypically. It is theorized that in some cases, these differences could lead to speciation and ultimately the evolution of a new species.

Speciation was first used to describe the process through which species evolve by Orator F. Cook, and Charles Darwin expanded on it in his 1859 magnum opus – On the Origin of Species. Specifically, it is peripatric speciation that mimics the Founder Effect. Peripatric speciation is what can happen when a smaller element of a larger population finds itself isolated and ceases to share genetic materials with its parent population. This isolation can often happen as a result of a bottleneck, when the size of a population is drastically reduced. This reduction is caused by external events such as famine, floods and drought. A bottleneck can also be caused by the population itself. Examples of this are genocide or human population planning.

By their very geography, islands have proved to be fertile grounds for scientists to

research the Founder Effect among flora and fauna. In particular, it is useful to observe the effect in places that have not been colonized before. Krakatoa is a good example of this kind of island. It was completely emptied of life after the eruption of 1883. Most of the island collapsed into the ocean, but what remained has been instrumental in understanding founder populations. Sometimes, scientists will introduce or re-introduce a species to an area in order to study its effects over a long period of time. However, this is not without controversy, as some believe it is not their place to 'play God' in such a manner.

A good example of this is to be found among the Amish populations in the United States. Genetic disorders, particularly among more isolated communities of Amish, are found at a higher rate than among the population at large. Some of these disorders include Dwarfism, where the individual concerned is much smaller than the average for their species. Angelman's Syndrome, which is characterized by a very small head and severe learning difficulties, is another common disorder. However, it should also be noted that the Amish population of Ohio suffer lower rates of cancer, thought to be a result of their healthier lifestyles, but according to researchers at The Ohio State University Comprehensive Cancer Center it may also be as a result of their genetic make-up.

There is a special type of Founder Effect known as a Serial Founder Effect. It occurs where human populations migrate over very great distances. The typical pattern for this kind of movement is characterized by periods of movement followed by periods of settlement. As the population moves on, it leaves behind less genetic diversity in the smaller population it leaves behind. This Serial Founder Effect is thought to have been at play during the first human migrations out of Africa.

The Founder Effect

1 ➡ Genes are ribbons of DNA that determine our traits. They are not fixed. Genes often mutate and can take several different forms, known as alleles. An often-cited example of this variation is that of eye color. Humans have a particular gene that determines eye color, but it is the variant of the gene, the allele, that determines what color the eye will be. This expression of a particular trait is known as a phenotype - an outwardly expressed, physical characteristic. Phenotypes visible to the average human come in the form of hair styles and eye color. The genetic code which determines these physical traits is known as the genotype.

2 ➡ Each individual gene consists of two alleles, one inherited from the mother, and one inherited from the father. These alleles can either be dominant or recessive. There will not necessarily be one dominant and one recessive allele for each gene. Recessive alleles only reveal themselves when two are present simultaneously. The Founder Effect refers to the decrease in genetic variance that takes place when a new colony is established by a very small population from a larger, parent population. This decrease in genetic variation can lead to the new population appearing distinctively different from the parent population. These differences are manifested both phenotypically and genotypically.
It is theorized that in some cases, these differences could lead to speciation and ultimately the evolution of a new species.

---

1 Which of the following best expresses the essential information in the highlighted sentence in paragraph 1? Incorrect choices change the meaning in important ways or leave out essential information.

(A) An allele is a variant of a gene, and it is responsible for eye color.

(B) Alleles are in fact mutations of an existing gene.

(C) All human beings are born with genes, and they are instrumental in deciding eye color.

(D) All of the genes in an individual are responsible for their eye color.

2 In paragraph 1, 'phenotype' is described as

(A) A type of gene that can mutate.

(B) An internal trait, responsible for deciding hair and eye color.

(C) External variations of a gene, visible to the human eye.

(D) The physical characteristics of an individual, determined by the genotype.

3 In paragraph 2, all of the following are true of the Founder Effect EXCEPT

(A) It could lead to the eventual evolution of a species.

(B) It essentially describes how small, cut off populations lack the genetic diversity of the larger population they have left.

(C) The Founder Effect manifested outwardly, in the phenotypical traits of the individual.

(D) Speciation is a result of The Founder Effect and is basically the differences in genetic material between two populations.

4 The word 'ceases' in paragraph 3 is closest in meaning to

Ⓐ stops

Ⓑ continues

Ⓒ start

Ⓓ stands

5 In paragraph 3, all of the following are true EXCEPT…

Ⓐ Peripatric speculation occurs as a result of the number of a particular species decreases radically.

Ⓑ Environmental disasters are a common cause for reductions in population density.

Ⓒ The evolution of species directly correlates to the number of shared genetic materials it has with the larger population.

Ⓓ Human intervention can lead directly to Peripatric speculation.

6 In paragraph 4, what can be implied about scientists?

Ⓐ At times, they manipulate environments in their research.

Ⓑ They are responsible for the lack of flora and fauna on some islands.

Ⓒ They are trying to repopulate species in areas where they are extinct.

Ⓓ They hope to study volcanic eruptions in pursuit of understanding The Founder Effect.

3 ➡ Speciation was first used to describe the process through which species evolve by Orator F. Cook, and Charles Darwin expanded on it in his 1859 magnum opus – *On the Origin of Species*. Specifically, it is *peripatric speciation* that mimics the Founder Effect. Peripatric speciation is what can happen when a smaller element of a larger population finds itself isolated and ceases to share genetic materials with its parent population. This isolation can often happen as a result of a bottleneck, when the size of a population is drastically reduced. This reduction is caused by external events such as famine, floods and drought. A bottleneck can also be caused by the population itself. Examples of this are genocide or human population planning.

4 ➡ By their very geography, islands have proved to be fertile grounds for scientists to research the Founder Effect among flora and fauna. In particular, it is useful to observe the effect in places that have not been colonized before. Krakatoa is a good example of this kind of island. It was completely emptied of life after the eruption of 1883. Most of the island collapsed into the ocean, but what remained has been instrumental in understanding founder populations. Sometimes, scientists will introduce or re-introduce a species to an area in order to study its effects over a long period of time. However, this is not without controversy, as some believe it is not their place to 'play God' in such a manner.

7   The author discusses some genetic disorders in paragraph 5 in order to
    Ⓐ Reinforce the fact that The Founder Effect could be a factor in these occurrences.
    Ⓑ Demonstrate how isolated the Amish communities are from the rest of the United States.
    Ⓒ Highlight a correlation between the genes of the Amishpopulation and a reduced risk of cancer.
    Ⓓ Inform us how the general population has a different genetic make-up to the Amish.

8   In paragraph 6, what can you infer about the first human migrations out of Africa?
    Ⓐ The people who initially migrated out of Africa showed signs of The Serial Founder Effect.
    Ⓑ The Serial Founder Effect played a role in why early humans decided to migrate.
    Ⓒ Those who left Africa in the early waves of migration had less genetic diversity than those who came later.
    Ⓓ It is reasonable to assume that genetic diversity among those who left Africa lessens the further away one travels, according to the Serial Founder Effect.

9   Look at the four places (A, B, C, D) that indicate where the following sentence could be added to paragraph 6.

    Additionally, African populations have been shown to possess the highest genetic diversity on Earth.

    Where would it best fit?

    Ⓐ   Ⓑ   Ⓒ   Ⓓ

5 ➡ A good example of this is to be found among the Amish populations in the United States. Genetic disorders, particularly among more isolated communities of Amish, are found at a higher rate than among the population at large. Some of these disorders include Dwarfism, where the individual concerned is much smaller than the average for their species. Angelman's Syndrome, which is characterized by a very small head and severe learning difficulties, is another common disorder. However, it should also be noted that the Amish population of Ohio suffers lower rates of cancer, thought to be a result of their healthier lifestyles, but according to researchers at The Ohio State University Comprehensive Cancer Center it may also be as a result of their genetic make-up.

6 ➡ **(A)** There is a special type of Founder Effect known as a Serial Founder Effect. It occurs where human populations migrate over very great distances. **(B)** The typical pattern for this kind of movement is characterized by periods of movement followed by periods of settlement. **(C)** As the population moves on, it leaves behind less genetic diversity in the smaller population it leaves behind. This Serial Founder Effect is thought to have been at play during the first human migrations out of Africa. **(D)**

10 **Directions**: The sentence below is an introductory sentence for a brief summary of the passage. Select THREE answer choices from the chart that represent important ideas in the passage. Some sentences are incorrect because they contain information that was not in the passage or contain information that is a minor detail.

Drag your answer choices to the spaces where they belong. To remove an answer choice, click on it. To review the passage, click on **VIEW TEXT**.

The Founder Effect is a special case of genetic drift, that involves the establishment of a new colony.

-
-
-

ANSWER CHOICES

A. Charles Darwin has become synonymous with his groundbreaking work, On the Origin of Species.

B. The Founder Effect could be a factor in the process through which new species evolve.

C. Genetic drift can be described as the change in frequency of a particular gene among a population.

D. The jar of marbles analogy is useful for explaining genetic drift.

E. It is often founded by very small, isolated populations who breed within their own social group

F. Genetic disorders are a common consequence, particularly among more isolated communities of Amish.

The Paleolithic Diet

The Paleolithic Diet, also known as the Paleo Diet, Caveman Diet, or Stone-age Diet, is an eating plan based on food choices similar to those consumed during the Paleolithic era (2.5 million to 10,000 years ago). Historically, the location of humans made the diets vary from region to region. Different variants of the diet exist; some rely on a plant-based diet, but many favor animal products. The diet usually includes hunter/gatherer food like lean meats, fish, fruits, vegetables, nuts, and seeds. The Paleo Diet limits foods that were produced on a farm including dairy products, legumes, and grains. Those who champion the Paleo diet claim this approach decreases the risk of chronic diet-related diseases and improves human performance.

The food intake of Paleolithic humans contained no dairy products and was high in grass-fed game protein from hunting and fishing. It was high in wild fruits, vegetables, and fungi, and low in starches and grains. Honey and fruits provided natural forms of sugar. According to many biologists, this nutrition most closely matches human biologic design because the human genome developed on this high-protein diet; our genes determine nutritional needs and were shaped by the environmental pressures of the Paleolithic environment. However, some experts argue against the Paleo nutrition theory. They postulate that the human genome has evolved rapidly since the Paleolithic era. They add that it is nearly impossible to reproduce a Paleo diet in the modern era. Hunter-gatherer populations also seemed to have poor health status.

Many people claim that the Paleo Diet helps manage or prevent their health problems ranging from auto-immune conditions like inflammatory bowel disease (IBD) and diabetes to anxiety, thyroid problems, poor digestion, and infertility. The diet is said to aid in treating with psoriasis, Hashimoto's thyroiditis, celiac, lupus, multiple sclerosis, chronic fatigue, fibromyalgia, Crohn's, ulcerative colitis, Alzheimer's, Parkinson's, obesity, and other health conditions. Also, those with blood sugar regulation and weight loss issues do well on the Paleo Diet. The Paleo Diet is also high in antioxidants, so it is said to fight and stave off disease.

Paleo Diet benefits include its high quantities of fruits and vegetables, which add antioxidants to the diet. This adds probiotics, giving the healthy bacteria in your gut a chance to flourish. The meal plan is also purported to increase and maintain more stable energy levels. It can improve sleep conditions. It also results in clearer skin, healthier looking hair, and increased mental clarity – leading to productivity and increased study. It is also said to decrease symptoms of depression or nervousness. It can also decrease bloating and gas. Eliminating sugar, processed foods, and unhealthy fats removes the sources of stress and inflammation from the digestive tract. Participants also claim sustained weight loss. Because of higher energy levels, experts believe that this inspires people to exercise more and the health benefits multiply.

Nevertheless, the Paleo Diet has drawbacks. Eliminating entire food groups restricts variety and makes eating a balanced diet difficult. Nutrient-dense and energy-providing foods to avoid on the diet include dairy products, oats, wheat, corn, rice, quinoa, soybeans, peanuts, lentils, potatoes, and chickpeas. Most low-cost food has at least one of these components, so the Paleo Diet is likely to be hard on one's budget. According to several clinical studies, the Paleo Diet is nutritionally insufficient in calcium, iron, and dietary fiber. Additionally, the longest living people in the world typically do not consume the Paleo Diet. Instead, they intake meat infrequently, and the basis of their diet consists of cereal grain or starch forms.

In some longitudinal experiments, Paleo Diet groups had significant improvements in glucose tolerance. Their systolic blood pressure went down temporarily and blood sugar levels decreased. HDL (good) cholesterol levels rose and LDL (bad) cholesterol fell – a trend which continue for a few weeks. Triglycerides went down and insulin AUC decreased, though both levels stabilized within a month. Experts reported an average reduction in liver fat of 49%, but with no significant consequence on the muscle cell fat content; the fat content of liver and muscle cells becomes a risk factor for metabolic disease. The diet improved waist circumference and glycemic control, and their body mass index (BMI) decreased.

PASSAGE 2

REVIEW
HELP
BACK
NEXT

HIDE TIME 00:54:00

Beginning

1 According to paragraph 1, what does the author imply about the Paleo Diet?

- (A) It is one of the oldest diets known to humanity
- (B) It is mostly dependent on consuming dairy products.
- (C) It could be a healthy diet choice that might help with illnesses
- (D) It is a vegetarian diet that might help with illnesses

2 The word 'champion' in the passage is closest in meaning to

- (A) address
- (B) accomplish
- (C) advocate
- (D) preach

3 According to paragraph 2, which of the following is NOT true of the Paleo Diet?

- (A) It avoids milk-based products
- (B) Human genes developed on this diet
- (C) Paleolithic peoples had robust health on the diet
- (D) Wild game, fruits, vegetables, and fungi are the preferred dietary choices

The Paleolithic Diet

1 ➡ The Paleolithic Diet, also known as the Paleo Diet, Caveman Diet, or Stone-age Diet, is an eating plan based on food choices similar to those consumed during the Paleolithic era (2.5 million to 10,000 years ago). Historically, the location of humans made the diets vary from region to region. Different variants of the diet exist; some rely on a plant-based diet, but many favor animal products. The diet usually includes hunter/gatherer food like lean meats, fish, fruits, vegetables, nuts, and seeds. The Paleo Diet limits foods that were produced on a farm including dairy products, legumes, and grains. Those who champion the Paleo diet claim this approach decreases the risk of chronic diet-related diseases and improves human performance.

2 ➡ The food intake of Paleolithic humans contained no dairy products and was high in grass-fed game protein from hunting and fishing. It was high in wild fruits, vegetables, and fungi, and low in starches and grains. Honey and fruits provided natural forms of sugar. According to many biologists, this nutrition most closely matches human biologic design because the human genome developed on this high-protein diet; our genes determine nutritional needs and were shaped by the environmental pressures of the Paleolithic environment. However, some experts argue against the Paleo nutrition theory. They postulate that the human genome has evolved rapidly since the Paleolithic era. They add that it is nearly impossible to reproduce a Paleo diet in the modern era. Hunter-gatherer populations also seemed to have poor health status.

4 According to paragraph 3, which of the following is true of the Paleo Diet?
- (A) It causes auto-immune illnesses among many other disorders
- (B) The diet can help alleviating most of the known diseases.
- (C) The diet controls blood sugar levels and helps with weight loss
- (D) Antioxidants are high due to the diet's capacity to fight all diseases.

5 What is the main purpose of paragraph 4 in the context of the passage?
- (A) It enumerates several physiological and physical advantages of the Paleo Diets.
- (B) It explains why the Paleo Diet involves disproportionately high amounts of fresh produces.
- (C) It defines what the Paleo Diet is and some of the ways it could backfire.
- (D) It explains in detail a few psychological benefits to the Paleo Diet.

6 Which of the sentences below best expresses the essential information in the highlighted sentence in the passage? Incorrect choices change the meaning in important ways or leave out essential information.
- (A) Cutting out sugar and processed foods makes people healthy
- (B) Eating sugar, processed foods, and unhealthy fats can make the digestive tract unhealthy
- (C) If a person eliminates the poor foods from the diet, it will decrease inflammation in the digestive system
- (D) Eliminating stress allows the person to eat more sugar, processed foods, and unhealthy fats

3 ➡ Many people claim that the Paleo Diet helps manage or prevent their health problems ranging from auto-immune conditions like inflammatory bowel disease (IBD) and diabetes to anxiety, thyroid problems, poor digestion, and infertility. The diet is said to aid in treating with psoriasis, Hashimoto's thyroiditis, celiac, lupus, multiple sclerosis, chronic fatigue, fibromyalgia, Crohn's, ulcerative colitis, Alzheimer's, Parkinson's, obesity, and other health conditions. Also, those with blood sugar regulation and weight loss issues do well on the Paleo Diet. The Paleo Diet is also high in antioxidants, so it is said to fight and stave off disease.

4 ➡ Paleo Diet benefits include its high quantities of fruits and vegetables, which add antioxidants to the diet. This adds probiotics, giving the healthy bacteria in your gut a chance to flourish. The meal plan is also purported to increase and maintain more stable energy levels. It can improve sleep conditions. It also results in clearer skin, healthier looking hair, and increased mental clarity – leading to productivity and increased study. It is also said to decrease symptoms of depression or nervousness. It can also decrease bloating and gas. Eliminating sugar, processed foods, and unhealthy fats removes the sources of stress and inflammation from the digestive tract. Participants also claim sustained weight loss. Because of higher energy levels, experts believe that this inspires people to exercise more and the health benefits multiply.

7 According to the author, all of the following are drawbacks of the Paleo diet EXCEPT.

   (A) It lacks the necessary nutritional content for people to maintain a healthy diet.

   (B) It is an expensive diet to maintain compared to other, low-cost diets.

   (C) It relies too heavily on fat-dense foods like peanuts and soybeans to maintain energy levels.

   (D) Because of its lack of plant foods, it does not contain adequate levels of essential dietary fiber.

8 In the paragraph below, there is a missing sentence. Look at the paragraph and indicate (A, B, C and D) where the following sentence could be added to the passage.

This is by-and-large the most recognizable aspect which throws people off starting the diet or maintaining it.

Where would the sentence best fit?

   (A)   (B)   (C)   (D)

9 According to paragraph 6, what can be inferred about the Paleo Diet?

   (A) It may be beneficial for people who are not able to withstand diets heavy in sugars.

   (B) It can help with many kinds of health problems, but it does not help reduce fat levels considerably.

   (C) It is effective when used for short periods of time, but not as a long-term advantage.

   (D) It increases muscle cell fat content in most healthy individuals.

5 Nevertheless, the Paleo Diet has drawbacks. **(A)** Eliminating entire food groups restricts variety and makes eating a balanced diet difficult. Nutrient-dense and energy-providing foods to avoid on the diet include dairy products, oats, wheat, corn, rice, quinoa, soybeans, peanuts, lentils, potatoes, and chickpeas. **(B)** Most low-cost food has at least one of these components, so the Paleo Diet is likely to be hard on one's budget. **(C)** According to several clinical studies, the Paleo Diet is nutritionally insufficient in calcium, iron, and dietary fiber. Additionally, the longest living people in the world typically do not consume the Paleo Diet. Instead, they intake meat infrequently, and the basis of their diet consists of cereal grain or starch forms. **(D)**

6 ➡ In some longitudinal experiments, Paleo Diet groups had significant improvements in glucose tolerance. Their systolic blood pressure went down temporarily and blood sugar levels decreased. HDL (good) cholesterol levels rose and LDL (bad) cholesterol fell – a trend which continue for a few weeks. Triglycerides went down and insulin AUC decreased, though both levels stabilized within a month. Experts reported an average reduction in liver fat of 49%, but with no significant consequence on the muscle cell fat content; the fat content of liver and muscle cells becomes a risk factor for metabolic disease. The diet improved waist circumference and glycemic control, and their body mass index (BMI) decreased.

VIEW TEXT

REVIEW

HELP

BACK

NEXT

HIDE TIME 00:54:00

10 **Directions**: An introductory sentence for a brief summary of the passage is provided below. Complete the summary by choosing the THREE answer choices that express the most important ideas in the passage. Some sentences do not belong in the summary because they express ideas that are not presented in the passage or are minor ideas in the passage.

Drag your answer choices to the spaces where they belong. To remove an answer choice, click on it. To review the passage, click on **VIEW TEXT**.

The Paleo diet is an ancient form of food restriction which decreases the risk of chronic diet-related diseases and increases performance, though there are some drawbacks.

-
-
-

ANSWER CHOICES

A Its positive effects on the reduction of symptoms are well-documented, most notably in chronic conditions and mental health problems.

B It can be used to treat symptoms of depression and is known to increase productivity through improving mental clarity.

C Because it contains many vegetables and fruits, it is high in antioxidants, which makes it better at fending off disease than a balanced diet.

D It helps improves mood and attitude, which make people happier results in the diet being more sustainable for the average person who struggles with dieting.

E The Paleo Diet is nutritionally deficient, and its food restrictions make eating a balanced diet difficult because of the lack of complex carbohydrates.

F Although beneficial, it is recommended people adopt the diet only temporarily, because it is expensive, lacks dietary requirements, and its effects are brief.

Parasites

Parasites live on or in a host organism. These opportunistic organisms get their food from or at the expense of their host. There are three main types of disease-causing parasites that infect humans: helminths, protozoa, and ectoparasites. It is estimated that between 75,000 and 300,000 helminth species exist. There is no credible way of estimating how many parasitic protozoa, fungi, bacteria, and viruses occur. Soil-transmitted helminth parasites infect more than 1.5 billion people worldwide (24% of the world's population). Parasites are fairly easy to acquire and extremely difficult to eliminate from the body.

One of the most plentiful parasites are protozoa. These microscopic, one-celled organisms can thrive outside in nature or inside a host. Inside humans or animals, they multiply at a rapid rate. This contributes to their survival and makes them more than a nuisance. A single organism can cause a serious infection because fecal-oral transmission (contaminated food or water or person-to-person contact) spreads the organism at an exponential rate. Bites from a mosquito or a fly transmit the organism into blood or tissue in animals and humans. Scientists classify these protozoa into four groups based on movement: flagellated protozoans or zooflagellates, amoeboid protozoans or sarcodines, ciliated protozoans or ciliates, and sporozoans.

Helminths are the second type of parasites. These large, multicellular organisms (visible to the naked eye in their adult stages) live free of hosts or are parasitic. Adult helminths cannot multiply in humans. Three main groups of helminths exist in humans. Flatworms (platyhelminths) include the trematodes (flukes) and cestodes (tapeworms). Adult forms of thorny-headed worms (acanthocephalans) reside in the gastrointestinal tract. They are the intermediaries between cestodes and nematodes. Adult forms of roundworms (nematodes) also reside in the gastrointestinal tract, blood, lymphatic system, or subcutaneous tissues. Also, immature (larval) states can infect various body tissues and cause disease.

The third type of parasites are called ectoparasites. These include vampiric arthropods such as mosquitoes (who depend on a blood from a human host). Ticks, mites, fleas, and lice that attach to the body or burrow into the skin, and remain there for relatively long periods

of time, are also classified as ectoparasites. They cause diseases in their own right, but are even more important as vectors, or transmitters, of many pathogens like typhus, various fevers, skin infections, Lyme disease, malaria, West Nile virus, dengue and yellow fever, chikungunya, and various forms of encephalitis.

A human or animal can contract a parasite in many ways. First, a possible host can ingest contaminated food or water. Second, a potential host can acquire a parasite through eating undercooked meat, especially underdone pork or raw fish (sushi). Walking barefoot in the dirt or grass can also cause parasitic infestation. Many parasites can be transmitted through exchange of saliva or through sexual contact. Finally, parasites can even be transmitted through bodily contact like handshakes.

Many symptoms can help identify a possible parasitic infection, especially after international travel. Symptoms of Irritable Bowel Syndrome (IBS) like constipation, diarrhea, gas, or bloating can show evidence of an infection. Nausea is also suspicious. Food poisoning signs, irregular digestion, insomnia, skin irritations or unexplained rashes, hives, rosacea or eczema can all be symptoms. Other symptoms include grinding teeth during sleep, aching muscles or joints, fatigue, exhaustion, mood changes, depression, or feelings of dissatisfaction after meals. If a doctor has diagnosed an iron-deficient anemia or symptoms of other autoimmune diseases, this can be infection from bacteria, virus, or parasites.

Parasites

1 ➡ Parasites live on or in a host organism. These opportunistic organisms get their food from or at the expense of their host. There are three main types of disease-causing parasites that infect humans: helminths, protozoa, and ectoparasites. It is estimated that between 75,000 and 300,000 helminth species exist. There is no credible way of estimating how many parasitic protozoa, fungi, bacteria, and viruses occur. Soil-transmitted helminth parasites infect more than 1.5 billion people worldwide (24% of the world's population). Parasites are fairly easy to acquire and extremely difficult to eliminate from the body.

1   According to paragraph 1, what best describes a parasite?

   (A) An organism that causes disease

   (B) An organism that is difficult to purge from the body

   (C) An organism that gets sustenance by consuming its host

   (D) An organism that is easy to obtain

2   According to paragraph 2, which of the following is NOT true of protozoa?

   (A) They are extremely small, single-celled organisms

   (B) They can cause serious infections in humans or animals

   (C) Some insects can transmit them to other hosts

   (D) They are multicellular organisms visible under a microscope

2 ➡ One of the most plentiful parasites are protozoa. These microscopic, one-celled organisms can thrive outside in nature or inside a host. Inside humans or animals, they multiply at a rapid rate. This contributes to their survival and makes them more than a nuisance. A single organism can cause a serious infection because fecal-oral transmission (contaminated food or water or person-to-person contact) spreads the organism at an exponential rate. Bites from a mosquito or a fly transmit the organism into blood or tissue in animals and humans. Scientists classify these protozoa into four groups based on movement: flagellated protozoans or zooflagellates, amoeboid protozoans or sarcodines, ciliated protozoans or ciliates, and sporozoans.

3   The word 'thrive' in the passage is closest in meaning to

   (A) reproduce

   (B) transcend

   (C) prosper

   (D) survive

4   The author mentions 'tapeworms' in the passage as an example of which of the following?

Ⓐ A type of helminth that is microscopic

Ⓑ A type of helminth in the flatworm family

Ⓒ A type of helminth in the thorny-headed worm family

Ⓓ A type of helminth in the roundworm family

5   What is the main idea of paragraph 4?

Ⓐ It elaborates on the last type of parasite that is mentioned earlier in the passage.

Ⓑ It lists the causes behind parasite-induced diseases.

Ⓒ It provides list of disease that can ectoparasites can cause.

Ⓓ It expands on the idea mentioned in the previous paragraph.

6   Which of the sentences below best expresses the essential information in the highlighted sentence in the passage? Incorrect choices change the meaning in important ways or leave out essential information.

Ⓐ Ectoparasites are vampiric arthropods that attach to the body or dig under the skin until they die.

Ⓑ Ectoparasites are blood-sucking arthropods that attach to the body or dig under the skin and live there for extensive periods.

Ⓒ Ectoparasites are vampiric arthropods that reside in one's skin for long durations of time.

Ⓓ Ectoparasites are blood-sucking arthropods that attach to the body or burrow into the skin, and they are transmitters for disease.

3 ➡ Helminths are the second type of parasites. These large, multicellular organisms (visible to the naked eye in their adult stages) live free of hosts or are parasitic. Adult helminths cannot multiply in humans. Three main groups of helminths exist in humans. Flatworms (platyhelminths) include the trematodes (flukes) and cestodes (tapeworms). Adult forms of thorny-headed worms (acanthocephalans) reside in the gastrointestinal tract. They are the intermediaries between cestodes and nematodes. Adult forms of roundworms (nematodes) also reside in the gastrointestinal tract, blood, lymphatic system, or subcutaneous tissues. Also, immature (larval) states can infect various body tissues and cause disease.

4 ➡ The third type of parasites are called ectoparasites. These include vampiric arthropods such as mosquitoes (who depend on a blood from a human host). Ticks, mites, fleas, and lice that attach to the body or burrow into the skin, and remain there for relatively long periods of time, are also classified as ectoparasites. They cause diseases in their own right, but are even more important as vectors, or transmitters, of many pathogens like typhus, various fevers, skin infections, Lyme disease, malaria, West Nile virus, dengue and yellow fever, chikungunya, and various forms of encephalitis.

7   According to paragraph 3, all the following are results of ways to contract a parasite EXCEPT:

   (A) A human or animal eats contaminated food or drinks contaminated water

   (B) A human or animal crosses an area of ground contaminated by parasites

   (C) A human or animal exchanges saliva or engages in bodily contact

   (D) A human or animal swims in water contaminated with parasites

8   In paragraph 5, there is a missing sentence. Look at the paragraph and indicate (A, B, C and D) where the following sentence could be added to the passage.

   Next, contaminated fruits and vegetables that have not been washed thoroughly can also be problematic.

   Where would the sentence best fit?

   (A)   (B)   (C)   (D)

9   Why does the author mention 'international travel' in the passage?

   (A) To suggest that the best way to be diagnosed with a parasitic infection is to speak to a local doctor in your country of travel.

   (B) To show the symptoms of parasitic infections occur mostly abroad.

   (C) To emphasize that traveling is one of the most common ways to be attacked with a parasite.

   (D) To suggest that people are likely to contract IBS and Nausea after international travel.

5 ⇨ A human or animal can contract a parasite in many ways. **(A)** First, a possible host can ingest contaminated food or water. Second, a potential host can acquire a parasite through eating undercooked meat, especially underdone pork or raw fish (sushi). **(B)** Walking barefoot in the dirt or grass can also cause parasitic infestation. **(C)** Many parasites can be transmitted through exchange of saliva or through sexual contact. Finally, parasites can even be transmitted through bodily contact like handshakes. **(D)**

6 ⇨ Many symptoms can help identify a possible parasitic infection, especially after international travel. Symptoms of Irritable Bowel Syndrome (IBS) like constipation, diarrhea, gas, or bloating can show evidence of an infection. Nausea is also suspicious. Food poisoning signs, irregular digestion, insomnia, skin irritations or unexplained rashes, hives, rosacea or eczema can all be symptoms. Other symptoms include grinding teeth during sleep, aching muscles or joints, fatigue, exhaustion, mood changes, depression, or feelings of dissatisfaction after meals. If a doctor has diagnosed an iron-deficient anemia or symptoms of other autoimmune diseases, this can be infection from bacteria, virus, or parasites.

10 **Directions**: An introductory sentence for a brief summary of the passage is provided below. Complete the summary by choosing the THREE answer choices that express the most important ideas in the passage. Some sentences do not belong in the summary because they express ideas that are not presented in the passage or are minor ideas in the passage.

Drag your answer choices to the spaces where they belong. To remove an answer choice, click on it. To review the passage, click on **VIEW TEXT**.

Parasites are opportunistic organisms which infect up to a quarter of the world's population, with little let-up.

-
-
-

ANSWER CHOICES

A Parasites—protozoa, helminths, and ectoparasites—get their food from or at the expense of their host, and they cause disease.

B Blood or tissue infestations are often transmitted to other humans or animals through the bite of insects

C It is possible to contract a parasite by eating contaminated food or engaging in body contact.

D Ectoparasites attach to the body or burrow into the skin and remain there causing disease.

E There are many different forms of symptoms of parasitic infections, including nausea or meal dissatisfactions.

F International travel is highly discouraged when patients experience symptoms of parasitic infections.

TOEFL

Reading
Actual Test

Actual Test
Geology

Plate Tectonics

Currently, it is almost universally accepted that all of the world's continents were once joined together in a supercontinent that came to be known as Pangaea, and that those continents continued to drift until they found themselves in the location they are at today. However, when this theory was first published by Alfred Wegener in 1912, it was not as readily accepted as it is today. The key observation that Wegener made was in recording how identical plant and animal fossils as well as rock formations were discovered on continents, which today are separated by hundreds of thousands of kilometers. His explanation was that they had evolved during the Paleozoic and early Mesozoic eras, when the continents were in much closer proximity.

While much of his work was accepted by the scientific community, indeed the idea of continental drift was not a completely new concept, Wegener could never satisfactorily explain the mechanical process which led to the drifting of the continents. It was not until later in the century, in the 1950s and 1960s, that evidence was produced for the process of continental drift and the theory of plate tectonics was advanced. A tectonic plate can be simply described as the vast tablets of rock that the continents lie on, and their interaction is known as plate tectonics. These huge tablets of thick rock, known as the upper mantle, along with the crust, form what is known as the lithosphere. This lithosphere 'floats' on the liquid mantle layer known as the asthenosphere.

It was really only when scientists started to map the ocean floor with echosounders and magnetometers that they were able to start explaining why the continents moved. These technologies were developed during World War 2, but they were employed immediately after the end of the War in pursuit of answers. Arguably, the most important discovery they made was the processes at work around mid ocean ridges. Here, divergent plate boundaries overlap and allow mantle to rise to the surface, first as magma and then as lava, as the plate boundaries move away from each other. This lava cools to form oceanic crust and lithosphere, which gradually move away from the oceanic ridge in what is known as sea floor spreading. Another feature of divergent plate-boundaries is known as a rift valley. Rift valleys are lowland faults located between two mountainous areas. These features occur where two tectonic plates are moving away from each other, and in the process, they separate and create these narrow valleys. The best-known example of this on Earth is probably the East African Rift, thought to have begun its development 22-25 million years ago.

As the diameter of the Earth remains constant, it stands to reason that older crust must be destroyed. This process occurs at subduction zones, where plates converge, and one plate is forced under another and is converted into magma. Often, this newly formed magma will erupt to the surface and over time can lead to the formation of volcanoes. At these points, deep ocean trenches are often formed, and violent earthquakes are common. A final type of tectonic activity is known as a transform plate boundary. Here, the two plates slip horizontally past one another. The huge stresses created at these points means that chunks of the Earth's crust can break off, and earthquakes are frequent. A famous example of a transform plate boundary is the San Andreas Fault in California, where the North American and Pacific plates are slowly pushing past each other.

One final point about plate tectonics that has been gaining traction in recent years is that the activity of these gargantuan slabs of solid and molten rock may be partially responsible for the development of life itself. Scientists theorize that the phosphorous contained in the Earth's mantle became concentrated and crystalized as the mantle cooled, due in part to plate tectonics. This refined form of phosphorous is known as apatite. Once the apatite, locked into igneous rock, reached the surface, it began to leach into the ocean waters, where phosphorous dependent primitive life began to thrive. This in turn led the primitive life forms to release oxygen into the atmosphere, helping to create viable circumstances for multi-cellular life.

PASSAGE 1

Q
REVIEW
?
HELP
<
BACK
>
NEXT

HIDE TIME 00:54:00

Beginning ▲

Passage 1 | Plate Tectonics

1 ➡ Currently, it is almost universally accepted that all of the world's continents were once joined together in a supercontinent that came to be known as Pangaea, and that those continents continued to drift until they found themselves in the location they are at today. However, when this theory was first published by Alfred Wegener in 1912, it was not as readily accepted as it is today. The key observation that Wegener made was in recording how identical plant and animal fossils as well as rock formations were discovered on continents, which today are separated by hundreds of thousands of kilometers. His explanation was that they had evolved during the Paleozoic and early Mesozoic eras, when the continents were in much closer proximity.

2 ➡ While much of his work was accepted by the scientific community, indeed the idea of continental drift was not a completely new concept, Wegener could never satisfactorily explain the mechanical process which led to the drifting of the continents. It was not until later in the century, in the 1950s and 1960s, that evidence was produced for the process of continental drift and the theory of plate tectonics was advanced. A tectonic plate can be simply described as the vast tablets of rock that the continents lie on, and their interaction is known as plate tectonics. These huge tablets of thick rock, known as the upper mantle, along with the crust, form what is known as the lithosphere. This lithosphere 'floats' on the liquid mantle layer known as the asthenosphere.

1   Which of the following best expresses the essential information in the highlighted sentence?
  Ⓐ Wegener's main observation was that he managed to study and record identical plant and animal life, as well as rock formations, from one hundred thousand kilometers away.
  Ⓑ Today, the continents are separated by hundreds of thousands of kilometers, which Wegener observed and recorded.
  Ⓒ Wegener noticed and recorded that identical rock formations and plant and animal fossils were found on different continents that are currently far apart from each other.
  Ⓓ Wegener discovered and recorded rock formations and plant and animal fossils from different continents.

2   According to the 1st paragraph, Wegener's explanation for finding the same fossils on different continents was that
  Ⓐ The continents were closer together when these fossils were formed.
  Ⓑ The continents continued drifting until they reached their current position.
  Ⓒ The fossils were formed during the Paleozoic and Mesozoic eras.
  Ⓓ Wegener recorded how identical fossils, as well as rock formations, appeared on different continents.

3   In paragraph 2, all of the following are true of continental drift EXCEPT
  Ⓐ Wegener could never explain the process behind continental drift.
  Ⓑ The idea of continental drift had not been suggested before Wegener.
  Ⓒ Evidence for how continental drift worked was not available in Wegener's time.
  Ⓓ Continental drift relates to the drifting of continents.

4   The word 'employed' in the passage is closest in meaning to:

   (A) hired
   (B) labored
   (C) accepted
   (D) utilized

5   Which of the following is true, according to paragraph 3?

   (A) Scientists' understanding of continental shifts increased with the development of ocean floor mapping technology.
   (B) Floor spreading occurs when cooled lava from plate surface begins to move away from plate boundaries.
   (C) It took more than 20 million years to form the East African Rift.
   (D) Technological development allowed scientists to enhance their knowledge about mid ocean ridges, one of the fundamental findings.

3 ➡ It was really only when scientists started to map the ocean floor with echosounders and magnetometers that they were able to start explaining why the continents moved. These technologies were developed during World War 2, but they were employed immediately after the end of the War in pursuit of answers. Arguably, the most important discovery they made was the processes at work around mid ocean ridges. Here, divergent plate boundaries overlap and allow mantle to rise to the surface, first as magma and then as lava, as the plate boundaries move away from each other. This lava cools to form oceanic crust and lithosphere, which gradually move away from the oceanic ridge in what is known as sea floor spreading. Another feature of divergent plate-boundaries is known as a rift valley. Rift valleys are lowland faults located between two mountainous areas. These features occur where two tectonic plates are moving away from each other, and in the process, they separate and create these narrow valleys. The best-known example of this on Earth is probably the East African Rift, thought to have begun its development 22-25 million years ago.

PASSAGE 1

Q
REVIEW

?
HELP

<
BACK

>
NEXT

HIDE TIME 00:54:00

More Available ▲

6   In paragraph 4, why does the author mention the San Andreas Fault?

　　Ⓐ In order to link transform plate boundaries with subduction zones.

　　Ⓑ To explain why earthquakes are common around plate boundaries.

　　Ⓒ To help the reader visualize the concept of a type of tectonic activity.

　　Ⓓ To inform the reader about how volcanoes are formed.

7   What can be inferred from paragraph 4?

　　Ⓐ Earthquakes in the vicinity of the San Andreas Fault in California are common.

　　Ⓑ There is a great deal of volcanic activity around California.

　　Ⓒ It is impossible for us to measure the depth of deep ocean trenches.

　　Ⓓ Volcanoes will always form where plates collide.

8   The word 'leach' in paragraph 5 is closest in meaning to

　　Ⓐ leak

　　Ⓑ filter

　　Ⓒ separate

　　Ⓓ pour

9   Look at the letters (A, B, C, and D) that indicate where the following sentence could be added to paragraph 5.

Geologists now wonder if this process is happening on other planets that, as of now, do not support life.

Where would it best fit?

　　Ⓐ　　　　Ⓑ　　　　Ⓒ　　　　Ⓓ

4 ➡ As the diameter of the Earth remains constant, it stands to reason that older crust must be destroyed. This process occurs at subduction zones, where plates converge, and one plate is forced under another and is converted into magma. Often, this newly formed magma will erupt to the surface and over time can lead to the formation of volcanoes. At these points, deep ocean trenches are often formed, and violent earthquakes are common. A final type of tectonic activity is known as a transform plate boundary. Here, the two plates slip horizontally past one another. The huge stresses created at these points means that chunks of the Earth's crust can break off, and earthquakes are frequent. A famous example of a transform plate boundary is the San Andreas Fault in California, where the North American and Pacific plates are slowly pushing past each other.

5 ➡ One final point about plate tectonics that has been gaining traction in recent years is that the activity of these gargantuan slabs of solid and molten rock may be partially responsible for the development of life itself. **(A)** Scientists theorize that the phosphorous contained in the Earth's mantle became concentrated and crystalized as the mantle cooled, due in part to plate tectonics. **(B)** This refined form of phosphorous is known as apatite. **(C)** Once the apatite, locked into igneous rock, reached the surface, it began to leach into the ocean waters, where phosphorous dependent primitive life began to thrive. This in turn led the primitive life forms to release oxygen into the atmosphere, helping to create viable circumstances for multi-cellular life. **(D)**

10 Directions: Select the appropriate phrases from the answer choices and match them to the correct type of plate activity. You will NOT use two of the answer choices.

Tectonic Activity.	Statements.
Divergent Plates.	
Convergent Plates.	
Transform Plates.	

Statements

1 Leads to the formation of oceanic crust and the lithosphere.

2 The diameter of the Earth always remains constant.

3 Has led to development of biodiversity o Earth.

4 The huge pressure generated can cause parts of the Earth's crust to break away.

5 Are responsible for a feature known as Rift Valleys.

6 Occurs at subduction zones and leads to the formation of volcanoes.

7 Deep ocean trenches can form, and earthquakes are common.

Rocks

Steamrolling from one technological innovation to the next, we can pinpoint the beginnings and ends of various humanistic cycles and land-changes. However, the slowest changes are the most natural and also have no discernible beginning or end. The 'rock cycle' is a term used to describe natural, everlasting geological process in which all rocks on the Earth's crust experience. More specifically, it deals with the metamorphosis of one rock to another, and the not-so-systematic phases it goes through - melting, cooling, eroding, compacting, and deforming. The rock cycle concerns three main types of rocks: sedimentary; igneous; and metamorphic.

This continuing recycling of rock forms has been occurring since the birth of our planet – it defines where we came from and what we will leave behind. Earth's first rocks were igneous, lava-born rocks, formed out the dense iron-rich basalt and the silicate-rich granite. The emergence of these rocks marked the beginning of life on earth, for their gradual erosion discharged essential nutrients into the biosphere. Such nutrients included sodium, potassium, iron, and calcium. These cardinal building-blocks allowed organisms to spawn and begin a 4.5 billion-year evolutionary chain – ultimately leading to homo sapiens. To this day, these same nutrients are considered the most primitive for human's neurological functioning, with many diseases and uncomfortableness stemming from a lack of them.

Sedimentary rocks are likewise important, particularly for the survival and progression of civilizations. Coal, a sedimentary rock from the Paleolithic-era, is not only the earliest known source of heat and energy for man but also the most infamous due to its prolific ability to pollute and destroy the natural world. However, energy sourcing from igneous rocks is more likely to be present in the future. Uranium mineralization and ore extraction from magmatic-hydrothermal systems is important in procuring uranium isotopes as fissionable materials for nuclear energy plants. This source of energy is becoming popular as a clean alternative to fossil fuels, such as coal. Uranium from igneous rocks is also easily dissolved and transported, making it an ideal candidate for a green future.

Rocks have been extracted and used as building materials as far back as archaeologists can uncover. Compared to woods and metals, rocks have an increased durability and hardness factor according to Mohr's scale and tend to undergo less erosion as a result of external factors, such as climate and fire. Igneous rocks, such as granite and syenites, are impervious and extremely hard and used in most modern construction works – particularly dams, bridges, and tunnels. Sedimentary rocks are a common requirement for all public buildings. Besides the obvious use of iron ore for steel, Bauxite is involved in forming bricks, tiles, and asphalt. Predating the Middle ages, limestone and sandstone were most dominant for their exceptional durability. The Great Pyramids of Giza are covered in an external shell of limestone.

Metamorphic rocks are formed deep inside the Earth's crust, usually after succumbing to an intense amount of heat and pressure. This typically happens as a result of tectonic processes or prehistorically, continental collisions. Upon the impact of two pieces, magma rises to the surface and melts sedimentary and igneous rocks. The results are not instantaneous – taking 30 million years – but *are* striking. When limestone is melted, calcites inside it recrystallize and transform into a dense, equigranular, crystal-filled rock. In a similar fashion, sandstone metamorphoses into quartzite. Its previously grainy texture becomes glossy, smooth, and easy to sculpt. Both marble and quartzite are used in the production of ornaments, statues, and kitchen interiors.

The most opulent stage of a rock's life is its prospective transformation into a precious gemstone. All three of the aforementioned rock types have the potential to become a gemstone, each diverse and distinct from the other. Sedimentary rocks are broken down into fragments, carried by wind and water, and become compacted over time - resulting in jasper, zircon, and opal stones. The more exciting, below-ground molten compression of metamorphic rocks shape sapphire, ruby, and jade, to mention a few. Nonetheless, it is igneous rocks which are the crème-de-la-crème for the jewel-lovers, over time becoming condensed into tanzanite, quartzites, and the most prestigious jewel: the diamond.

Rocks

1 ➡ Steamrolling from one technological innovation to the next, we can pinpoint the beginnings and ends of various humanistic cycles and land-changes. However, the slowest changes are the most natural and also have no discernible beginning or end. The 'rock cycle' is a term used to describe natural, everlasting geological process in which all rocks on the Earth's crust experience. More specifically, it deals with the metamorphosis of one rock to another, and the not-so-systematic phases it goes through – melting, cooling, eroding, compacting, and deforming. The rock cycle concerns three main types of rocks: sedimentary; igneous; and metamorphic.

2 ➡ This continuing recycling of rock forms has been occurring since the birth of our planet – it defines where we came from and what we will leave behind. Earth's first rocks were igneous, lava-born rocks, formed out the dense iron-rich basalt and the silicate-rich granite. The emergence of these rocks marked the beginning of life on earth, for their gradual erosion discharged essential nutrients into the biosphere. Such nutrients included sodium, potassium, iron, and calcium. These cardinal building-blocks allowed organisms to spawn and begin a 4.5 billion-year evolutionary chain – ultimately leading to homo sapiens. To this day, these same nutrients are considered the most primitive for human's neurological functioning, with many diseases and uncomfortableness stemming from a lack of them.

---

1   All of the following are mentioned in paragraph 1 EXCEPT
  Ⓐ The rock cycle is never-ending.
  Ⓑ It is not ascertainable when each cycle begins and ends.
  Ⓒ Melting is the first stage in the rock cycle.
  Ⓓ It is easier to determine humanistic changes than rock changes.

2   Which of the sentences below best expresses the essential information in the highlighted sentence in the passage? Incorrect choices change the meaning in important ways or leave out essential information.
  Ⓐ The rock cycle will keep going continuously until all humans die and are not able to affect the cycle anymore.
  Ⓑ The rock cycle began when earth was formed and has continued ever since that moment.
  Ⓒ The rock cycle began before, and will outlast, all humans on earth.
  Ⓓ The rock cycle signifies the origins of life and will continue even after all life has gone.

3   Why does the author mention building-blocks?
  Ⓐ To compare the rock composition to that of building materials
  Ⓑ To explain the impact that Earth's first rocks had on the growth of life.
  Ⓒ To highlight the fact that sodium, potassium, iron, and calcium are the most important elements.
  Ⓓ To start the discussion of the development of homo sapiens.

4 What does the author imply about coal as an energy source?

   Ⓐ It is important to replace it with a cleaner, more renewable energy source.

   Ⓑ Nuclear energy is still secondary to coal because of its inherent dangers.

   Ⓒ There are other ways in which we can extract coal, but they are not as popular as the ones currently employed.

   Ⓓ Coal was the most important discovery ever made by humans.

5 According to paragraph 4, which of the following is true of igneous rocks?

   Ⓐ They have been used in the construction of modern bridges and dams.

   Ⓑ They are the hardest rocks in the world.

   Ⓒ They are not used nowadays in modern construction works.

   Ⓓ It was introduced into construction in the Middle ages.

6 The word 'impervious' in the passage is closest in meaning to…

   Ⓐ sturdy

   Ⓑ resilient

   Ⓒ resistant

   Ⓓ robust

3 ➡ Sedimentary rocks are likewise important, particularly for the survival and progression of civilizations. Coal, a sedimentary rock from the Paleolithic-era, is not only the earliest known source of heat and energy for man but also the most infamous due to its prolific ability to pollute and destroy the natural world. However, energy sourcing from igneous rocks is more likely to be present in the future. Uranium mineralization and ore extraction from magmatic-hydrothermal systems is important in procuring uranium isotopes as fissionable materials for nuclear energy plants. This source of energy is becoming popular as a clean alternative to fossil fuels, such as coal. Uranium from igneous rocks is also easily dissolved and transported, making it an ideal candidate for a green future.

4 ➡ Rocks have been extracted and used as building materials as far back as archaeologists can uncover. Compared to woods and metals, rocks have an increased durability and hardness factor according to Mohr's scale and tend to undergo less erosion as a result of external factors, such as climate and fire. Igneous rocks, such as granite and syenites, are impervious and extremely hard and used in most modern construction works – particularly dams, bridges, and tunnels. Sedimentary rocks are a common requirement for all public buildings. Besides the obvious use of iron ore for steel, Bauxite is involved in forming bricks, tiles, and asphalt. Predating the Middle ages, limestone and sandstone were most dominant for their exceptional durability. The Great Pyramids of Giza are covered in an external shell of limestone.

7 Which of the following is true, according to paragraph 5?

  Ⓐ Metamorphic rocks need to overcome heat and pressure in order to form deep inside the Earth's crust.

  Ⓑ Limestones are the immediate outcome of continental collisions.

  Ⓒ Limestone and sandstone are metamorphic rocks.

  Ⓓ Metamorphic rocks can form regardless of tectonic processes.

8 In the paragraph below, there is a missing sentence. Look at the paragraph and indicate (A, B, C and D) where the following sentence could be added to the passage.

When melted, the grains inside it recrystallize and form complex mosaics of crystals.

Where would the sentence best fit?

  Ⓐ   Ⓑ   Ⓒ   Ⓓ

9 What is the relationship of paragraph 6 to paragraph 5?

  Ⓐ Paragraph 6 provides further examples of how rocks can become beautiful objects through compression, which is the focus of paragraph 5.

  Ⓑ Paragraph 5 discusses the formation of metamorphic rocks, while paragraph 6 focuses on the materialistic value of such rocks.

  Ⓒ Paragraph 6 provides contradictory evidence to paragraph 5's explanation of rock formation.

  Ⓓ Paragraph 6 provides further evidence of the processes of rock compression and transformation when coming into contact with intense heat and pressure.

5 ➡ Metamorphic rocks are formed deep inside the Earth's crust, usually after succumbing to an intense amount of heat and pressure. This typically happens as a result of tectonic processes or prehistorically, continental collisions. Upon the impact of two pieces, magma rises to the surface and melts sedimentary and igneous rocks. **(A)** The results are not instantaneous – taking 30 million years – but *are* striking. When limestone is melted, calcites inside it recrystallize and transform into a dense, equigranular, crystal-filled rock. **(B)** In a similar fashion, sandstone metamorphoses into quartzite. **(C)** Its previously grainy texture becomes glossy, smooth, and easy to sculpt. **(D)** Two such crystalline structures – marble and quartzite – are used in the production of ornaments, statues, and kitchen interiors.

6 ➡ The most opulent stage of a rock's life is its prospective transformation into a precious gemstone. All three of the aforementioned rock types have the potential to become a gemstone, each diverse and distinct from the other. Sedimentary rocks are broken down into fragments, carried by wind and water, and become compacted over time - resulting in jasper, zircon, and opal stones. The more exciting, below-ground molten compression of metamorphic rocks shape sapphire, ruby, and jade, to mention a few. Nonetheless, it is igneous rocks which are the crème-de-la-crème for jewel-lovers, over time becoming condensed into tanzanite, quartzites, and the most prestigious jewel: the diamond.

VIEW TEXT

REVIEW

HELP

BACK

NEXT

HIDE TIME 00:54:00

10 Directions: Complete the table below to summarize information about the three types of rock as discussed in the passage. Match the appropriate statements to either type as appropriate.

Rock Type	Statements.
Igneous	• •
Sedimentary	• •
Metamorphic	•

Statements

1 Provided the essential nutrients necessary for organisms to spawn.

2 Is considered the most useful rock type for its multiple benefits and prospect for the future.

3 Was mandatory for the construction of the structures pre-Middle age.

4 Can be broken down to create jasper and opal stones.

5 Were earth's first rocks.

6 Used in its final marble form for ornamental purposes.

7 Often required in the construction of municipal buildings.

Gold Mining

The extraction of materials from the earth is a process familiar to societies throughout the world. Coal is mined for its ability to retain heat once it has begun to burn. Uranium is taken for its ability to power nuclear plants. Copper was mined for millennia to create weapons once it was combined with tin to form a bronze alloy. More recently it has been widely used to make wire because of its high conductivity. Some materials are not mined for their practical applications but purely on the value we assign to them based on their aesthetic qualities. Gold is probably the outstanding example of this kind of material.

It is hard to say definitively when humans first put such a high value on gold and began to mine it in earnest. The oldest confirmed gold mine archaeologists have discovered is at the prehistoric site Sakdrisi in Georgia. This mine is thought to have been in operation since at least the 3rd century BC, making it the oldest known site of gold production in the world. Of course, it is entirely possible and probable that some form of gold mining was occurring simultaneously at another place or at an earlier point in time.

There are several different types of gold deposits that miners work with. The first of these is known as a placer deposit. These types of deposits are usually found in stream beds where heavier gold has settled below less dense deposits of alluvium. Generally, this kind of deposit is mined using water due to its location on riverbeds and the fact that tunneling is not an option due to the looseness of the material. The exception to this is where the ground around the deposit is permanently frozen.

Panning, sluicing, dredging, and the rocker box are all used to separate the small fragments of gold from the alluvium. Panning, sluicing, and the rocker box are essentially variations on the same design. They extract gold from the rest of the collected material by relying on the action of gravity. Gold is generally heavier than the material in which it sits, and so it can be manipulated away from the throw away sand and rock to be collected. Dredging uses a hose to suck material up to the deck where it is separated using one of the methods mentioned above. Some older dredges used a bucket line to scoop up soil and transport it to a sluice.

Igneous rock mining involves tunneling into the earth and extracting ore, which is later processed in order to retrieve gold. This type of mining is responsible for most of the world's gold. It is generally only performed by large companies due to the expertise and equipment required for its successful execution. Once the rock encased gold has been hewn from the mine, it must be sent to be processed using either mercury or cyanide.

Mercury extraction has almost stopped completely, and it is generally only used in smaller placer deposit mines, but cyanide processing is still very much in use. A sodium cyanide solution is mixed with the gold ore as well as zinc. The zinc is then dissolved leaving behind a sludge that is up to 99% pure. Clearly with the heavy use of so many chemicals, there is ample opportunity for potential accidents. Many environmental disasters have occurred as a result of gold mining throughout the years and have led to much greater precautions being taken by the large mining companies.

Unfortunately, many mines in developing countries tend to employ children to do a lot of the manual labor required for gold mining. They are exposed to numerous dangers such as pit collapses, chemical exposure and noise pollution. Many organizations will now only sell gold that they can prove was ethically produced, though to what extent it is actually possible to do this is still open for debate. Gold mining does not create the conditions for child labor to exist, but it does produce a product that needs to be scrutinized by consumers.

Gold Mining

1 ➡ The extraction of materials from the earth is a process familiar to societies throughout the world. Coal is mined for its ability to retain heat once it has begun to burn. Uranium is taken for its ability to power nuclear plants. Copper was mined for millennia to create weapons once it was combined with tin to form a bronze alloy. More recently it has been widely used to make wire because of its high conductivity. Some materials are not mined for their practical applications but purely on the value we assign to them based on their aesthetic qualities. Gold is probably the outstanding example of this kind of material.

2 ➡ It is hard to say definitively when humans first put such a high value on gold and began to mine it in earnest. The oldest confirmed gold mine archaeologists have discovered is at the prehistoric site Sakdrisi in Georgia. This mine is thought to have been in operation since at least the 3rd century BC, making it the oldest known site of gold production in the world. Of course, it is entirely possible and probable that some form of gold mining was occurring simultaneously at another place or at an earlier point in time.

---

1 According to paragraph 1, which of the following is true of copper?

- Ⓐ It was used straight from the ground to create weapons.
- Ⓑ It was mixed with bronze to form an alloy.
- Ⓒ It was used to make weapons after being mixed with tin.
- Ⓓ Copper wiring is not very conductive.

2 Which of the following best expresses the essential information in the highlighted sentence in paragraph 1? Incorrect choices change the meaning in important ways or leave out essential information.

- Ⓐ Mining is conducted by very practical corporations and is considered a beautiful undertaking.
- Ⓑ Sometimes, mining is undertaken in order to extract precious stones from the Earth.
- Ⓒ Certain materials whose value is only based on what is measured by humans exist.
- Ⓓ Not all materials we mine are used for something practical but solely for how they look.

3 The phrase 'in earnest' in paragraph 2 is closest in meaning to

- Ⓐ devotedly
- Ⓑ soberly
- Ⓒ casually
- Ⓓ impatiently

4   Which of the following is NOT mentioned in paragraph 3 in relation to gold deposits?

    Ⓐ Gold is heavier than the material that it is usually found with.

    Ⓑ Placer deposits are often found near glaciers.

    Ⓒ Placer deposits are mined using water.

    Ⓓ Frozen ground means using alternative methods to mine the ground.

5   What can be inferred from paragraph 3 about gold?

    Ⓐ Gold is a precious metal which is only found on old stream beds.

    Ⓑ Alluvium is made of a lighter material than gold.

    Ⓒ A majority of deposits that miners work is known as placer deposits.

    Ⓓ Loose material makes tunneling a viable option for extracting material.

6   What function does paragraph 4 serve as a whole?

    Ⓐ It elaborates on an idea discussed in paragraph 3.

    Ⓑ It provides a specific example of a method defined in paragraph 3.

    Ⓒ It lists a number of different ways gold mining has evolved.

    Ⓓ It contradicts paragraph 3's notion that mining is a simple process.

3 ➡ There are several different types of gold deposits that miners work with. The first of these is known as a placer deposit. These types of deposits are usually found in stream beds where heavier gold has settled below less dense deposits of alluvium. Generally, this kind of deposit is mined using water due to its location on riverbeds and the fact that tunneling is not an option due to the looseness of the material. The exception to this is where the ground around the deposit is permanently frozen.

4 ➡ Panning, sluicing, dredging, and the rocker box are all used to separate the small fragments of gold from the alluvium. Panning, sluicing, and the rocker box are essentially variations on the same design. They extract gold from the rest of the collected material by relying on the action of gravity. Gold is generally heavier than the material in which it sits, and so it can be manipulated away from the throw away sand and rock to be collected. Dredging uses a hose to suck material up to the deck where it is separated using one of the methods mentioned above. Some older dredges used a bucket line to scoop up soil and transport it to a sluice.

7 In paragraph 5, there is a missing sentence. Look at the paragraph and indicate (A, B, C and D) where the following sentence could be added to the passage.

Smaller enterprises or illicit operations will almost exclusively employ one of these methods to mine gold deposits.

Where would the sentence best fit?

Ⓐ   Ⓑ   Ⓒ   Ⓓ

8 Which of the following is true according to paragraph 6?

Ⓐ It is impossible to extract mercury today.

Ⓑ Zinc is the primary cause of accidents involving the use of many chemicals.

Ⓒ In order to reduce environmental disasters, it is mandatory to caution large mining companies.

Ⓓ Unless done on a small scale, extracting mercury is not a common practice nowadays.

5 ➡ **(A)** Igneous rock mining involves tunneling into the earth and extracting ore, which is later processed in order to retrieve gold. **(B)** This type of mining is responsible for most of the world's gold. It is generally only performed by large companies due to the expertise and equipment required for its successful execution. **(C)** Once the rock encased gold has been hewn from the mine, it must be sent to be processed using either mercury or cyanide. **(D)**

6 ➡ Mercury extraction has almost stopped completely, and it is generally only used in smaller placer deposit mines, but cyanide processing is still very much in use. A sodium cyanide solution is mixed with the gold ore as well as zinc. The zinc is then dissolved leaving behind a sludge that is up to 99% pure. Clearly with the heavy use of so many chemicals, there is ample opportunity for potential accidents. Many environmental disasters have occurred as a result of gold mining throughout the years and have led to much greater precautions being taken by the large mining companies.

9   What is the author's purpose in discussing child labor in paragraph 7?

(A) To explain that not all gold mining is done in ethical ways.

(B) To raise awareness of the poor conditions some children are forced to work in.

(C) To convince the reader not to purchase gold or gold products.

(D) To highlight the differences that exist between rich and poor countries.

7 ➡ Unfortunately, many mines in developing countries tend to employ children to do a lot of the manual labor required for gold mining. They are exposed to numerous dangers such as pit collapses, chemical exposure and noise pollution. Many organizations will now only sell gold that they can prove was ethically produced, though to what extent it is actually possible to do this is still open for debate. Gold mining does not create the conditions for child labor to exist, but it does produce a product that needs to be scrutinized by consumers.

10 Directions: Complete the table below to summarize information about the three types of rock as discussed in the passage. Match the appropriate statements to either type as appropriate.

Mining Type	Statements.
Igneous	• •
Placer Deposit	• • •

Statements

1 Relies largely on gravity to separate the gold from other materials.

2 Uses certain chemicals to extract gold from rock.

3 Is a very safe method of mining both for people and the environment.

4 Are generally found in stream beds.

5 Usually, this type of mining requires a lot of expertise.

6 Children are often exploited in this kind of mining.

7 Can use tunneling to extract gold only if the ground is permanently frozen.

TOEFL

Reading

Actual Test

TOEFL

Reading

Actual Test

토플마스터 **TOEFL MASTER**

THE TOEFL iBT
READING ACTUAL TEST
SERIES 1

토플마스터

TOEFL MASTER

THE
TOEFL iBT
READING ACTUAL TEST
2nd Edition

SERIES 1

토플 Reading 30점 만점을 위한 최종 실전서 (총 9회분)

Jordan Jamie Green
Claire Park

Profreaders
Laura Joo
Jin Oh Bae

Answers &
Explanations

새롭게 시행된 New TOEFL iBT 완벽반영
TOEFL에 나오는 주요 토픽 별 실전 테스트 시리즈
토플전문강사가 직접 집필한 친절한 해설

HERMONHOUSE

토플마스터 TOEFL MASTER

TOEFL
READING
ACTUAL TEST
SERIES 1

Answers & Explanations

⊘ ANSWERS

PASSAGE 1

| 1 C | 2 B | 3 B | 4 A | 5 B |
| 6 D | 7 B | 8 C | 9 A | |

10 B, D, F

PASSAGE 2

| 1 A | 2 C | 3 C | 4 C | 5 D |
| 6 A | 7 C | 8 D | 9 B | |

10 A, C, D

PASSAGE 3

| 1 B | 2 D | 3 A | 4 A | 5 C |
| 6 D | 7 B | 8 C | 9 B | |

10 C, D, E

Imminent 임박한	Consternation 깜짝 놀람
Proportionate 균형 잡힌	Siege 포위
Degenerative 퇴행성의	Underscore 밑줄 긋다
Alleged 주장된	Errant 잘못된

PASSAGE 1 : Phobias

1
[정답] **C**

[Fact] 문제의 핵심인 fear가 일어나는 원인을 서술하고 있는 문장을 찾아야 한다. 첫 번째 단락 두 번째 문장 "This biochemical response"에서 this가 가리키는 것은 그전 문장의 주어인 "Fear"이다. 따라서 두 번째 문장 "...response occurs when humans are presented with some kind of imminent danger…"(이러한 화학적 반응= fear는 사람이 곧 다가올 듯한 위험에 처했을 때 일어나는 반응이다)에서 내용을 유추해야 한다. 보기 C에 있는 immediately threatening는 지문에 있는 imminent danger와 동의어 격이기 때문에 정답이다.

2
[정답] **B**

[Fact] 질문의 키워드인 optophobia 문장을 살펴보면, "...this [optophobia] could put one in danger"(옵토포비아=눈 뜨기 공포증은 사람을 위험에 처하게 만들 수 있다)라고 나와 있다. 따라서 "put one in danger"(위험에 처하게 할 수 있다)와 같은 의미인 put

someone at risk라고 나와 있는 보기 B가 정답이다.

3
[정답] **B**

[Fact] 질문의 키워드긴 astraphobia 문장을 살펴보면 "Astraphobia is the fear of thunderstorms"(번갯불 공포증은 번개/뇌우에 대한 공포증이라)라고 나와 있다. 따라서 보기 B가 정답이다. 보기 A는 본문의 내용 "Astraphobia is the fear of thunderstorms. It is not just a fear of thunderstorms, but a prolonged and crippling anxiety surrounding them"(번갯불 공포증은 번개에 대한 공포증뿐만 아니라, 번개에 대한 지속적이고 심한 불안감을 뜻한다)을 보고 정답으로 착각할 수 있다. 하지만 본문에서는 지속적이고 심한 불안감이라고 나와 있는 반면, 보기 A는 지속적이고 심한 공포(fear)라고 되어 있으므로 오답이다.

4
[정답] **A**

[Inference] 3단락 첫 번째 문장의 "What exactly causes a person to develop a phobia?"(사람이 공포증을 갖게 되는 정확한 원인은 무엇인가?) 질문에서 원인에 대한 내용이 나온다는 걸 알 수 있다. 그다음 문장들을 읽어보면 "there is no precise answer"(명확한 대답=원인은 없다)라고 나와 있다. 이는 아직도 과학자들이 정확한 원인 방법을 알아가고 있는 단계라고 유추해 볼 수 있는 대목이므로 "Scientists' understanding of the causes of phobias is still developing"(공포증을 유발하는 원인들에 대한 과학자들의 이해도는 아직도 진행 중이다)이라고 나와 있는 보기 A가 정답이다.

5
[정답] **B**

[Rhetorical Purpose] 3단락에서 arachnophobia가 예시로 쓰인 이유를 물어보는 질문이다. 따라서 이 예시가 나오게 된 context를 정확하게 이해하는 게 중요하다. 단락의 마지막 문장을 보면 "Most people would be afraid of spiders to some extent after such [terrified and afraid] an event"(대부분의 사람들은 거미와 관련된 두려웠던 사건 때문에 거미를 무서워하게 될 수 있다)라고 시작되지만, "but"을 기준으로 문장 후반부에는 "some individuals might develop arachnophobia, which is a continuing and intense anxiety related to anything to do with spiders"(어떤 사람들에겐 거미에 대한 지속적이고 강력한 불안감을 초래하는 거미공포증으로 이어질 수 있다)라고 설명한다. 따라서 거미공포증을 예시로 쓴 이유는 stressful events(="terrified and afraid" 됐던 사건들)의 결과로 이어질 수 있는 설명을 하기 위함이므로 정답은 보기 B이다.

6
[정답] **D**

[Sentence Insertion] 삽입 문장에서 정답의 단서는 transition word인 "However"이다. '그러나'로 시작하기에 적절한 위치를

파악하는 게 첫 번째 단계이고, 그다음으로 확인해 봐야 할 부분은 However의 뒷부분, "what we do know is that degenerative changes to human behavior could be related to developing phobias in later years"(변화는 대부분 퇴행성이고 나중에 공포증으로 이어질 가능성이 있다는 부분은 알고 있다=밝혀진 바이다) 내용이 들어가기에 적합한 위치여야 한다. C 문장에서는 "it is not always possible to give a definite answer about why someone acts the way they do"(사람들의 행동에 대한 설명을 정확하게 하는 건 아직 어렵다)라고 공포증을 표명하는 것의 어려움을 논하고 있다. 따라서 이 뒤에 그럼에도 불구하고 밝혀진 바에 대해 문장을 삽입하는 게 자연스럽다. 따라서 D가 정답이다.

7

[정답] **B**

[Vocabulary] 지문의 burdened(부담을 갖는)는 phobia로 부정적인 영향을 받은 사람들을 수식하기 때문에 보기 B의 afflicted(고통받는)가 정답이다.

＊affected: 영향을 받은
＊thwarted: 좌절한
＊Irritated: 짜증난

8

[정답] **C**

[Rhetorical Purpose] 음영 문구 'treatment will be specific to the presenting case'(치료 방법은 주어진 상황에 맞춰서 진행된다)가 언급된 직전 문장을 보면 "There are several broad ways physicians treat those burdened by phobias"(공포증 환자들을 치료하는 데는 다양한 치료법이 있다)라고 나와 있다. 하지만 다음 문장이 "Obviously"(분명히)로 시작하기 때문에 다양한 치료법도 있지만, 환자에게 필요한 적합하고 적절한 치료법도 있다는 내용을 서술하고 있으므로 보기 C가 정답이다.

9

[정답] **A**

[Rhetorical Purpose] 5단락의 핵심내용은 phobia 환자들 치료법에 관한 설명이다. 그중 구체적으로 exposure theory에 대한 설명과 구체적인 예시로 이어지기 때문에 정답은 A "It presents one method of treatment employed to patients with phobia"(5단락은 공포증 환자에게 사용되는 치료법 중 하나를 제시한다)이다.

10

[정답] **B, D, F**

[Summary] 지문의 중심내용은 phobia에 대한 일반적인 설명이다. 보기 B는 1단락에 나와 있는 Phobia와 fear의 차이 설명과 일치하고, 보기 D는 2~3단락에서 phobia가 생기는 과정에 대한 설명과 일치하며, 보기 F는 4단락에서의 Phobia가 생길 수 있는 마지막 이유, 유전적 원인에 대한 해석과 일치한다. 따라서 정답은 B, D, F이다.

PASSAGE 2 : Pavlovian Conditioning

1

[정답] **A**

[Fact] 문제의 키워드 classical conditioning(고전적 조건부여)에 관한 첫 번째 문장을 보면 "Pavlovian conditioning, also known as classical conditions"(파블로프의 조건반사, 혹은 고전적 조건부여)라고 이 두 가지 용어를 동의어 격으로 간주하고 있다. 그리고 같은 문장 마지막 부분을 보면 "..was accidently discovered by the Russian physiologist Ivan Pavlov"(accidently=우연치 않게 러시아인 이반 파블로브에 의해 발견되었다)라고 나와 있다. 따라서 accidently의 동의어인 unexpected (예상치 못한)로 다르게 표현한 A가 정답이다.

2

[정답] **C**

[Vocabulary] 지문의 triggered는 "feeding"이 "saliva"를 자극한 것이기 때문에 동의어인 activated, 보기 C가 정답이다.

＊Dribbled: 질질 흘리다, 똑똑 떨어지다
＊Responded: 응답하다
＊Tripped: 넘어지다

3

[정답] **C**

[Negative Fact] 문제의 키워드 Pavlov's dogs에 대한 내용을 살핀 후 지문에 나온 내용을 제거하면 된다. 보기 A는 지문의 "many of the animals were mutts or mongrels"(대부분의 [실험에 사용된] 동물은 잡종견들이었다)와 일치한다. 같은 이유로 정답은 C(specific breed=혈통이 있는)이다. 보기 B는 지문의 "As many as 30 canines were used in his classical conditioning tests before he got his surgical procedure correct."(고전적 조건부여 실험에서 원하는 결과를 낳는데까지 많게는 30마리의 개들이 사용되었다)와 일치한다. 보기 D는 지문의 "...Pavlov consistently employed thieves who regularly stole collared pets in their alleged collection of street dogs…"(파블로프는 주인 있는 개까지 훔쳐 떠돌이 개라고 주장하기까지 했다)와 일치한다.

4

[정답] **C**

[Negative Fact] 문제의 키워드 results of numerous research studies in classical conditioning(고전적 조건부여 실험 결과들)과 관련된 문장과 내용을 살펴보면 다음을 알 수 있다. 보기 A는 두 번째 문장 "Phobias, repulsion, nausea, rage, and sexual arousal can be responses shown by the effects of classical conditioning."(공포증, 혐오감, 메스꺼움, 분노, 그리고 성적인 욕망과 같은 반응들이 고전적 조건부여의 효과로 나타났다)과 일치한다. 보기 B는 "For example, conditioned nausea … can affect people greatly in their daily lives"(예를 들어, 조건적 메스꺼움은

사람들의 일상에도 크게 영향을 미칠 수 있다)와 일치한다. 보기 D 는 단락 마지막 문장인 "Classical conditioning can eliminate this trauma by reconditioning the subject"(고전적 조건반사는 대상을 recondition 함으로써 이러한 트라우마를 제거할 수 있다)와 일치 한다. 따라서 보기 A, B, D는 지문의 내용과 일치하므로 오답이다. 그러나 보기 C는 지문에 언급되지 않은 내용이므로 정답이다.

5   [정답] **D**

[Vocabulary] 지문의 trauma는 이전 문장에 언급된 conditioned nausea 같은 증상을 뜻하기 때문에, 일반적인 고통, 힘듦을 나타 낸다. 따라서 정답은 보기 (D) suffering(고통)이다.

＊test: 시험
＊Mentality: 정신
＊situation: 상황

6   [정답] **A**

[Sentence Simplification] 음영 표시된 문장 전체가 핵심 정보 로서 "Behaviorism stresses the role of environmental influences in manipulating behavior, to the near exclusion of native or inherited influences,"(행동주의는 타고난 혹은 유전적 영향을 제 외한 나머지 환경이 행동을 조작하는 데에 역할을 강조한다)를 보 기 A의 "Rather than focusing on intrinsic or inherited influences, behaviorism underscores the effect that the environment has on behavior,"(내재적 혹은 유전적 영향에 포커스를 맞추기보다는, 행동주의는 환경이 행동에 미치는 영향을 강조한다)로 paraphrase 되었고, "and it becomes essentially a focus on learning as we learn new behaviors through classical conditioning."(그리고 행 동주의는 우리가 고전적 조건부여를 통해 새로운 행동을 배울 때 연구의 중심이 된다)는 보기 A의 뒷부분 "and focuses on learning new behaviors through classical conditioning"(그리고 [행동주의 는] 고전적 조건부여를 통해 새로운 행동을 배우는 데에 포커스를 맞춘다)와 일치한다.

따라서 정답은 보기 A이다.

7   [정답] **C**

5단락 첫 번째 문장의 핵심은 이 단락의 중점이 "Before Conditioning"(반응/훈련 전) 단계라는 걸 알 수 있다. 그 세부적 인 내용은 바로 뒤이어 "In this phase, an unconditioned stimulus produces an unconditioned response in the subject"(이 단계에 는, 조건 없는 자극이 대상으로부터 조건 없는 반응을 초래하게 만 든다)라고 나와 있다. 이어서 같은 설명을 하고 있으므로, 정답은 보기 C이다.

8   [정답] **D**

[Sentence Insertion] 삽입 문장에서 정답의 단서는 "All of these factors"(이 모든 요소들은)로, 5단락에서 설명하고 있는 Before Conditioning에 부합하는 모든 요소들에 대한 설명이 다 나 온 뒤, 맨 마지막에 위치하는 게 흐름상 자연스럽다. 따라서 정답은 마지막 D이다.

9   [정답] **B**

[Rhetorical Purpose] 음영 문구 'neutral stimulus'(중립자극)가 언급된 문장을 살펴보면, "During this [During Conditioning] part of conditioning"(반응/훈련 중 단계에는) "a neutral stimulus is connected to an unconditioned stimulus. After this happens, it becomes known as a conditioned stimulus."(중립자극이 조건 없 는 자극과 연결되어 있다. 그 후, 중립자극은 조건자극으로 이루어 진다)라고 나와 있다. 즉, 중립자극은 조건자극 이전에 선행되는 단 계("particular stage")를 설명하고 있으므로 정답은 B이다.

10   [정답] **A, C, D**

[Summary] 지문의 중심내용은 파블로프의 조건반사에 대한 설 명과 실험 과정, 다양한 단계에 대한 묘사이다. 보기 A는 4단락부 터 시작되는 behaviorism에 관한 설명과 중요성에 대한 내용과 일 치하고, 보기 C는 3단락에서 파블로프의 조건반사가 다른 연구에 미치는 영향에 대한 설명과 일치하고, 보기 D는 1~2단락의 중심 내용인 파블로프의 조건반사(=고전적 조건) 설명과 실험내용의 중 요성과 일치한다. 따라서 정답은 A, C, D이다.

1

정답 **B**

[Fact] 문제의 키워드 dopamine(도파민)이 나와 있는 1단락 두 번째 문장을 보면 "Dopamine was actually synthesized in a laboratory...before it was discovered in the human brain"(도파민은 사실 인간의 뇌에서 발견되기 전, 실험실에서 만들어낸 합성물질이다)이라고 나와 있다. 따라서 synthesized(합성된)와 동의어인 made라고 paraphrase 되어 있는 보기 B가 정답이다.

2

정답 **D**

[Negative Fact] 문제의 키워드 dopamine과 관련된 문장에서 나온 내용들을 제거하면 된다. 보기 A는 지문의 첫 번째 문장 "dopamine plays a key role."(도파민은 중요 역할을 한다)과 일치한다. 보기 B는 마지막 문장 "...proved that dopamine also acted as a neurotransmitter."(~는 도파민이 신경 전달 물질 역할을 한다는 것을 증명했다)와 일치한다. 보기 C는 두 번째 문장 "Dopamine was actually synthesized in a laboratory … before it was discovered in the human brain..."(도파민은 사실 인간의 뇌에서 발견되기 전에 실험실에서 합성되었다)과 일치한다. 따라서 보기 A, B, C는 지문의 내용과 일치하므로 오답이다. 그러나 보기 D는 지문에 언급된 내용을 틀리게 서술했기 때문에 (George Barger와 James Ewens가 발견한 게 아니다. 이들은 실험실에서 도파민을 synthesize 한 인물들이다) 이것이 정답이다.

3

정답 **A**

[Sentence Simplification] 음영 표시된 문장 전체가 핵심 정보로서 "Dopamine originates in the Ventral Tegmental Area(VTA)"(도파민은 VTA에서 나오며)를 보기 A의 "dopamine is released from the Ventral Tegmental Area"(도파민은 VTA에서 생성된다)로 다르게 표현됐다. 음영 표시 문장의 단어들을 동의어를 사용하여 바꾸어 표기한 A가 정답이다. 본문의 multiplies = proliferates(번성하다); 본문의 stored = remains(저장되다, 남다)

4

정답 **A**

[Fact] 질문의 키워드인 Mesocortical Dopamine Pathway가 나와 있는 문장과 다음 이어지는 문장을 보면 "This pathway [Mesocortical Dopamine Pathway] also starts in the VTA"(이 통로는 [Mesocortical Dopamine Pathway] VTA에서 시작된다)라고 나와 있다. 따라서 보기 A(initiated=시작되다)가 정답이다.

5

정답 **C**

[Vocabulary] 지문의 undetermined는 도파민이 맡고 있는 "precise role"(정확한 역할)이 아직 알려지지 않음을 설명하고 있기 때문에 동의어인 보기 C의 unknown(알려지지 않은)이 정답이다.

＊inoperable: 수술할 수 없는, 실행할 수 없는
＊unchanging: 변하지 않는
＊unstable: 안정적이지 않은

6

정답 **D**

[Rhetorical Purpose] 음영 문구 "gaming disorder"(게임 장애)가 언급된 문장을 보면 "Two examples of this addiction are gambling addictions and gaming disorder,"(이러한 중독의 두 가지 예시는 도박중독과 게임중독이 있다)라고 "this addiction"에 대한 예시로 나온 걸 확인할 수 있다. 앞 문장에서는 behavioral addiction(행동 중독)을 "...does not offer any apparent reward other than the increase in dopamine in the brain"(뇌에서 도파민 증가 이외엔 명확한 보상이 없다) 이라고 정의내렸기 때문에 보기 D가 정답이다.

7

정답 **B**

[Inference] 5단락에서 문제의 키워드 도파민과 addiction(중독)에 관한 첫 번째 문장을 살펴보면 "Dopamine is thought to affect the neurological biomechanisms for behavioral addiction"(도파민은 행동중독에 영향을 미치는 신경 생체학에도 영향을 미치는 거라고 알려져 있다)이라고 나와 있다. 그리고 그 과정에 대한 내용은 같은 문장 뒷부분을 확인하면 되는데, "...by rewarding certain actions with the release of greater quantities of the hormone"(특정 행동에 대해 더 많은 양의 호르몬을 분비한다)이라고 나와 있다. 또한 5단락 중간을 보면 "Gradually, they will come to associate these activities with the pleasure of dopamine release"(점점 도파민 분비가 곧 즐거움으로 직결될 것이다)라고 나와 있다. 따라서 이 모든 내용을 담고 있는 B(뇌의 도파민 수치가 높을수록 더 많은 행복을 느끼고, 이는 중독을 초래할 가능성을 증가시킨다)가 정답이다.

8

정답 **C**

[Fact] 문제의 키워드 addiction treatment(중독 치료)에 관한 설명이 나오는 6단락 세 번째 문장을 보면 "Medication is therefore supplemented to help patients combat withdrawal symptoms and function in their daily lives"(따라서 약물치료는 환자들의 금단증상을 이겨내고 일상생활을 할 수 있도록 도와주는 역할을 한다) 라고 나와 있다. 따라서 정답은 C이다.

9

[Sentence Insertion] 삽입 문장에서 정답의 단서는 "Even"(심지어 ~ 도)과 "still"(~더라도) 부사들이다. 문장의 내용이 "심지어 환자들이 정신적으로 중독을 헤쳐나가려고 결심하더라도, 그들의 몸은 익숙해져 있던 높은 수치의 도파민을 갈망할 것이다."이므로 withdrawal symptoms(금단증상)에 대한 내용이 나온 후, 이어진다면 글의 흐름이 자연스럽다. 따라서 정답은 B이다.

10

[정답] **C, D, E**

[Summary] 지문의 중심내용은 addiction(중독)에 있어서 도파민의 역할과 우리 몸에 미치는 영향이다. 보기 A와 B는 각각 서론에서 도파민의 등장에 대한 설명과 도파민의 이동 경로에 대한 설명이다. 지엽적인 설명이므로 답이 아니다. 보기 F는 중심내용에서 도파민이 중독 증세에 미치는 영향에 대해 이야기하고 있지만 chemical addiction(화학적 중독)의 withdrawal symptom(금단 증세)에 대한 설명으로 보기 E에 비해 지엽적인 설명이므로 정답에서 제외된다. 보기 C는 1~2단락의 중심내용인 도파민 소개와 어디에서 그리고 어떻게 흘러나오는지에 대한 설명과 일치하고, 보기 D는 3단락의 reward system 내용과 일치하고, 보기 E는 4~5단락의 도파민과 중독의 상관관계에 대한 설명과 일치한다. 따라서 정답은 C, D, E이다.

Test 02 | Sociology

✓ ANSWERS

PASSAGE 1

1 B	2 C	3 D	4 A	5 B
6 D	7 B	8 A	9 C	
10 A, B, E				

PASSAGE 2

1 C	2 A	3 B	4 A	5 D
6 C	7 A	8 C	9 D	
10 B, C, E				

PASSAGE 3

1 B	2 D	3 C	4 B	5 B
6 A	7 C	8 A	9 D	
10 B, D, F				

Virtually 사실상
Advent 출현, 도래
Compulsory 강제적인, 의무의
Coercive 강제적인
Constrained 제어된
Delinquent 비행, 직무태만의
Prevail 만연하다
Knead (반죽·찰흙 등을) 이기다[치대다]

Subversion 파괴, 전복, 멸망
Adherent 접착성의
Grunge 지저분한
Adhere to (법이나 규칙 따위)를 준수하다
Functionalist 구조 기능주의자
Subliminal 잠재의식의
Indispensable 필수적
Preside 주재하다

PASSAGE 1 : Suburbs

1

[정답] **B**

[Sentence Insertion] 삽입 문장에서 정답의 단서는 시간의 흐름을 유추할 수 있는 "then"(그제서야)이다. 지문의 "very beginnings of the industrial revolution"(산업혁명 초기에) 문장 후에 "mass exodus of people from the country to the city began in earnest"(본격적으로 사람들이 대규모로 시골에서 도시로 이동하기 시작했다)가 들어가면 가장 자연스럽다. 산업혁명 때문에 대규모 이동이 일어났다고 글의 흐름이 이어진다. 따라서 정답은 B이다.

2

[정답] **C**

[Fact] 첫 번째 단락에서 "In modern usage, the term describes

an outlying district of a city that is predominantly residential"(오늘날 이 단어는 [교외 지역] 대부분 거주지로 구성되어 있는 도시의 외부 지역을 묘사할 때 쓰이고 있다) 문장의 내용과 일치하는 보기는 C이다.

3
[정답] D

[Negative Fact] 문제의 키워드인 America after World War 2 (세계 2차 전쟁 후 미국) 내용이 있는 2단락 첫 번째 문장부터 살펴보면 다음을 알 수 있다. 보기 A는 "there was a vast housing shortage in America"(미국에는 엄청난 주택난에)와 일치한다. 보기 B는 "these men who wished to settle down and start a family"(이들[돌아온 군인들]은 자리를 잡고 가정을 꾸리기 위해 집이 필요했다)와 일치한다. 보기 C는 "Millions of American servicemen had returned home, and it was estimated that no fewer than five million new homes would be required to accommodate these men"(수백만 명의 군인들이 집으로 돌아왔고, 적어도 500만 채의 새로운 집이 이들을 수용하기 위해 필요했다)와 일치한다

4
[정답] A

[Rhetorical Purpose] 음영 문구 "40% of American households didn't own a mode of transport"(미국 가구의 40%는 교통수단을 갖고 있지 않았다)가 언급된 문장의 앞부분을 살펴보면, "Back when suburbs were just beginning to take off"(교외 지역이 막 퍼지기 시작했을 때)라고 이전의 상황을 설명해 주고 있는 걸 알 수 있다. 그리고 다음 문장에서는 "Over the course of the following decade, having a car would become more than just a convenience – it would become an absolute necessity for modern life"(금후 수십 년 동안, 차를 소유하는 것은 편의 그 이상이었다 – 현대 생활의 필수품이 되었다)라고도 나와 있다. 해당 내용을 조합해 보면 사람들의 차 소유 변화가 교외 지역의 확산에 기여했다는 원인(factor)으로 설명하기 위함이다. 따라서 답은 보기 A이다.

5
[정답] B

[Inference] 3단락의 핵심내용은 교외 지역이 갑자기 성장하게 된 원동력이다. "Yet, another factor appeared as a cause in the rapid rise of suburbs in America; the automobile."(그러나, 미국 교외 지역의 급성장에는 또 다른 원인이 있었다. 바로 자동차이다.) 이라는 내용에 이어 바로 다음에 미국인의 40%가 교통수단을 갖고 있지 않았다고 나와 있다. 따라서 이들은 suburb boom이 일어나기 전까지는 교통수단이 없었다고 유추해 볼 수 있다.

6
[정답] D

[Sentence Simplification] 음영 표시된 문장 전체가 핵심 정보로서 "Millions of people left the cities to live the American Dream in the suburbs, but millions of people who didn't have the means to follow them were forced to stay behind"(수백만 명의 사람들이 아메리칸 드림을 쫓아 도시에서 교외 지역으로 떠났지만 그럴 방법이 없는 또다른 수백만 명의 사람들은 남아있어야 했다) 문장에서 "but millions of people who didn't have the means to follow them were forced to stay behind" 부분이 보기 D에 있는 "Those who could not afford the move to the suburbs were forced to stay in the cities"(교외로 갈 수 없는 사람들은 도시에 남아있을 수밖에 없었다)로 간략하게 바꾸어 쓰였다. 따라서 답은 보기 D이다.

7
[정답] B

[Vocabulary] 지문의 disillusioned (환멸을 느낀)의 동의어를 찾으면 된다. 따라서 답은 보기 B이다.
＊Shortsighted 근시안적인, 선견지명이 없는
＊Disenchanted 환멸을 느낀
＊Discharged 해방된, 해고된
＊Discouraged 낙담한

8
[정답] A

[Vocabulary] 지문의 strikingly (두드러지게, 눈에 띄게)의 동의어를 찾으면 된다. 따라서 답은 보기 A이다.
＊Noticeably 두드러지게, 눈에 띄게
＊Impactfully impactful = '영향력 있는'이라는 뜻으로 부사 형태인 impactfully는 사실 사용되지 않는다
＊Physically 육체적으로, 물리적으로
＊Consciously 의식하면서

9
[정답] C

[Fact] 문제의 키워드 "changes of suburb"(교외 지역의 변화)에 대한 언급이 있는 5단락 마지막 문장을 보면 "These changes indicate that the suburbs of tomorrow will be strikingly different from those we know today."(이러한 변화는 내일의 교외 지역은 오늘의 교외 지역과는 눈에 띄게 달라질 것을 의미한다) 라고 나와 있다. 이는 보기 C(미국의 교외 지역과 도시들은 또다른 변화의 시기를 겪고 있다)와 일치한다.

10
[정답] A, B, E

[Summary] 지문의 중심내용은 세계 2차 전쟁의 종결이 미국에서 교외 지역 성장에 기여했다(set stage)는 사실이다. 보기 A는 2

단락 중심내용인 전쟁 후 미국의 급증하는 거주지 부족 문제에 대한 해결책으로 개발가들(developers)이 큰 땅을 사들여 집을 짓기 시작했다는 내용과 일치하고, 보기 B는 3단락의 중심내용인 교외 지역에 거주하는 인구의 급증과 그로 인한 결과들에 대한 내용과 일치하고, 보기 E는 4~5단락의 내용인 미국인들이 교외 지역으로 이동하면서 도심에서 일어나는 문제점들과 오늘날의 추세에 대한 내용과 일치한다. 따라서 정답은 A, B, E이다.

PASSAGE 2 : Youth Culture

1
[정답] C

[Sentence Simplification] 음영 표시된 문장 전체가 핵심 정보로서 "Their logic is that prior to compulsory schooling"(그들의 논리는 의무 교육 이전에)을 " Before compulsory schooling"(의무 교육 이전에)으로, "and they spent a lot of their time interacting with adults."(그리고 그들은 어른들과 오랜 시간을 보냈다.)를 "the youth spent more time with adults"(청소년들은 어른들과 더 많은 시간을 보냈다)로 간략하게 바꾸어 표현한 보기 C가 정답이다.

2
[정답] A

[Fact] 문제의 키워드 youth culture(청소년 문화)에 대한 내용이 나와 있는 1단락 마지막 문장을 보면 "Others argue that youth culture as we understand it today has only been around since some time in the mid-1950s, particularly in American society."(우리가 지금 알고 있는 청소년 문화는 1950년대 중반이 되어서야 특히 미국 사회에 들어선 것으로 보는 사람들도 있다.)라고 나와 있고, 보기 A에는, 그것(청소년 문화)은 존재한 지 70년 정도밖에 되지 않았다고 틀림없이 말할 수 있다고 나와 있어서 정답이다.

3
[정답] B

[Negative Fact] 문제의 키워드 youth culture (청소년 문화)에 대한 내용을 읽어보고 언급된 내용을 지우면 된다. 보기 A는 "It was in the 1950s that youth cultures began to make themselves known on a national level~"(1950년대가 되어서야 청소년 문화가 국가적인 차원으로 보여지기 시작했다)와 일치한다. 보기 C는 "They maintain that youth culture is no different from 'adult' culture, and that separating the two is not necessary."(그들은 청소년 문화는 '성인' 문화와 크게 다르지 않다고 생각하며 이 둘을 분리하는 게 의미가 없다고 본다.)와 일치한다. 보기 D는 "This association with civil unrest and defiance against the establishment led to them being considered delinquent by society at large."(사회적 불안과 반항과 관련됨으로써 청소년 문화는 대체로 사회의 비행집단으로 여겨져 왔다.)와 일치한다.

4
[정답] A

[Vocabulary] 지문의 adhere to (~을 고수하다)의 동의어를 찾으면 된다. 따라서 답은 보기 A이다.
* maintain 유지하다
* protect 보호하다
* Bond with ~을 형성하다
* Attach to ~ 에 붙이다

5

[Fact] 문제의 키워드 "the United States and England"(미국과 영국)가 언급된 문장을 보면 "The United States and England are good examples of this kind of society."(미국과 영국은 이러한 사회의 좋은 예시이다)라고 나와 있고, 여기서 가리키는 "this kind of society"는 앞에 나온 "it develops among peer groups"(이것=청소년 문화는 친구들 사이에서 커져 간다)를 말한다. 또한 그 이전에는 "the family is not really the unit within which a young person's identity is formed."(가족은 청소년들의 정체성을 형성하는 유닛이 아니다) 라고 나와 있다. 종합해 보면 보기 D가 정답이다.

6   [정답] **C**

[Rhetorical Purpose] 문제의 키워드 modernizing societies 문장을 살펴보면 "Predominantly rural, modernizing societies are a good example of this."(대부분, 시골이나 현대화가 되어가는 사회가 이것의 좋은 예시이다) 라고 나와 있고 여기서 가리키는 this는 4단락 첫 번째 문장에 나온 앞에 언급되었던 "Conversely, societies within which the youth do not progress through life in such a predictable manner are less inclined towards forming sub or youth cultures."(반면에, 예측과 다르게 청소년들이 커가면서 성장하지 않는 사회들은 sub-youth 혹은 청소년 문화를 형성할 가능성이 낮다) 라고 나와 있다. 따라서 보기 C가 정답이다.

7   [정답] **A**

[Inference] 5단락에서 문제의 키워드 punk movement에 대한 언급된 부분을 살펴보면 "Once it becomes infiltrated and mass produced it can often mean the beginning of the end."(한번 스며들기 시작하고 대량생산이 되면 대부분 끝의 시작을 알린다) 라는 내용이 나와 있다. 따라서 인기를 끌어 mass produce가 되는 순간 (= "interest it garderned from large companies" 대기업의 이목을 끌었던 펑크의 인기는 오래 가지 못할 것) 인기가 사라질 것이라고 paraphrase 해놓은 보기 A가 정답이다.

8   [정답] **C**

[Sentence Insertion] 삽입 문장에서의 단서는 "In fact"(사실상)이기 때문에 앞에 나온 내용을 뒷받침해줘야 한다. 5단락 "Even the music of the era was a response to the often lengthy and overblown psychedelia of the 1960s."(심지어 이 당시의 음악조차도 60년대의 거창하고 부풀려진 사이키델리아 아트에 대한 반응이었다) 이 내용 후에 펑크밴드는 음악적 재능은 연주에 필요 없다고 생각했다는 "overblown" 사상을 반영하기 때문에 C에 들어가면 자연스럽다.

9   [정답] **D**

[Vocabulary] 지문의 commodity (상품, 물건)의 동의어를 찾으면 된다. 따라서 답은 보기 D이다.

＊Artifact 유물
＊Mechanism 메커니즘, 구조
＊Export 수출
＊Product 상품

10   [정답] **B, C, E**

[Summary] 지문의 중심내용은, 청소년 문화란 정의 내리기 어렵고 문화의 진화를 묘사하기 어렵다는 내용이다.

보기 B는 1단락의 중심내용인 청소년 문화가 어떻게 시작되는지에 대한 두 부류에 대한 내용과 일치한다.

보기 C는 5단락의 중심내용인 청소년 문화가 있는 곳엔 그것에 대한 대항이 있다는 내용과 일치한다.

보기 E는 6단락의 중심내용인 펑크뮤직 예시의 설명과 일치한다.

1 [정답] **B**

[Sentence Simplification] 음영 표시된 문장 전체가 핵심 정보로서 "Despite its apparent lighthearted nature,"(유쾌한 본질에도 불구하고)를 "beyond entertainment"(오락거리 그 이상으로)로, 심리학자들은 "consider it more powerful than simply a pleasant form of distraction,"(대중문화를 즐겁게 해주는 오락 그 이상의 힘이 있다고 여긴다)를 "Psychologists believe that mass media's role in society"(심리학자들은 대중문화가 사회에 미치는 역할)로 간략하게 바꾸어 표현한 보기 B가 정답이다.

2 [정답] **D**

[Fact] 문제의 키워드 functionalist perspective (기능주의자의 관점)의 내용이 담겨있는 2단락 마지막 문장을 보면 "This ideology is largely accepted by psychologist as a positive motivator and accepted by society."(이러한 사상 = 기능주의자 관점은 긍정적인 원동력 역할을 하고 사회에서 순응하는 방법으로 심리학자들로 하여금 받아들여지고 있다) 라는 것을 알 수 있다. 따라서 보기 D는 지문의 내용과 일치하므로 정답이다.

3 [정답] **C**

[Rhetorical Purpose] 3단락 첫 문장을 살펴보면 "Commercial advertisements are considered an extension of the functionalist approach"(상업 광고는 기능주의적 방법의 연장선으로 여겨진다) 라고 명시되어 있다. 이는 전 단락의 functionalist perspective에 이어 구체적인 예시를 통해 그들의 approach를 설명한다는 것을 알 수 있다. 또한 해당 내용이 "average child"에 미치는 영향에 대한 언급도 나와 있다. 따라서 보기 C가 정답이다.

4 [정답] **B**

[Fact] 음영 표시가 된 문장을 살펴보면 "underdeveloped mind"(=아직 성숙하지 못한 아이들)에 미치는 영향에 대해 설명한다. 그리고 그다음 문장을 이어서 보면 "Their misunderstanding leads to the normalization of unhealthy eating habits, brand—loyalty, and an increased desire to obtain the latest novelties."라고 나와 있는데 여기서 말하는 their는 앞에 나온 Underdeveloped mind, 즉 아이들을 가리키는 것이고, 문장 뒤에는 다양한 negative consequences(ex/ unhealthy eating habits, brand loyalty, increased desire to obtain)가 나와 있다. 따라서 보기 B가 정답이다.

5 [정답] **B**

[Negative Fact] 문제의 키워드 conflict perspective로 시작되는 4단락 첫 번째 문장부터 살펴보면 된다. 보기 A는 첫 번째 문장인 "the portrayal of divisions in society through the media"(미디어를 통해 보여지는 사회의 다방면)와 일치한다. 보기 C는 "The process in which the information is selected, filtered, and presented to consumers is well—documented, is known as gatekeeping."(게이트키핑 이론처럼 결정권자가 뉴스의 내용을 선택할 수 있다는 내용의 중요성)이 언급되는데, 게이트키핑은 그 의미에서도 알 수 있듯이 미디어의 상충되는 면모를 보여주는 이론이기 때문에 C와 일치한다. 보기 D는 "...with those making the decisions ranging from media corporations to high—ranking government officials."(미디어 관계자들부터 고위관직자들의 결정에 따른다)라는 내용과 일치한다.

6 [정답] **A**

[Vocabulary] 지문의 presiding (주도하는) 의 동의어를 찾으면 된다. 따라서 답은 보기 A이다.

＊dominant 지배적인
＊Xenophobic 외국 공포증의
＊formidable 무시무시한
＊Established 인정받는

7 [정답] **C**

[Rhetorical Purpose] 음영 표시된 5단락 첫 번째 문장을 살펴보면 "Despite the harmful results of gatekeeping, the conflict perspective also highlights the important role mess media has as an agent of socialization"(게이트키핑의 해로운 점에도 불구하고 conflict perspective는 '사회화 agent'로서 중요한 역할을 강조한다)이라고 나와 있기 때문에 'positive role'(긍정적인 역할)을 보여주기 위함이다. 따라서 보기 C가 정답이다.

8 [정답] **A**

[Inference] 5단락 마지막 문장을 보면 "Unfortunately, such open coverage has given a platform for people to spread radical ideologies and glorify violence and hatred."(open coverage는 사람들로 하여금 급진적인 사상을 심어줄 수 있고, 폭력과 증오를 숭배할 수 있도록 할 수도 있다)라고 "unfortunate" 한 부분에 대한 언급이 있다. 따라서 모든 결과가 긍정적이진 않다고 서술하고 있는 보기 A가 정답이다.

9

D

[Sentence Insertion] 삽입 문장의 단서는 "However controversial"(얼마나 논쟁이 많든)이다. 앞에 controversial 한 내용이 나와야 하는데, 5단락 마지막 부분에서 unfortunately로 시작하는 문장에서 주의해야 하는 부분에 대해 나왔기 때문에 마지막 문장 뒤로 삽입되면 가장 자연스럽다. 따라서 정답은 보기기 D이다.

10

[정답] **B, D, F**

[Summary] 지문의 중심내용은 대중문화가 우리 사회에 미치는 영향과 그 영향력의 다양한 방식에 대해 설명하고 있다. 보기 B는 2단락의 중심내용인 대중문화가 사회의 규범에 미치는 영향에 대해 언급한 내용과 일치하고, 보기 D는 4단락의 부정적인 영향에 대한 언급과 5단락의 긍정적 영향을 복합적으로 다루는 문장이고, 보기 F는 1단락의 대중문화 소개내용과 일치한다. 따라서 정답은 B, D, F이다.

Test 03 — Anthropology

✓ ANSWERS

PASSAGE 1

1 C	2 C	3 B	4 C	5 D
6 A	7 C	8 B	9 B	

10 B, C, F

PASSAGE 2

1 B	2 A	3 C	4 D	5 D
6 C	7 B	8 D	9 A	

10 A, C, E

PASSAGE 3

1 C	2 D	3 A	4 B	5 A
6 C	7 A	8 D	9 B	

10 A, C, D

Occult 신비한, 숨은 (=Cryptic)	Erect 똑바로 서다
Dismember 절단하다	Relevant 관련 있는, 적절한
Exaltation 고귀한, 고양된	Testament 유언, 증언,증거
Ingestion 섭취,삼키다.	Ingenuity 독창성,기발한 재주,재간
Affliction 고통	Liminal 경계의
Trance 황홀경,무아지경	Reveler 흥청망청

PASSAGE 1 : Shamanism

1

[정답] **C**

[Fact] 1단락에서 shaman을 소개하는 문장을 보면 샤먼은 "interacts with the spirit world through altered states of consciousness."(의식이 바뀐 상태에서 정신적 세계와 소통한다) 라고 나와 있다. 다음 문장을 이어서 보면 그들은 "fix some personal or community problem."(개인적 문제가 공동체의 문제를 고친다) 라고 나와 있다. 따라서 정답은 보기 C이다.

2

[정답] **C**

[Inference] 음영단어 Occult가 언급된 문장을 보면 샤먼은 "directs these spiritual energies into the material world for healing or for some other occult purpose"(~이러한 에너지를 치유의 목적이나 초자연적인 의도를 가지고 물질적 세계로 이끈다) 라고 나와 있다. 본문의 "healing or for some other occult purpose"을 보기의 "supernatural (초자연적인) or mystical (신비로운) intention"으로 paraphrase 됐다. 따라서 보기 C가 정답이다.

3
[정답] **B**

[Fact] 문제의 키워드긴 initiatory crisis가 포함된 2단락 첫 번째 문장을 보면, "Often, the shaman obtains his or her power through an initiatory crisis or divine madness."(대부분 샤먼은 initiatory crisis 나 divine madness를 통해 힘을 얻는다)라고 나와 있고, 그다음 문장을 보면 "...shamans believe that they speak to the spirit world…"(샤먼은 그들이 정신적 세계와 소통할 수 있다고 믿는다)라고 나와 있다. 따라서 정답은 보기 B이다.

4
[정답] **C**

[Negative Fact] 문제의 키워드는 "results of shamanic experience"(샤먼 경험의 결과들)이다. 보기 A는 "The shamans believe that the spirit world calls to them"(샤먼은 정신적 세계가 그들을 부른다고 믿는다)와 같은 내용이다. 보기 B는 "Sometimes shaman report distressing experiences like~"(샤먼들은 대부분 고통을 받는 경험을 한다고 말한다)와 일치한다. 보기 D는 "anyone without this self-cure should only be known as a "normal healer."(이러한 자가치료 과정을 거치지 않은 샤먼은 normal healer로 불린다)와 일치한다. 따라서 정답은 보기 C이다.

5
[정답] **D**

[Sentence Simplification] 음영 표시된 문장 전체가 핵심 정보로서 "Exaltation places the shaman outside himself or herself into a state of transcendence"(행복감=exaltation은 샤먼이 초월의 상태로 놓이게 해준다)가 the shaman reaches a state of transcendence by moving beyond his or her current state and into ecstasy (샤먼은 본인의 상태 그 이상을 넘어선 초월의 상태에 도달하고 황홀감을 경험한다)로, "to attain a possible cure"(치료하기 위해)는 "In order to obtain a possible cure"(낫기 위해서)로 표현한 보기 D가 정답이다.

6
[정답] **A**

[Vocabulary] 지문의 mundane (지극히 평범한) 의 동의어를 찾으면 된다. 따라서 답은 보기 A이다.
* Normal 평범한
* Original 원래의
* Spiritual 정신적의
* Conscious 의식하는, 자각하는

7
[정답] **C**

[Negative Fact] 5단락에서 나와 있지 않은 내용을 고르면 된다. 보기 A는 "Extreme exhaustion or fasting can put one into a spell."(극심한 피로감이나 금식은 주문에 걸리게 할 수 있다)와 일치한다. 보기 B는 "All of these ways aid the shaman in finding the secret knowledge needed to heal the sick…"(이 모든 방법은 샤먼이 아픈 사람들을 치유하게 만들 수 있는 비밀의 지식을 갖게 도와준다)와 일치한다. 보기 D는 "Drunkenness or the ingestion of sacred plants can also put the shaman into trance."(술에 취하거나 신성한 식물을 섭취함으로써 샤먼은 무아지경 상태로 빠질 수 있다)와 일치한다.

8
[정답] **B**

[Sentence Insertion] 삽입 문장의 단서는 문장 앞머리의 "This state of intoxication"(이러한 취한 상태)이다. 앞에 Drunkenness or the ingestion of sacred plants (술에 취하거나 신성한 식물을 섭취함으로써) 내용이 나온 뒤 삽입하면 가장 자연스럽다. 따라서 정답은 B이다.

9
[정답] **B**

[Rhetorical Purpose] 음영 표시 문구가 포함된 문장을 보면 "Often these community trances are said to heal mass afflictions, to change the weather in the case of a drought, or to guide the destiny of the tribe." [대부분 이런 공동체 트랜스 (무아지경) 상태는 많은 사람들의 고통을 치유하고, 가뭄 때 날씨를 변화시킬 수 있고, 부족의 운명을 이끌 수 있다고 한다.]라는 내용이 있는데 이는 앞 문장의 "Sometimes, the people from his or her community dance"(때로는 공동체 사람들이 함께 춤을 출 수 있다.) 내용에 대한 부연 설명이다. 따라서 샤먼만 트랜스 상태에 빠지는 게 아닌, 다른 사람들도 빠질 수 있다는 사실을 보여주기 위함이다. 매력적인 보기 D가 답이 되지 않는 이유는 community trance와 shamanic trance의 차이에 대해서 직접적으로 비교하는 내용이 언급되지 않기 때문이다. 따라서 보기 B가 정답이다.

10
[정답] **B, C, F**

[Summary] 지문의 중심내용은 샤먼이 공동체에 미치는 중요한 역할과 샤먼이 그들의 임무를 수행하기 위해 사용하는 여러 기술에 대한 묘사이다. 보기 B는 마지막 6단락의 샤먼이 고통받는 사람 혹은 공동체를 치유하는 방법에 대한 설명이고, C는 2~3단락의 샤먼이 되기 전 겪는 육체적 고통과 나을 수 있는 방법에 대한 이야기이며, F는 4단락에서 샤먼이 겪는 'exaltation' 상태에 대한, 그로 인해 얻는 'wisdom'에 대한 설명과 일치한다.

1 [정답] B

[Rhetorical Purpose] 질문의 키워드인 pre-Roman civilizations 내용이 언급된 문장을 찾아야 한다. 1단락 끝에서 두 번째 문장을 보면 "Building on the legacy of those civilizations that had come before them – the Ancient Greeks, Egyptians, Persians, and others, the Romans developed a unique cultural identity."[로마는 이전에 있던 문명들의(그리스, 이집트, 페르시아, 등등) 유산을 기반으로 해서 그들만의 독특한 문화적 정체성을 만들었다]라고 나와 있다. 보기 C가 오답인 이유는 이전 문명의 영향력이 없었다면 절대로 그만큼 강력해지지 못했을 것이라고 하는 해설("never have become so powerful")때문에 오답이다. 따라서 로마인들은 온전히 그들만의 문화를 만든 게 아니라고 서술하고 있는 보기 B가 정답이다.

2 [정답] A

[Sentence Simplification] 음영 문장 전체가 핵심내용으로서 "From the founding of Rome – the city which became the capital – sometime around 800 B.C.E., to the fall of the Western Roman Empire in 476 C.E."(800BCE에 건국된 로마는 476CE 로마제국의 멸망까지) 라고 time span 이 언급된 부분을 "The Roman Empire was in existence for approximately 1300 years"(로마제국은 대략 1300년 동안 존재했다)로, "the Romans were responsible for some of the most important technological innovations in history and their influence on art, architecture, laws, language, and politics has been far-reaching and long-lasting."(로마는 오랫동안 역사적 기술발전과 예술, 건축, 법, 언어, 그리고 정치까지 이어 다양한 분야에 영향을 미쳤다)은 "their culture has remained relevant to the present day."(그들의 문화는 오늘날까지 영향력이 있다)로 간략하게 표현된 보기 A가 정답이다.

3 [정답] C

[Fact] 질문에서 키워드는 founding fathers(건국의 아버지들)와 structure of Government(정부의 형태)이다. 2단락을 보면 "they [founding fathers] borrowed heavily from the traditions of the Romans."(그들은 로마의 전통에 크게 의존했다)라고 나와 있다. 그리고 그 이유는 그다음 문장인 "The founding fathers adopted the idea that each of the three branches of government served as a check and balance to the others, so they kept that the same."(건국의 아버지들은 3권분립으로서 견제와 균형을 유지하고자 했고, 따라서 이를 유지했다)이라고 나와 있다. 따라서 정답은 보기 C이다.

4 [정답] D

[Negative Fact] 문제의 키워드 Roman architecture에 대한 내용을 검토하고 3단락에 나온 내용을 지우면 된다. 보기 A는 "The staggering number of Roman ruins scattered around"(상당한 수의 로마의 유물들이 세계적으로 흩어져 있다) 라는 내용과 일치하고, 보기 B는 "The delicate balance between science and art that the Romans managed to find with many of their building projects continues to inspire modern architects."(로마사람들은 과학과 예술의 수평을 잘 맞췄고, 그들의 건축물들은 오늘날의 건축학에도 영감을 주고 있다) 라는 내용과 일치하고, 보기 C 는 "The Romans experimented with different kinds of building materials."(로마인들은 다양한 재료를 시험 삼아 건축물에 사용했다)와 일치한다. 따라서 언급되지 않은 보기 D가 정답이다.

5 [정답] D

[Rhetorical Purpose] 4단락의 목적을 물어보고 있는 질문이다. 이를 풀기 위해선 4단락의 핵심내용을 파악하면 된다. concrete 의 발견, 다양한 layer와 arches를 사용하는 기법 등 "wide implication"(폭넓은 결과들)에 대한 내용이다. 따라서 정답은 보기 D이다.

6 [정답] C

[Fact] 4단락 마지막 문장을 보면 "...their buildings managed to blend the man-made with the natural world that surrounded them."(로마인들은 인간이 만든 작품과 그들을 둘러싸고 있는 자연계를 병합했다) 이라고 나와 있다. 따라서 "balance between artificial and natural world"라고 paraphrased 되어 있는 보기 C가 정답이다.

7 [정답] B

[Sentence Insertion] 삽입 문장의 단서는 As are those of Cicero (Cicero의 것들도 ~이다) 이다. A 문장에서 "The works of Virgil and Ovid are still standard reading in schools all around the world today"(Virgil이나 Ovid의 작품들도 아직 전 세계적으로 학교에서 다루고 있다) 내용 뒤에 들어가면 가장 자연스럽다. 따라서 정답은 B이다.

8 [정답] D

[Rhetorical Purpose] 음영 표시된 문구의 문장을 살펴보면 The works of Virgil and Ovid are still standard reading in schools all around the world today"(Virgil이나 Ovid의 작품들도 아직 전 세계적으로 학교에서 다루고 있다)이라고 나와 있고, 바로 직전 문장에는 "Rome was home to some of the greatest writers of the ancient world."(로마에는 고대사회의 훌륭한 작가들이 있었다)라고 나와 있다. 따라서 여러 유명한 작가들이 오늘날까지 미치는 영향에 대해 설명을 하고 있다고 할 수 있다. 따라서 정답은 보기 D이다.

9
[정답] **A**

[Inference] 질문의 키워드인 Romans에 대한 문장을 살펴볼 필요가 있다. 7단락 앞의 두 문장을 보면 "The span of time from the founding of Rome to the end of the Western Roman Empire is roughly the same span of time that separates us from the Song Dynasty. Life in ancient Rome was strikingly different from what it was at the tail end of the Roman period."(로마의 건국부터 로마제국의 멸망까지의 기간은 우리와 송나라와의 격차와 비슷하다. 로마의 처음은 끝과 매우 달랐다) 내용과 보기 A가 일치한다.

10
[정답] **A, C, D**

[Summary] 지문의 중심내용은 로마가 역사적으로 가장 오래된 문명 중 하나였다는 것과, 오늘 우리 사회에 가장 많은 영향을 미쳤다는 내용이다. 보기 A는 2단락의 로마의 문화적 유산이 오늘날까지 영향을 미치고 있다는 내용과 일치하고, 보기 C는 4단락의 구체적인 건축 자재의 발명인 콘크리트에 대한 내용과 일치하고 B는 순서가 서로 다르므로 맞지 않고 E는 안 나온 내용이며 Eastern이 아니라 Western Empire이다. 따라서, 정답은 A,C,D이다.

PASSAGE 3 : Halloween

1
[정답] **C**

[Sentence Simplification] 음영 표시된 문장 전체가 핵심 정보로서 "In the Scots language, the word eve is pronounced even, and it is believed that All Hallows Eve was shortened to Halloween over time."(스코틀랜드 언어로는 eve라는 단어는 even으로 발음이 되고, All Hallows Eve라는 표현이 시간이 지나면서 Halloween으로 줄어들었다) 는 내용과 일치하는 건 보기 C이다.

2
[정답] **D**

[Fact] 1단락 두 번째 문장을 보면 죽은 이들을 기념하는 날이 있는 국가들은 "predominantly Western Christian countries,"(대부분이 서양 크리스천 국가들)이라고 나와 있다. 따라서 정답은 보기 D이다.

3
[정답] **A**

[Vocabulary] 지문의 permeable (침투할 수 있는) 의 동의어를 찾으면 된다. 따라서 답은 보기 A이다.

* penetrable 관통할 수 있는
* absorbent 흡수력 있는
* spongy 흡수력 있는
* Accessible 접근 가능한

4
[정답] **B**

[Negative Fact] 2단락에서 나온 내용을 제거하면 된다. 보기 A는 첫 번째 문장 "The roots of Halloween are thought to go back to the Gaelic festival known as Samhain."(핼러윈은 Samhain이라고 알려져 있는 Gaelic 축제로부터 비롯된다고 알려져 있다)와 일치한다. 보기 C는 "The first mention of Samhain in the written record comes from the 10th century Gaelic tale Tochmarc Empire. It is from this and similar mythological stories that some of the practices we still observe today were inherited."(10세기 기록된 내용과 신화 이야기들로부터 우리가 지금도 목격하고 있는 관행을 상속받았다고 할 수 있다)와 일치한다. 보기 D는 "The first mention of Samhain in the written record comes from the 10th century Gaelic tale Tochmarc Empire. It is from this and similar mythological stories that some of the practices we still observe today were inherited."(Samhain이 처음으로 언급된 것은 10세기에 기록된 Gaelic 이야기이고, 여기에서 오늘날 기념하고 있는 여러 관습들이 비롯됐다고 알려져 있다)와 일치한다. 따라서 언급되지 않은 보기 B가 정답이다.

5

[정답] **A**

[Fact] 3단락 첫 번째 문장을 보면 "Bonfires are believed to have been a central feature of Samhain and they have remained an integral part of Halloween tradition up to the present day."(모닥불은 Samhain 축제에서 중요한 부분을 차지하고 있고, 핼러윈 전통부터 오늘날까지 중요한 요소로 존재하고 있다) 내용과 일치하는 보기 A가 정답이다.

6

[정답] **C**

[Rhetorical Purpose] 질문의 키워드인 'trick of treating'이 언급된 문장을 보면 "Another favored activity of revelers during Halloween is to dress up in costumes and go from door to door 'trick or treating'."(핼러윈을 즐기는 사람들이 좋아하는 액티비티 중 하나는 의상을 입고 동네를 돌아다니며 trick or treating을 하는 것이다) 라고 나와 있다. 그리고 그 뒤의 내용도 첫 번째 문장을 뒷받침해 주고 있다. 예를 들어 costumes와 guising에 대한 내용도 첫 번째 문장과 관련된 추가 설명들이다. 따라서 정답은 보기 C 이다.

7

[정답] **A**

[Fact] 질문의 키워드인 guising이 언급된 문장을 보면 된다. "Many of the costumes on display will invariably be supernatural in theme. This tradition closely resembles that of 'guising' and 'mumming'."(의상들은 대부분 초자연적인 주제와 관련이 되어 있고, 이 전통은 'guising'과 'mumming'와 비슷하다)의 내용이 담긴 보기 A가 정답이다.

8

[정답] **D**

[Negative Fact] 5단락에서 나오지 않은 내용을 고르면 된다. 보기 A는 "By the first decade of the twentieth century, it had spread throughout North America, regardless of the ethnicity or religion of those celebrating it."(20세기에 들어서서는 핼러윈은 북미로 퍼졌고, 즐기는 이들의 민족성이나 종교와 상관없이 즐기게 되었다)와 일치하고, 보기 B는 "the holiday only reached the New World in the nineteenth century."(19세기에는 핼러윈이 뉴월드=아메리카 대륙에까지 퍼졌다)와 일치하고, 보기 C는 마지막 문장인 "Today, Americans spend between 2.5 and 3 billion dollars on candy and chocolate for Halloween"(오늘날 미국인들은 25.3~30억 달러를 핼러윈 사탕과 초콜릿을 사는 데 쓴다)와 일치한다. 따라서 정답은 나오지 않은 보기 D이다.

9

[정답] **B**

[Sentence Insertion] 삽입해야 하는 문장에서의 키워드는 "This"이다. 삽입 문장은 이런 이유 때문에 대부분의 이민자들이 모국어를 사용하고 그들의 문화와 친밀했던 성향 때문일 것이라는 내용이다. 따라서 B 문장 직전 내용 (아일랜드나 스코틀랜드 이민자들이 핼러윈 문화를 정착시켰고 그들이 사는 동네에서만 실행됐다)와 일치한다.

10

[정답] **A, C, E**

[Summary] 지문의 중심내용은 오늘날의 핼러윈은 다양한 시대와 전통에서 비롯됐다는 것이다. 보기 A는 2단락의 핼러윈의 기원에 관한 내용과 일치하고, 보기 C는 3~4단락의 구체적인 핼러윈 활동 내용의 기원에 관한 내용과 일치하며 보기 E는 5단락의 핼러윈이 19세기에 New World로 전파된 내용과 일치한다. 보기 B는 모든 활동이 Gaelic festival에 기원을 뒀다는 설명으로 다양한 시대와 전통에서 비롯된 핼러윈에 대한 잘못된 설명이므로 오답이다. 보기 D는 천주교 전도사들에 의해 선택(selected)되었다는 내용이 언급된 적이 없으므로 오답이다. 보기 F는 문단 5에서 Irish and Scottish immigrants에 의해 전파되었다는 설명이 있으므로 천주교 전도사들에 의해 전파되었다는 설명은 오답이다.

ANSWERS

PASSAGE 1

1 D	2 C	3 B	4 B	5 B
6 C	7 B	8 B	9 C	

10 A, C, E

PASSAGE 2

1 B	2 C	3 C	4 A	5 D
6 C	7 C	8 B	9 D	

10 A, B, D

PASSAGE 3

1 C	2 B	3 C	4 C	5 B
6 B	7 C	8 B	9 A	

10 B, C, D

Occult 신비한, 숨은 (=Cryptic)
Dismember 절단하다
Exaltation 고귀한, 고양된
Ingestion 섭취, 삼키다.
Affliction 고통
Trance 황홀경, 무아지경

Erect 똑바로 서다
Relevant 관련 있는, 적절한
Testament 유언, 증언,증거
Ingenuity 독창성, 기발한 재주, 재간
Liminal 경계의
Reveler 흥청망청

PASSAGE 1 : Machu Picchu

1 [정답] D

[Fact] 질문의 키워드인 impressive(놀라운)과 일치하는 문장을 찾으면 된다. 15세가 당시의 이용가능한 도구의 부족 및 구조물의 정교함을 감안하면 Machu Picchu는 믿을 수 없는 공학적,고고학적 위업으로 간주된다. 따라서, absence of machinery는 시대를 앞서간 건축을 의미한다고 볼 수 있으므로 답은 D이다. A의 경우 내용은 맞으나 질문이 researcher의 의견을 묻는 것으로 A는 researcher 가 아닌 author의 의견이다. 따라서 정답은 D이다.

2 [정답] C

[Inference] 질문의 키워드인 rocks와 관련된 내용을 확인해 본다. 2단락에서는 무거운 돌을 옮기는 게 힘들었을 거라는 설명을 이어가고 마지막 문장을 보면 "Archaeologists have since unearthed skeletal remains at the foot of the valley, buried

under enormous stones,"(고고학자들은 엄청난 크기의 돌에 묻혀 있는 해골을 찾기도 했다) 내용을 보면 일을 하다 죽은 사람들이 있었다는 걸 말해주고 있다. 따라서 hazardous라는 표현을 담고 있는 보기 C가 정답이다.

3 [정답] B

[Vocabulary] 지문의 arduous (고된) 의 동의어를 찾으면 된다. 따라서 답은 보기 B이다.

* Physical 육체적인
* Demanding 힘든
* Substantial 엄청난
* Time-consuming 시간이 오래 걸리는

4 [정답] B

[Fact] 질문의 키워드 stonemason (석공)과 관련된 문장에서 단서를 찾으면 된다. 3단락 첫 번째 문장을 보면 "...stonemasons to pound and shape each rock and then lower them into place."(석공들은 돌을 치고 모양을 만들어서 낮은 위치로 옮겼다)라고 나와 있고, 그 뒤에 문장에서는 "This process was intricate…"(이러한 과정은 섬세하고…) 에 대한 평가가 나온다. 따라서 정답은 보기 B이다.

5 [정답] B

[Negative Fact] 4단락에서 나오지 않은 내용을 고르면 된다. 보기 A는 "...Machu Picchu was constructed intentionally on a network of tectonic faults…"(마추픽추는 고의적으로 지각단층에 건설되었다)와 일치하고, 보기 C는 "Consequently, the corrosion of the stone walls was avoided…"(따라서 이 돌로 구성된 벽들은 부식을 피할 수 있었으며…)와 일치하며, 보기 D는 마지막 문장에서 "...regarded by historians as a symbol of engineering ingenuity..."(역사학자들은 이를 기발한 공학기술의 상징물이라고 여긴다) 와 일치한다. 따라서 언급되지 않은 B가 정답이다.

6 [정답] C

[Sentence Simplification] 음영 표시된 문장 전체가 핵심 정보로서 "The completion of such an irrigation system is regarded by historians as a symbol of engineering ingenuity on behalf of the Incas."(역사학자들은 이와 같은 관개 조직의 완성은 잉카사람들의 기발한 공학기술의 상징물이라고 여긴다) 가 " The Incas built an irrigation system which historians consider to be resourceful and creative."(잉카인들은 역사학사들이 지략 있고 기발하다고 여기는 관개 조직을 만들었다)로 paraphrase 되었다. 따라서 보기 C가 정답이다.

7   [정답] B

[Negative Fact] 5단락에서 마추픽추의 위치 선정에 대하여 나오지 않은 이유를 고르면 된다. 보기 A는 "supply of sustenance"(자양물 공급)와 일치하고, 보기 C는 "some form of defense"(방어의 형태)와 일치하며 보기 D는 "and streams"(개울가)와 근접하다는 내용을 통해 걸러낼 수 있다. 따라서 정답은 나오지 않은 보기 B이다.

8   [정답] B

[Vocabulary] 지문의 adversaries(적들)의 동의어를 찾으면 된다. 따라서 답은 보기 B이다.

* Peers 친구들
* Enemies 적들
* Neighbors 이웃들
* Strangers 낯선이들

9   [정답] C

[Sentence Insertion] 삽입 문장에서의 키워드는 "This" 이다. '이것'은 "acted like a slow-running faucet"(천천히 흐르는 수전과 같은 역할을 했으며) 이는 "upheld dampness and increased cultivation in the compounds."(눅눅함을 유지하고 경작을 증가시켰다) 따라서 '이것'은 이전 문장에 나오는 "water"라는 걸 알 수 있다. 따라서 정답은 C이다.

10   [정답] A, C, E

[Summary] 지문의 중심내용은 안데스 산맥에 있는 마추픽추의 위대한 건축 그리고 기계공학의 업적에 대한 설명이다. 보기 A는 본문 전체 내용에 해당되는 내용이다. "…overcame many tribulations…"는 수많은 시련을 극복했다는 뜻으로서, 본문에 언급됐던 다양한 어려움들을 가리키는 표현이다. 보기 C는 5단락의 마추픽추의 지리학적 위치에 대한 내용과 일치하며, 보기 E는 2~3단락의 마추픽추 구조물 설명 내용과 일치한다. 보기 B는 험난한 기후로 stone wall 없이는 농경이 발달하지 못했을 것이라는 내용으로 본문과 일치하지 않아 오답이다. 보기 D는 "carving"에 대한 언급이 없으므로 오답이다. 보기 F는 "fantastic condition"이라는 부분이 본문과 일치하지 않아서 오답이다.

PASSAGE 2 : Hagia Sophia

1   [정답] B

[Fact] 질문의 키워드는 designated mosque이다. 1단락 중간을 보면 "…subsequently became a designated mosque"(… 후에 지정된 모스크가 되었다) 라고 나와 있다. 직전 문장에는 "It was previously an Eastern Orthodox (Christian) church from its construction in 537 through to the capture of Constantinople by the Ottoman Empire in 1453…"라고 시기가 나와 있기 때문에 보기 B가 정답이다.

2   [정답] C

[Fact] 질문의 키워드는 brick and mortar walls이다. 2단락을 보면 "Forty windows were built into the dome structure, which had the purposes of creating a light, airy interior space, and lessening the use of heavy brick and mortar walls."(40개의 창문이 돔 건설물에 지어졌고 이는 빛을 비추고, 내부 공간이 바람이 잘 통하게 하고 벽돌과 회반죽 벽의 사용을 줄였다)라고 나와 있다. 따라서 정답은 C이다.

3   [정답] C

[Fact] 2단락 두 번째 문장을 보면 "It is an outstanding specimen of Byzantine Architecture…"(훌륭한 비잔틴 건축물의 표본이다)라고 Hagia Sophia를 묘사한다. 따라서 정답은 보기 C이다.

4   [정답] A

[Fact] 3단락의 첫 번째 문장을 보면 "The numerous mosaics in the structure have caused a certain amount of controversy."(건축물에 있는 다양한 모자이크는 상당한 논쟁을 펼치게 했다)라고 나와 있고, 보기 A에서 were not immune to (be immune to = ~에 영향을 받지 않는)이라는 표현을 사용해 paraphrase 했다.

5   [정답] D

[Vocabulary] 지문의 secular (세속적인)의 동의어를 찾으면 된다. 따라서 답은 보기 D이다.

* Artistic 예술적인
* Educational 교육적인
* Spiritual 정신적인
* Non-religious 비종교적인

6

[Sentence Simplification] 음영 표시된 문장 전체가 핵심 정보로서 The Muezzin은 "...would use an external gallery built on the minaret to be heard by as many worshipers as possible."(뾰족탑에 설치된 외부 갤러리를 사용해서 최대한 많은 숭배자들이 [기도를] 들을 수 있게 했다)을 보기 C "The Muezzin used an outside gallery in order to be heard by more worshippers."로 paraphrase 했다.

7

[정답] **C**

[Rhetorical Purpose] 글 전체에서 4단락의 목적을 물어보는 질문이다. 4단락 첫 번째 문장에서부터 "Another notable feature of the building are the four minarets which enclose the building."(건물을 에워싸고 있는 네 개의 뾰족탑이 중요한 특징이다) 라고 되어 있다. 따라서 보기 C가 정답이다.

8

[정답] **B**

[Negative] Fact 5단락의 runic graffiti 설명으로 나와 있지 않은 내용을 고르면 된다. 보기 A는 "...some runic graffiti has been found on this level[auditorium]."(룬 문자의 그래피티는 강당에서 발견되었다) 와 일치하고, 보기 C는 "Some have speculated that it may have been a member of the Varangian Guard who were responsible for the graffiti..."(어떤 이들은 그래피티가 Varangian Guard 멤버 중 하나의 작품이라고 추론한다) 와 일치하며, 보기 D는 그래피티가 발견된 강당은 "Empress and her court"(여제와 궁중)을 위한 장소라고 나와 있고, 그다음 문장은 "Interestingly,~"(흥미롭게도)로 시작된다는 점에서 추론해 볼 수 있는 내용이다. 따라서 언급되지 않은 보기 B가 정답이다.

9

[정답] **D**

[Structure] 본문이 어떤 흐름으로 전개되는지를 물어보는 질문이다. 1단락에서 Hagia Sophia에 대한 overview로 시작되고, 그다음 문단들에서 외관과 내부에 대한 구체적인 묘사가 이어진다. 따라서 정답은 보기 D이다.

10

[정답] **A, B, D**

[Summary] 지문의 중심내용은 독특한 건축물 양식을 한 Hagia Sophia가 오늘날까지 기독교와 이슬람교 모두에서 중요한 문화적 유산으로 남아있다는 설명이다. 보기 A는 1단락의 Hagia Sophia에 관한 소개 내용과 일치하고, 보기 B는 2~3단락의 Hagia Sophia 구조 설명 내용과 일치하며 보기 D는 5단락의 Hagia Sophia graffiti와 관련된 논쟁 내용과 일치한다.

PASSAGE 3 : La Sagrada Familia

1

[정답] **C**

[Inference] 1단락 두 번째 문장에 보면 Sagrada Familia는 건축가인 Francisco de Paula del Villar 가 맡게 된 건축물이라고 나와 있다. 하지만 그다음 문장을 보면 가우디에게 작품이 넘어오면서 "...Gaudi transformed the project with his innovative architectural..."(가우디는 그만의 혁신적인 스타일로 프로젝트를 맡았다) 라고 나와 있다. 따라서 여러 건축가의 손을 걸쳤기 때문에 하나 이상의 건축물적 스타일을 embodies(구현하다)한다고 표현할 수 있다.

2

[정답] **B**

[Negative Fact] 2단락에 언급되지 않은 내용을 고르는 문제이다. 보기 A는 2단락의 첫 문장 "The Sagrada Familia was started as a Roman Catholic church, [···] and finally a minor basilica in 2010"과 일치한다. 보기 B는 "···it will stand as the tallest religious building in Europe"에서 보듯이 완성될 경우에는 가장 높은 건물이 된다는 것으로 현재는 가장 높은 건물이 아니므로 본문의 내용과 일치하지 않는다. 보기 C는 "...construction of the basilica has taken longer than that of the Great Pyramids."(바실리카의 건설은 피라미드를 건설하는 것보다 오래 걸렸다) 와 일치하며 마지막 보기 D는 첫 번째 문장의 "...finally a minor basilica in 2010"(2010년도에 minor basilica로 임명되었다) 와 일치한다. 따라서 본문과 일치하지 않는 내용인 보기 B가 정답입니다.

3

[정답] **C**

[Vocabulary] 지문의 artificial (인공의, 인위적인) 의 동의어를 찾으면 된다. 따라서 답은 보기 C이다.

＊Replicated 복제된
＊Ordinary 평범한
＊Manufactured 제작된
＊Superficial 피상적인

4

[정답] **C**

[Negative Fact] 문장에서 Gaudi는 Nativity Facade는 직접 만들었다고 나오지만 Passion Facade와 Glory Facade는 나중에 지어진 거라고 나와 있다. 따라서 정답은 C이다.

5

[정답] **B**

[Sentence Simplification] 음영 표시된 문장 전체가 핵심내용으로서 "Finally, Gaudi installed a 4x4 magic square of 15 numbers on a wall of the basilica; the magic constant—the sum of all numbers horizontally or vertically—is 33,"(마지막으로, 가우디는 4x4의 매직 스퀘어 15개의 숫자를 바실리카 벽에 설치했으며, magic constant [마법의 정수] – 가로세로 숫자의 합 – 는 33" 이 "Gaudi included a magic square with the sum of all the numbers horizontally or vertically"(가우디는 가로세로 숫자의 합인 매직 스퀘어를 포함시켰고)로 간단하게 paraphrase 되었고, 본문의 "Christ's age when he was crucified."(예수가 십자가에 못 박혔을 때의 나이)를 "adding up to Christ's age when the religious figure died"(예수가 돌아가셨을 때의 나이를 합산한…)으로 표현했다.

6   [정답] **B**

[Fact] 3~4단락을 전체적으로 확인해야 하는 질문이다. 3단락에서 건축물의 설명을 보면 일부는 "too abstract"(너무 추상적)이라는 표현이 있다. 이는 implicit(암시적)이라고 표현될 수 있다. 반면에 각각의 외관에 눈에 보이는 것들을 디자인한 것은 explicit(눈에 보이는, 명백한) 내용의 표현이라고 할 수 있다. 따라서 보기 B가 정답이다.

7   [정답] **C**

[Rhetorical Purpose] 질문의 키워드인 "school"이 나온 부분을 보면 되는데, 가우디는 "built a school on the site for the children of construction workers." 건설현장에서 일하는 사람들의 아이들을 위해 그곳에 학교를 설립했다"라고 나와 있고, 현장에서 일하는 아버지들이 밤낮으로 일할 때 아이들이 있을 수 있는 곳이라고 설명이 나와 있다. 이는 가우디의 사려 깊음(thoughtfulness)과 혁신적인 아이디어(innovation)를 보여주는 대목이다. 따라서 보기 C가 정답이다.

8   [정답] **B**

[Sentence Insertion] 삽입 문장의 키워드는 'This' 이다. 뒤의 내용은 일하는 것들 더 생산력 있게 도와주었다 이기 때문에, 학교를 설립해서 일하는 아버지들이 일에 더 몰두할 수 있게 해준 내용 뒤에 나오면 자연스럽다. 따라서 보기 B가 정답이다.

9   [정답] **A**

[Inference] 6단락 첫 번째 문장을 보면 그의 누추한 모습 때문에 "mistaken for a beggar."(거지로 오해를 받았다) 라고 나와 있고, 트램카에 치였을 때도, "Because he looked like a beggar and he had no identification papers, help came slowly."(그는 거지처럼 보였고 신원을 확인할 수 없었기 때문에 도움의 손길이 늦게 왔다) 라는 내용이 있다. 따라서 그의 외적인 모습은 그의 불운한 죽음에 어느 정도 기여했다고 할 수 있다. 따라서 보기 A가 정답이다.

10   [정답] **B, C, D**

[Summary] 본문의 핵심내용은, Sagrada Familia는 가우디의 건축적인 경이로움과 헌신을 보여준다는 것이다. 보기 B는 5단락의 학교의 건설에 관한 내용과 일치하고, 보기 C는 1~3단락에서의 사그라다 파밀리아의 묘사와 웅장함을 나타내는 내용과 일치하며 보기 D는 4단락의 "symbolism" 내용과 일치한다. 보기 A는 서론에서 소개되는 Sagrada Familia의 특징으로 지엽적인 내용이므로 오답이다. 보기 E는 가우디의 죽음에 대한 내용으로 가우디의 헌신에 대한 내용과 직접적인 연관이 없으므로 오답이다. 보기 F는 본문에서 언급되지 않은 내용이므로 오답이다.

ANSWERS

PASSAGE 1

1 C	2 D	3 C	4 A	5 A
6 B	7 D	8 D	9 D	
10 B, C, D				

PASSAGE 2

1 B	2 B	3 D	4 D	5 D
6 B	7 B	8 A	9 C	
10 A, D, E				

PASSAGE 3

1 A	2 A	3 B	4 C	5 B
6 A	7 C	8 D	9 D	
10 B, C, F				

Detonate 폭파하다
Isotopic 동위원소의
Implosion (진공관의)내파(opp. explosion)
Erratically 엉뚱하게
Havoc 큰 파란, 큰 혼란

Harness 마구(를 채우다)
Malignment 악성의
Leukemia 백혈병
Disinfection 소독,살균
Incineration 소각

PASSAGE 1 : The Manhattan Project

1
[정답] **C**

[Sentence Simplification] 음영 표시된 문장 전체가 핵심 정보로서 "This discovery prompted a warning from two eminent Hungarian–American scientists to President Franklin D. Roosevelt"(이러한 발견은 두 명의 저명한 헝가리–미국계 과학자들로 하여금 루즈벨트 대통령에게 주의를 주게 했다)가 "Franklin D. Roosevelt received a warning from two scientists"(루즈벨트는 두 명의 과학자들로부터 경고를 받았다)로 paraphrase 되었고, "the discovery could lead to the development of a devastating new kind of weapon in Nazi Germany"(그 발견은 나치독일이 파괴력 있는 새로운 무기를 만들 수 있을 거라고)가 "who alerted him of the development of a new weapon"(새로운 무기의 개발을 알렸다)로 paraphrased 되었다.

2
[정답] **D**

[Fact] 1단락 두 번째 문장을 보면 "It was initiated partially in response to the accidental discovery of nuclear fission by German scientists"(맨하튼 프로젝트는 독일 과학자가 우연치 않게 핵분열을 발견하게 되면서 시작된 원인도 있다) 라고 나와 있다. 따라서 정답은 보기 D이다.

3
[정답] **C**

[Vocabulary] 지문의 escalation(상승)의 동의어를 찾으면 된다. 따라서 답은 보기 C이다.

＊Intensification 강화
＊Leap 도약, 점프
＊Rise 상승
＊Aggravation 악화

4
[정답] **A**

[Negative Fact] 2단락에서 나오지 않은 내용을 걸러내면 된다. 보기 B는 "...the British program for nuclear research was at a more advanced stage than that of the United States"(핵 연구는 당시에 영국이 미국보다 앞서있었다) 와 일치한다. 보기 C는 "The aim of the project was to create a bomb capable of detonating using nuclear fission before Nazi Germany."(프로젝트의 목표는 독일나치보다 먼저 핵분열을 사용해 폭탄을 만드는 것이었다) 와 일치한다. 보기 D는 "Nuclear research was already being conducted at several universities around the United States"(핵 연구는 미국 전역에 걸쳐 여러 대학에서 실험이 진행되고 있었다) 와 일치한다. 따라서 언급되지 않은 보기 A가 정답이다.

5
[정답] **A**

[Main Idea] 3단락 전체의 역할, 즉 핵심내용을 물어보는 질문이다. 3단락 첫 번째 문장을 보면 "Nuclear material was essential in the development of the 'Little Boy' and 'Fat Man' bombs which were the results of the Manhattan Project."('리틀보이'와 '팻맨' 폭탄을 만드는 데에 있어서 핵물질은 중요했다.) 라고 나와 있고, 그 후에 "The Manhattan Project developed weapons grade materials from two of these elements, plutonium and uranium."(맨하튼 프로젝트를 통해 개발된 무기는 이들 중 두 개의 요소를 필요로 했는데, 플루토늄과 우라늄이다) 라고 나와 있다. 그리고 이어서 이 두 요소에 "two important materials" 대한 설명이 나와 있으므로 정답은 보기 A이다.

6
[정답] **B**

[Rhetorical Purpose] 질문의 키워드인 production and

acquisition of uranium 설명이 나온 내용을 찾으면 된다. 4단락 첫 번째 문장부터 "The production of uranium-235 and plutonium-239 would prove to be the biggest undertakings of the whole Manhattan Project."(uranium-235과 plutonium-239의 생산은 이 프로젝트의 가장 큰 일이었다) 라고 나와 있고, 그 뒤 문장에서는 "It is estimated that 80~90% of the project's budget was expended on this pursuit."(예산 중 80~90%가 이러한 목표를 위해 사용되었다)라고 생산의 중요성에 대해 강조하고 있다. 따라서 정답은 보기 B이다.

7 [정답] D

[Inference] 질문의 키워드인 Shinkolobwe mine에 관한 내용을 찾으면 된다. 우라늄을 조달해 오는 과정에 대한 중요성을 설명하면서 "Most of the uranium used in the Manhattan Project was taken from the Shinkolobwe mine in the Congo."(프로젝트에 사용된 대부분의 우라늄은 콩고에 있는 Shinkolobwe mine에서 가져오게 되었다) 라고 나와 있다. 따라서 모든 우라늄의 출처가 Shinkolobwe 는 아니라는 뜻이므로 정답은 보기 D이다.

8 [정답] D

[Fact] 맨하튼 프로젝트를 통해서 두 가지 종류의 폭탄을 개발하게 되었는데, 그 두 번째 종류는 "...implosion type device with a plutonium core."(플루토늄 코어를 사용하는 내파 종류의 장치) 라고 나와 있다. 내파 타입의 특징 중 하나는 "...explosion is focused inward…"(폭파가 안쪽으로 일어난다)라고 나와 있으므로 정답은 보기 D이다.

9 [정답] D

[Sentence Insertion] 삽입 문장의 키워드는 "This test"(이러한 시험)이다. 삽입 문장의 또다른 단서는 "dropped live"라는 표현인데, 이전 문장에서 "trial run"(시운전)에 대한 내용이 나오고, 그 후에 실제(Live)로 폭격한 내용이 나오면 자연스럽다. 따라서 정답은 보기 D이다.

10 [정답] B, C, D

[Summary] 본문의 핵심내용은 맨하튼 프로젝트가 전쟁 당시의 프로젝트로서 핵무기 발전에 기여한 중요한 역할을 한 사건이라는 부분이다. 보기 B는 2단락의 프로젝트의 "aim"(목적)과 관련된 핵심내용이고, 보기 C는 3~4단락의 nuclear material로 쓰인 중요한 원소에 관한 내용이고, 보기 D는 맨하튼 프로젝트를 통해 미국이 얻게 된 두 가지 폭탄 종류에 대한 설명인 5단락의 핵심내용이다.

PASSAGE 2 : Magnetic Fields

1 [정답] B

[Fact] 1단락 두 번째 문장을 보면 "It illustrates the magnetic influence on an electric charge of other charges or magnetized materials."(이것은 자화된 물질이나 전하가 다른 전하에 미치는 자기 영향을 보여준다)라고 나와 있다. 따라서 'the impact a charge has on other charges'라고 다르게 표현한 보기 B가 정답이다.

2 [정답] B

[Vocabulary] 지문의 exerts (힘을 가하다) 의 동의어를 찾으면 된다. 따라서 답은 보기 B이다.

＊attempts 노력하다
＊applies (힘 등을) 가하다
＊Pulls 당기다
＊Pushes 밀다

3 [정답] D

[Negative Fact] 2단락에서 나오지 않은 내용을 고르면 된다. 보기 A는 "The north and south ends of two magnets attract, while two north ends or two south ends repel."(자석의 북/남쪽은 서로 이끌고, 북쪽끼리 혹은 남쪽끼리는 서로 밀어낸다) 와 일치한다. 보기 B는 "Two subsets of magnets exist: permanent and electromagnetic."(자석에는 두 가지 부류가 있다: 영구자석과 전자기 자석이다)와 일치한다. 보기 C는 "Permanent magnets have continuous magnetism while electromagnets require electricity to retain their magnetism."(영구자석은 지속적인 자력이 필요하고, 전자기자석은 자력을 위해 전기를 필요로 한다)와 일치한다. 따라서 언급되지 않은 보기 D가 정답이다.

4 [정답] D

[Negative Fact] 3단락에 언급되지 않은 보기를 고르면 된다. 보기 A와 B는 "The magnetic field's south pole is near the Earth's geographic north pole, and the north pole is near the geographic south pole. This makes compass use possible for navigation"(자기장의 남극은 지구의 북극 근처에 있고, 자기장의 북극은 지구의 남극 근처에 있다. 이는 운행을 할 때 나침반 사용을 가능케 한다)와 일치한다. 보기 C는 "The Earth's magnetic field, also known as the geomagnetic field, forms the magnetosphere."와 일치한다.

5

D

[Sentence Simplification] 음영 표시된 문장 전체가 핵심내용이다. 본문은 "Some~ zones" 이 부분 때문에, "so ~ storms"(~이다)라고 인과관계가 cause → effect 순서로 표현되어 있다. 정답 D는 거꾸로, "Astronomers~storms(~이다)까지의 내용과 "because~ionosphere"의 인과관계를 BECAUSE로 effect → cause 순서로 다르게 paraphrase 해놨다. 따라서 "so"를 기준으로 한 내용과 "because"를 기준으로 한 내용이 순서만 다를 뿐 같기 때문에 정답은 보기 D이다.

6

B

[Fact] 질문의 키워드인 음영 표시된 dipole과 관련된 내용을 보면 된다. 문장에서는 전후의 지시어를 살펴보는 것이 중요하다. This offset field라는 지시어를 통해서 dipole를 지칭하고 있다.

7

B

[Sentence Insertion] 삽입 문장에서의 단서는 "In other words"(즉, 다시 말해)이다. 앞선 문장에서 "the dipole goes straight through the planet"(쌍극자는 행성을 관통한다) 과 관련된, 혹은 이 내용 다르게 표현한 문장을 고르면 된다. 이 내용은 본문의 "A central axis defines the dipole's orientation"(중심축은 쌍극자의 방향을 나타낸다) 내용 뒤에 나오면 자연스럽다. 따라서 보기 B가 정답이다.

8

A

[Rhetorical Purpose] 질문에서 음영 표시된 문장 주변 내용을 먼저 확인하면 된다. 이전 문장에서 "...the horizontal plane points erratically(=변덕스럽게)" 그리고 "...local deviations(=탈선) happen."이라고 나와 있다. 이처럼 움직임을 종잡을 수 없고, 이로 인해 탈선이 일어난다는 내용을 다르게 표현한(=instability) 보기 A가 정답이다.

9

C

[Fact] 질문의 키워드는 "variable"(변수)이다. 7단락 중간을 보면 "...it varies depending upon the position on the Earth's surface and time."(지구 표면에서의 위치와 시간에 따라 다르다)라고 varies 라는 동사를 써서 변수에 대한 설명이 시작된다. 그리고 그다음 문장부터 이에 대한 설명이 이어지는데, "Second is the magnetic inclination, also known as the angle of dip. It is the angle made against the horizontal plane on the Earth's surface" 여기에서 "angle of dip"를 정의내리면서 "angle made against the horizontal plane"이라는 표현을 쓴다. 이는 보기 C와 일치한다.

10

A, D, E

[Summary] 본문의 핵심내용은 자기장이 지구에 여러 방면으로 중요하다는 내용이다. 보기 A는 7단락의 "three variables"(=magnetic declination, magnetic inclination, magnetic field)를 요약한 내용이고, 보기 D는 4~5단락의 지구의 자기장에 관한 내용과 일치하고, 보기 E는 6단락에서 언급되는 "local deviation"과 그에 따른 나침반의 한계에 관한 내용과 일치한다.

보기 B는 지구의 자기장에 대한 지엽적인 설명으로 오답이고 보기 C 또한 자기력에 대한 설명으로 자기장에 대해 이야기하는 핵심내용과 어긋난다. 보기 F는 본문의 내용과 일치하지 않으므로 오답이다.

1
[정답] **A**

[Fact] 질문의 키워드는 'gamma rays'이다. 1단락 두 번째 문장 앞부분에서 gamma rays는 "Discovered shortly after x-rays in 1900" 1900년에 x-ray의 발견 이후로 발견되었고, 그 이유는 "because of their shared properties,"(그들의 유사한 성질 때문)이라고 나와 있다. 따라서 정답은 보기 A이다.

2
[정답] **A**

[Sentence Simplification] 음영 표시된 문장 중 앞 내용 ("Fortunately, the strongest gamma rays are emitted by matters some millions of lightyears away, deep in outer space – such as black holes, supernova explosions, and the collision of neutron stars") 이 보기 A의 (Emitted by matter deep in space) 부분으로 paraphrase 되었다. 마찬가지로 음영 표시 문장의 뒷부분 (meaning most humans are largely safe from such a lethal exposure.) 은 보기의 (the most lethal gamma rays are too distant to significantly affect humankind)로 간략하게 paraphrase 되었다.

3
[정답] **B**

[Vocabulary] 지문의 benign (상냥한, 온순한) 은 "humans are safe from radiation"(인간은 방사선으로부터 안전하다)의 의미로 사용됐다. 따라서 방사선의 양이 인간에게 해를 끼치지 않는다의 의미이므로 답은 보기 B이다.

＊Insignificant 중요하지 않은
＊Nonthreatening 위협적이지 않은
＊Substantial 상당한
＊kind 친절한

4
[정답] **C**

[Negative Fact] 3단락에 나오지 않은 내용을 걸러내면 된다. 보기 A는 첫 번째 문장을 보면 된다. Gamma ray가 방출되는 소스에 대한 설명에서, "...as well as the natural, radioactive decay of uranium"(또한, 자연적으로 발생하는 우라늄의 방사성 붕괴…)라는 원인이 언급된다. 보기 B는 "...can emit levels of radiation that are harmful if absorbed over many years." 내용과 일치하고, 보기 D는 마지막 문장에 나오는 "DNA alteration"(DNA 변이)에 대한 내용과 일치한다. 따라서 나오지 않은 내용은 보기 C이다.

5
[정답] **B**

[Vocabulary] trial-and-error는 시행착오라는 뜻이다. 따라서 본문에 나온 "through trial-and-error" 는 시행착오를 통해서~ 라는 표현이므로, 보기 B(성공적인 결과가 나올 때까지 실험해보기)와 일치한다.

6
[정답] **A**

[Rhetorical Purpose] 음영 표시된 'photo-testing 이 포함된 문장 앞부분을 살펴보면, "Despite being experts in knowledge of the use of radiation in a medical setting,"(의학적인 상황에서 방사능을 다루는 전문가들이었지만)이라고 시작이 된다. 전문가였음에도 불구하고 방사능을 소량 사용한 'photo-testing' 때문에 몇몇은 죽게 됐다. ("The consequences with this approach would result in their death…")라고 나온다. 따라서 과학자들이 부작용에 대해 완전히 알고 있다는 사실을 반박(=dispute)하고 있으므로 보기 A가 정답이다.

7
[정답] **C**

[Main Idea] 4~5단락의 핵심내용과 연결되는 흐름을 이해하면 된다. 4단락에서는 방사능의 위험에 대해 설명됐다. 예를 들어 전문가들이 소량을 테스트했음에도 불구하고 죽었다는 얘기도 나왔다. 5단락의 main idea는 첫 번째 문장인 "Moderate levels of gamma radiation…"(적절한 양의 gamma rays) 이라고 시작이 되고, 적절한 양을 사용했을 때 부작용 없이 다양한 쓰임에 대한 내용이다. 따라서 정답은 보기 C이다.

8
[정답] **D**

[Vocabulary] 지문의 unfathomable (가늠할 수 없는) 의 동의어를 찾으면 된다. 따라서 답은 보기 D이다.

＊Implausible 그럴듯하지 않은, 가능성 없는
＊Uninhibited 억제되지 않은
＊Immediate 즉각적인
＊Inscrutable 가늠할 수 없는, 이해하기 힘든

9
[정답] **D**

[Sentence Insertion] 삽입 문장의 키워드는 "The aftereffects of these blasts"(이러한 폭발의 여파…)이다. 앞 문장에서 blasts와 관련된 설명이 나온 후 삽입하면 자연스럽다. 6단락 마지막 문장을 보면 "initial blast"에 대한 설명임을 알 수 있다. 따라서 정답은 보기 D이다.

[Summary] 지문의 핵심내용은 감마선은 인류 역사상 가장 유
용하면서 위험한 발견 중 하나임에 대한 설명이다. 보기 B는 4~5
단락에서의 "medical sector"에서 사용된 gamma radiation 설명
과 일치하고, 보기 C는 3단락의 gamma radiation의 원천과 그 양
이 인간에겐 안전하다는 내용과 일치하며, 보기 F 또한 5단락의 내
용과 일치한다. A의 경우에는 실제 지문에서 읽은 내용이 아니므로
답이 아니다. B와 D는 둘 다 detail 한 내용을 담고 있지만 D가 너
무 detail 한 내용이므로 답에서 제외된다. 그리고 E의 내용도 역시
너무 detail 한 내용이다. 2개의 answer choice 가 비슷할 경우에
는 조금 더 포괄적인 내용을 골라야 한다. 즉, Summary 문제의 경
우 단순히 True and False를 골라내면 안 되고 중요한 아이디어인
major point를 선택하고 minor point를 제외해야 한다.

| Test 06 | Astronomy |

✅ ANSWERS

PASSAGE 1

| 1 C | 2 C | 3 A | 4 B | 5 A |
| 6 D | 7 A | 8 B | 9 C | |

10 A, C, D.

PASSAGE 2

| 1 A | 2 D | 3 B | 4 B | 5 B |
| 6 B | 7 C | 8 D | 9 B | |

10 C, E, F

PASSAGE 3

| 1 C | 2 D | 3 B | 4 A | 5 A |
| 6 A | 7 C | 8 A | 9 B | |

10 D, E, F

Conflagration 큰불, 대화재
Combustible 가연성의
Plethora 과잉
Arson 방화
Troposphere 대류권
Avenue 방안

Prosecute 기소하다, 추진하다
Immemorial 아득한 옛날부터
Circumstellar 별 주위를 맴도는
Sublimate 바람직한 방향으로 돌리다
　　　　　(=Channel)
Perihelion 근일점
Rapidity 속도

PASSAGE 1 : Wildfires

1   [정답] **C**

[Negative Fact] 1단락에서 언급되지 않은 내용을 고르면 된
다. 보기 A와 D는 "Wildfires are classified as uncontrolled
conflagrations that begin in rural areas."(들불은 시골에서 시작되
는 컨트롤 되지 않은 화재라고 분류된다) 내용과 일치한다. 보기 B
는 "Wildfires are often named for the type of matter which fuels
them"(들불은 보통 시작하게 만든 연료의 종류에 따라서 이름이
붙여진다) 와 일치한다. 따라서 언급되지 않은 C가 정답이다.

2   [정답] **C**

[Fact] 질문의 키워드는 causes of wildfires(들불의 원인들)이다.
본문의 "plethora of ways in which fires can start"(불길이 시작되
는 여러 가지 원인들) 문장을 보면 된다. 사람들의 부주의로 시작된
이유들과 더불어, 마지막 문장에는 arson(방화)도 이유이기 때문에

보기 C가 정답이다.

3 [정답] **A**

[Sentence Simplifcafication] 음영 표시된 문장 전체가 핵심 내용으로서, 본문의 "Evidently, regions with drier climates are more prone to experiencing naturally occurring wildfires than cooler regions."(명백히도, 건조한 지역은 선선한 지역에 비해서 자연적으로 발생하는 들불에 취약하다) 내용이 보기 A(자연적인 들 불은 추운 지역보다 건조한 지역에서 시작된다)로 paraphrase 되었다.

4 [정답] **B**

[Rhetorical Purpose] 1단락에서 들불에 대한 묘사를 할 때 글쓴이는 uncontrollable 하다고 표현했다. 3단락의 핵심내용은 왜 들불이 다루기 힘든 이유인지, 그 종류에 대한 설명이므로 보기 B가 정답이다.

5 [정답] **A**

[Rhetorical Purpose] highlight 되어 있는 문장 아래를 보면 wildfire have been a feature of many ecosystems since they first started to develop이라고 나와 있다.

answer choice A와 같은 내용이다. 그래서 A가 정답이다.

6 [정답] **D**

[Sentence Insertion] 삽입 문장의 키워드는 "Wildfires also have the effect"(들불은 또한 이러한 효과도 있다) 이다. 앞에 Effect에 대한 설명이 미리 나온 후 (많은 식물이 불을 통해 resistance 저항을 기른다는 얘기) 나오면 자연스럽다. 따라서 보기 D가 정답이다.

7 [정답] **A**

[Inference] plants에 관련된 문장을 찾으면 된다. 4단락 마지막 문장을 보면 "Many plants rely on fires to spread or have developed resistances to high temperatures in order to survive the annual wildfire season."(많은 식물들은 매년 들불로부터 살아남기 위해 높은 온도에 대한 저항력을 퍼트리거나 키운다)라고 나와 있다. 따라서 모든 식물들이 들불이 자주 일어나는 서식지에서 살아남을 수 있는 조건을 갖고 있다고 볼 수 없다. 따라서 보기 A가 정답이다.

8 [정답] **B**

[Fact] 5단락의 내용은 들불이 대기에 미치는 영향에 대한 서술인데, 들불이 공기 입자에 영향을 미칠 수 있고, 사람들의 "cardio-vascular"(심장혈관 질환) 문제를 일으킬 수 있다고 나와 있다. 따라서 정답은 보기 B이다.

9 [정답] **C**

[Vocabulary] 지문의 eradicate (근절하다) 의 동의어를 찾으면 된다. 따라서 답은 보기 C이다.
*Kill 죽이다
*Erase 지우다
*Eliminate 제거하다
*Abolish 폐지하다

10 [정답] **A, C, D**

[Summary] 본문의 핵심내용은 들불은 식물들이 있었을 때부터 존재했고, 불이 발생하는 장소에 다시 활기를 찾게 하는 중요한 역할을 한다는 내용이다. 보기 A와 C는 1~2단락의 들불의 원인에 대한 내용과 일치하고, 보기 D는 5단락의 들불의 "real and long-lasting effect" 관련된 내용과 일치한다.

PASSAGE 2 : The Telescope

1
[정답] **A**

[Fact] 질문의 키워드는 our ancestors이다. 1단락 두 번째 문장을 보면 "...the setting of the sun and the onset of dusk brought a sense of trepidation to our ancestors."(해가 지고 땅거미가 내리면 우리의 조상들은 trepidation=두려움을 느꼈다)라고 나와 있다. 따라서 보기 A가 정답이다. 보기 B는 그럴듯해 보이지만 small fires 주변에서 이야기를 나누었다는 직접적인 언급은 없고 본문에서 엉성하게 두 내용이 연달아 있는 문장으로 이어져 있으므로 정답이 되기에는 불충분하다.

2
[정답] **D**

[Vocabulary] 지문의 elude(피하다)의 동의어를 찾으면 된다. 따라서 답은 보기 D이다.
*Flee 도망가다
*Lose 느슨해지다
*Dodge (몸을 숙여) 피하다
*Evade 피하다, 회피하다

3
[정답] **B**

[Sentence Simplification] 음영 표시된 문장 전체가 핵심 정보로서 "Early astronomers were limited by a lack of instruments, so in ancient times, astronomy consisted solely of observing celestial objects with the naked eye."(고대의 천문학자들은 도구가 없었기 때문에, 천문학은 천체를 눈으로 관찰하는 게 유일한 방법이었다)를 보기 B로 " When people first started observing the sky, they had to do so without tools, and used their eyes."(사람들이 처음으로 하늘을 관찰했을 때, 그들은 도구 없이 해야 했기 때문에 눈으로 관찰할 수밖에 없었다) 간략하게 paraphrase 했다.

4
[정답] **B**

[Main Idea] 2단락의 핵심내용을 정확히 이해하고 전체 패시지의 흐름과 연결시켜 본다. 이다음 3단락부터 본격적으로 telescope에 대한 설명이 이어지고, 2단락 마지막 문장에서도 단서를 얻을 수 있다. "...but the science of astronomy was changed forever with the invention of the telescope"(천문학은 망원경의 발명으로 영원히 바뀌었다)를 보면 망원경의 발명 이전의 과학계에 대한 설명임을 알 수 있다. 따라서 보기 B가 정답이다.

5
[정답] **B**

[Negative Fact] 3단락의 내용 중 망원경의 설명과 일치하지 않는 것을 고르면 된다. 보기 A는 마지막 문장의 "...the principles

on which it operates will remain very much the same"(망원경의 원리는 거의 다 비슷하다) 와 일치하고, 보기 C는 "...the internal components will be unvaried"(망원경의 내부는 다르지 않다) 와 일치하며 보기 D는 "Others are incredibly powerful and so large that they occupy an entire building…"(다른 망원경들은 너무 강력하고 거대해서 빌딩 전체를 차지한다)와 일치한다. 따라서 나오지 않은 내용은 보기 B이다.

6
[정답] **B**

[Fact] 질문의 키워드는 origin of the telescope이다. 4단락 두 번째 문장을 보면 "...many historians agree that the earliest verifiable proof we can point to supports the theory that the man behind the design for the first telescope was a Dutchman by the name of Hans Lippershey who attempted to patent his idea in 1608."(많은 역사학자들은 증명할 수 있는 증거로 보았을 때 처음으로 망원경을 디자인한 사람은 Hans Lippershey라는 네덜란드인이 1608년도에 그의 아이디어를 특허를 내려고 했을 때를 지목한다)와 일치한다. 따라서 정답은 보기 B이다.

7
[정답] **C**

[Sentence Insertion] 삽입문장의 단서는 "Another individual"이다. 앞에 먼저 어떠한 'Individual'에 대한 설명이 나오고 '또 다른 사람'이라는 표현이 들어가면 자연스럽다. 4단락의 내용상 Hans Lippershey가 그 첫 번째 인물이기 때문에 삽입문장은 C에 들어가야 된다.

8
[정답] **D**

[Inference] 작가의 태도에 대해 물어보는 질문은 tone을 파악하면 도움이 된다. 그리고 특정 톤/무드는 단어 선택으로 만들어지기 때문에 워딩을 잘 보자. 5단락 마지막 문장을 보면 망원경은 "secrets"를 발견할 수 있는 기회를 제공했으며, 인류 역사상 있었던 궁금증에 대해 "answer" 할 수 있게 해주었다고 말한다. 따라서 작가는 망원경의 발명을 "praise" 한다라고 볼 수 있으므로 정답은 보기 D이다. 보기 C는 "…it can only be predicted that future improvements to existing telescopes will grant us access to new wonders in years to come"에 따라 답에 근접한 것 같지만 future development of telescopes가 가져올 미래에 대해 낙관적인 태도를 보이는 것이지 telescope의 발전 자체에 대한 낙관적인 태도가 아니므로 오답이다.

9
[정답] **B**

[Rhetorical Purpose] 작가의 의도를 파악해야 하는 질문이다. 6단락에서 여러 질문이 나열되어 있는 건, 정답을 물어보는 질문이 아닌, 독자로 하여금 생각하게 만드는 rhetorical questions이다. 이

러한 질문들은 결국 망원경의 발명으로 인해 일부 해결되었기 때문에 보기 B (1단락에 언급됐던 미스터리를 다시 한번 상기시켜주고, 그 미스터리를 푸는데 망원경이 큰 역할을 했다는 사실을 상기시킨다) 가 정답이다.

10 [정답] C, E, F

[Summary] 본문의 핵심은 인류는 늘 구름 뒤에 무엇이 있는지를 궁금해 했으며, 망원경의 발명으로 인해 오래된 질문들에 대해 점차 대답할 수 있게 되었다는 내용이다. 보기 C는 2단락 마지막 부분에 언급된 "the science of astronomy was changed forever with the invention of the telescope"과 마지막 단락에서 인간의 존재에 대한 여러 질문들을 내포하고 있는 부분과 일치하며, 보기 E는 6단락의 여러 질문과 일치하는 문장이며, 보기 F는 4단락의 망원경의 발명에 관한 핵심내용이다.

PASSAGE 3 : Pluto

1 [정답] C

[Fact] 질문의 키워드는 Pluto's discovery이다. 플루토(명왕성)의 발견에 대한 문장을 읽어보면 "The discovery brought to scientists a sense of excitement and curiosity…"(명왕성의 발견은 과학자들로 하여금 흥분과 호기심을 같이 유발했다) 라고 나와 있다. 따라서 mixed feelings =복잡한 감정이라고 간략하게 paraphrase 해놓은 보기 C가 정답이다.

2 [정답] D

[Negative Fact] 2단락에서 나오지 않은 내용을 걸러내면 된다. 보기 A는 명왕성의 낮은 온도로 인해 "…making it near-impossible for the planet to harbor living organisms"(생명체가 살기는 거의 불가능하다) 내용과 일치하고, 보기 B는 마지막 문장의 "… jagged mountains which bear some resemblance to those on Earth"(뾰족한 산들은 지구의 산 모양과 비슷하다) 와 일치하며 보기 C는 첫 번째 문장의 "…comprising predominantly of nitrogen ice and rock, with the former accounting for 98%."(대부분 질소 얼음과 질소 돌로 구성이 되어있는데, 전자는 98%나 차지한다) 와 일치한다. 따라서 나오지 않은 내용은 보기 D이다.

3 [정답] B

[Sentence Simplification] 음영 표시된 문장 전체가 핵심내용으로서 과학자들이 발견한 내용 중 "…at perihelion(=근일점), its gassy atmosphere freezes solid, with ices sublimating only at aphelion – its closest position on its solar-orbit"[근일점에서 가스 형태의 대기는 고체로 얼고, 얼음은 aphelion(=원일점)으로 승화된다. 그리고 원일점은 태양의 궤도와 가장 가까운 지점이다.]를 다르게 표시한 B(명왕성의 대기는 태양에서 멀어질수록 얼고, 얼음은 태양과 가까워질수록 증발한다)가 정답이다.

4 [정답] A

[Vocabulary] 지문의 scrupulous (꼼꼼한, 세심한) 의 동의어를 찾으면 된다. 따라서 답은 보기 A이다.

＊Thorough 꼼꼼한
＊Continuing 지속되는
＊Prolonged 늘려진
＊Multiple 다양한, 다수의

5 [정답] A

[Main Idea] 단락의 핵심내용은 대부분 첫 번째 문장에 담겨있다. 3단락 첫 번째 문장을 보면 "…Hubble observations have revealed unexpected substances on Pluto's surface that may contain the building blocks for life: carbon."(허블을 통해 명왕성 표면에 예상치 못한 물체를 관찰했는데, 이 물체는 모든 생명의 기반이 되는 탄소이다) 라고 나와 있다. 따라서 life가 명왕성에 있을 수도 있다는 추측이 핵심내용이다. 정답은 보기 A이다.

6 [정답] A

[Negative Fact] 4단락에서 언급되지 않는 관찰 내용을 고르면 된다. 보기 B는 "...Pluto may have begun as an ocean planet, before going through multiple ice ages and 're-freezing' repeatedly"(명왕성은 바다가 있는 행성이었다가, 여러 빙하기를 걸치면서 다시 freeze 되는 과정을 걸쳤을 거라고 주장한다)와 일치하고, 보기 C는 첫 번째 문장의 "signs of water-filled cracks below Pluto's icy surface"(명왕성의 얼음 표면 아래에 물로 찬 틈)과 일치하며 보기 D는 앞서 언급한 "Pluto may have begun as an ocean planet…"(명왕성은 바다가 있는 행성이었다가…)와 일치한다. 따라서 정답은 보기 A이다.

7 [정답] C

[Rhetorical Purpose] 음영 표시가 된 표현이 언급된 문장을 보면 "The water some hundred kilometers below the surface could have interacted with the warm radioactive core…"(수면 아래 몇백 킬로미터 깊은 곳의 물은 방사성 코어와 결합되었을 가능성도 있다)라고 나와 있다. 이 설명은 생명체가 명왕성에 있을 수도 있다는 이야기이므로 보기 C가 정답이다.

8 [정답] A

[Sentence Insertion] 삽입문장의 내용이 키워드 역할을 한다. "화산작용은 생명이 살 수 있다는 행성의 조건을 보여준다" 내용이 먼저 서술이 되고 나머지 volcanic activity에 대한 설명이 나오면 자연스럽다. 따라서 이 삽입문장은 topic sentence 역할로서 보기 A에 들어가야 한다.

9 [정답] B

[Inference] 질문의 단서는 "evidence scientists have presented"(과학자들이 제시한 단서들)이다. 6단락 두 번째 문장에서는 좀 더 발전된 망원경과 우주 탐사선과 같은 기술이 명왕성에 대한 이해도를 높여 줄 거라고 기대한다고 나와 있다. 더불어 마지막 문장에서는 명왕성이 태양에서 멀어지면서 새로운 데이터를 수집하기 어려워지고 있다고 한계점에 대해서도 언급한다. 종합적으로 봤을 때 아직 명왕성에 대한 연구는 지속되고 있고, 생명체가 살고 있다는 것을 확실하게 밝히기에는 부족한 점이 있다는 것을 알 수 있다.

10 [정답] D, E, F

[Summary] 본문의 핵심은 이전에는 과학자들이 살 수 없는 행성이라고 여긴 명왕성에서 생명체가 살 수 있는 단서를 찾은 내용이다. 보기 D는 4단락의 명왕성에서 물의 발견을 통해 이론적으로는 생명체가 번성할 수 있다는 내용과 일치하고, 보기 E는 5단락의 cryovolcanoes 내용과 일치하며, 보기 F는 3단락의 UV light의 목격과 이로 인해 명왕성에 생명이 살 수도 있을 가능성에 관한 내용과 일치한다.

✓ ANSWERS

PASSAGE 1

1 A	2 C	3 C	4 B	5 C
6 D	7 A	8 A	9 D	
10 A, B, C				

PASSAGE 2

1 B	2 C	3 C	4 B	5 A
6 D	7 C	8 C	9 B	
10 A, B, F				

PASSAGE 3

1 D	2 B	3 A	4 C	5 B
6 C	7 B	8 D	9 A	
10 A, B, F				

Asphyxiate 질식(사)시키다 (=suffocate)	**Atrocity** 잔혹행위
	Charlatan 돌팔이
Heinous 악랄한, 극악무도한	**Extricate** 해방되다, 탈출하다
Deploy 배치하다	**Alloy** 합금
Sparingly 조금씩 아껴 쓰는	**Esoteric** 소수만 이해하는
Stockpile 비축 량,비축	**Complementary** 상호 보완적인
Defoliant 고엽제	**Rudimentary** 기본적인
Incendiary 방화의, 선동적인	

PASSAGE 1 : Chemical Warfare Ethics

1
[정답] **A**

[Fact] 토플에서 Fact를 찾는 문제에서는 반드시 evidence sentence 즉 증거문장이 있어야 한다. 질문의 키워드 chemical warfare(화학전)에 대해서 가장 잘 묘사한 내용을 찾는 게 핵심이다. 따라서, "and they all have strong ethical arguments against using them" 라는 명확한 evidence sentence 가 있는 A가 정답이다.

2
[정답] **C**

Vocabulary 지문의 misery(고통, 빈곤)의 동의어를 찾으면 된다. 앞 문장에서 "victims … are unprepared and defenseless"(화학전 희생자들은 대부분 준비되지 않은 상태이거나 방어를 할 수 없는 상태이다) 라고 희생자들을 수식하고 있다. 따라서 답은 보기 C이다.

＊Mistrust 불신   ＊Depression 우울

＊heartache 심적 고통   ＊torment 고뇌

3
[정답] **C**

[Negative Fact] 2단락에 언급되지 않은 내용을 고르면 된다. 보기 A는 "The use of chemical weapons reaches back to antiquity."(화학 무기는 아주 오래전부터 사용되어 왔다.)와 일치하고, 보기 B는 "The gases rarely killed people, but they did mutilate or injure them."(가스는 사람들을 죽이지 않았지만 다치게 하거나 불구로 만들었다.)와 일치하며, 보기 D는 "…many of these treaties appeared after the two world wars"(나라 간의 조약은 두 번의 세계 전쟁 이후 나타났다)라고 나와 있으며 그다음 문장에는 "In WW1 in particular"(특히 세계 1차 대전 때에는)이라는 표현이 있으므로 세계 1차, 2차 전쟁에서 쓰였음을 암시한다. 따라서 보기 C가 정답이다.

4
[정답] **B**

[Negative Fact] 3단락에 언급되지 않은 내용을 고르면 된다. 보기 A는 "The Axis powers used them sparingly, and the Allies never brought them out." 내용과 일치하며 보기 C는 "…Japanese forces used them more extensively against their Asian enemies…" 와 일치하고 마지막 보기 D는 "the Nazis did use Zyklon B and carbon monoxide gas against noncombatants in the Holocaust"와 일치한다. 3단락 마지막 문장을 보면 "This incident remains the deadliest poison gas use in history."이라고 분명히 나와 있기 때문에 보기 B는 틀린 내용 (정답)이다.

5
[정답] **C**

[Sentence Simplification] 음영 표시된 문장 전체가 핵심내용으로서 "Between 1962 and 1971, during the Vietnam War, the United States military applied nearly 20,000,000 U.S. gallons of "rainbow herbicides" and defoliants in Vietnam, eastern Laos, and parts of Cambodia."(베트남 전쟁 당시 – 1962~1951 – 미국은 20,000,000갤런의 "rainbow herbicides"와 고엽제를 베트남과 동 라오스 그리고 캄보디아 일부에 사용했다.)라는 내용의 핵심을 빠뜨리지 않고 paraphrase 한 문장은 보기 C이다.

6
[정답] **D**

[Fact] 음영 표시된 "incendiaries"(소이탄)이 나오는 문장 위주로 확인해 보면 작가가 왜 이러한 예시를 썼는지 파악할 수 있다. 화학자들이 발명한 여러 가지 중 하나로 언급되고 있고, incendiary는 "방화의"라는 뜻이다. 따라서 어휘와 맥락을 모두 고려해 봤을 때 incendiaries는 불을 붙게 하는 무기라고 볼 수 있으므로 보기 D가 정답이다.

7

[정답] **A**

[Sentence Insertion[삽입문장은 화학 무기는 엄청난 해를 가할 수 있다는 내용이다. 5단락의 핵심내용을 잘 정리해놓은 문장이며, A 문장의 첫 번째 단어 대명사 They가 삽입문장의 "Chemial weapons"와 일치한다는 것을 확인할 수 있다. 따라서 정답은 보기 A이다.

8

[정답] **A**

[Rhetorical Purpose] 음영 표시된 문장의 앞부분을 자세히 살펴보면 "Sadly, many scientists and chemists become entangled in political pressures, economic interests, and professional ambition…"(슬프게도, 대부분의 과학자들과 화학자들은 정치적 압박, 경제적 이익, 그리고 직업에 대한 열정에 모두 연루되어 있다) 라고 나와 있다. 이 말은 그들이 사회적인 영향력에서 자유롭지 못하다는 얘기이므로 보기 A가 정답이다.

9

[정답] **D**

[Inference] 질문의 키워드는 화학자들과 과학자들의 의무감이다. 그들의 책임도 중요하지만 과학에 종사하는 모든 사람들도 (professionals active in chemistry and the associated sciences) 책임이 있고, 도덕적인 행동을 가이드하는 "many organizations"도 책임이 있다. 따라서 보기 D가 정답이다.

10

[정답] **A, B, C**

[Summary] 본문의 핵심은 화학 무기가 발명됨과 동시에 논쟁에 휩싸였고 윤리적이지 못하다는 내용이다. 보기 A는 1단락의 화학전 설명에 관한 핵심내용이고, 보기 B는 2~3단락의 세계 1, 2차 전쟁 때 쓰인 화학 무기에 대한 핵심내용이며 보기 C는 마지막 6단락의 과학자들의 "codes of ethics and conduct" 에 대한 핵심내용이다.

PASSAGE 2 : Alchemy

1

[정답] **B**

[Inference] alchemy(연금술)에 대해 작가가 암시하는 바를 이해해야 한다. 1단락 첫 번째 문장을 보면 "Alchemy is the precursor of chemistry"(연금술은 화학의 선구자이다)라고 화학 보다 앞선 학문이라고 나와 있는 표현과, 동양에서는 "first mentions of alchemy originate from 73 to 49 BC China"(BC73~49 중국에서 처음으로 연금술이 사용됐다고 언급된다) 라고 나와 있다. 따라서 연금술을 굉장히 오래된 (=ancient) 학문이라는 것을 뜻하고 보기 B가 정답이다.

2

[정답] **C**

[Vocabulary] 지문의 rudimentary (기본의) 의 동의어를 찾으면 된다. 따라서 답은 보기 C이다.

＊rude 무례한 ＊Raw 날것의
＊basic 기본적인 ＊Uncomplicated 단순한, 복잡하지 않은

3

[정답] **C**

[Negative Fact] 연금술사들에 대해 언급되지 않은 보기를 걸러내면 된다. 보기 A는 "The alchemists guarded their knowledge in cyphers and perplexing symbolism…"[연금술사들은 그들의 지식을 암호와 복잡한 부호들로 사용(=보호)했다]와 일치하고, 보기 B는 "…alchemists played an important role in early chemistry and medicine"(연금술사들은 초기 화학과 의학에 있어 큰 역할을 했다)와 일치하고, 보기 D는 "…invented the basic laboratory methods, theory, vocabulary, and experimental methods…"(연금술사들은 기본적인 연구 방법과 이론, 언어 그리고 실험방법들을 개발해냈다)의 내용과 일치한다. 따라서 언급되지 않은 내용은 보기 C이다.

4

[정답] **B**

[Fact] 3단락의 두 번째 문장을 보면 "In most cases this included the changing of "base metals"(typically lead) into "noble metals"(usually gold)"(대부분 [transmutation]은 납과 같은 천한 금속을 금과 같은 고귀한 금속으로 변화시킨다)라고 나와 있다. 따라서 B가 정답이다.

5

[정답] **A**

[Fact] 질문의 키워드는 Arab's understanding of elemental system (아랍인들의 기초 체계에 대한 이해도)이다. 그들은 8 가지의 elements를 사용했다고 나와 있고, 그다음 문장을 보면 "western alchemsits"(서양 연금술사들도) "…used this understanding for advances in medicine…"(이러한 지식을 가지고 의학을 발전하는 데에 사용했다)라고 나와 있다. 따라서 보기 A가 정답이다.

6 [정답] **D**

[Sentence Simplification] 음영 표시된 문장 전체가 핵심내용으로서 "Western alchemists—including the father of modern medicine Paracelsus—used this understanding for advances in medicine, metallurgy, and even astronomy, and Asian alchemists even invented gunpowder and fireworks based off this system."(서양의 연금술사들 – 근대 의학의 아버지 파라켈수스를 포함한 – 은 이러한 지식을 가지고 의학, 금속공학, 심지어는 천문학 발전에까지 사용했다. 그리고 동양의 연금술사들은 심지어 화약과 폭죽을 만들기도 했다)가 좀 더 간결하게 paraphrase 된 문장은 보기 D이다.

7 [정답] **C**

[Sentence Insertion] 삽입문장의 단서는 Some alchemists (어떤 연금술사들은) 이라는 표현이다. 앞에 B 문장을 보면 "…alchemists being labeled as charlatans who dealt with superstitious methods of "magic.""(연금술사들은 미신과 관련된 마술 방법을 사용하는 사기꾼들이라고 불리었다) 라는 내용이 나온다. 이처럼 그들의 평판이 좋지 못했던 내용과 바로 이어지는 삽입문장 (어떤 연금술사들은 그들의 연구 때문에 죽임을 당하기도 했다) 가 나오면 자연스럽다. 따라서 정답은 보기 C이다.

8 [정답] **C**

[Fact] 음영 표시된 단어가 나온 문장을 먼저 잘 이해하면 된다. 6단락 첫 번째 문장을 보면 "The important contributions made by the alchemists are innumerable"(연금술사들이 기여한 중요한 업적은 innumerable=무궁무진하다) 라고 나와 있으므로 정답은 보기 C이다.

9 [정답] **B**

[Main Idea] 지문에서 내용의 흐름을 이해하는지 물어보는 질문이다. 7단락의 핵심내용은 "Modern scholars still like to divide alchemy between its practical scientific applications and its esoteric spiritual characteristics…"(오늘날 학자들은 연금술을 과학적인 응용인지 아니면 소수만 이해하는 영혼/정신적인 성질을 띠고 있는지에 대해 의견이 분분하다) 에서 알 수 있듯이 연금술의 평가에 대한 내용이다. 따라서 보기 B가 정답이다.

10 [정답] **A, B, F**

[Summary] 본문의 핵심내용은 연금술의 역사와 다양한 흥미로운 발견들에 관한 얘기이다. 보기 A는 1단락의 연금술에 대한 기원에 대한 내용과 일치하고, 보기 B는 2~3단락의 연금술사들이 화학과 의학분야에서 중요한 역할을 맡았던 것, 그리고 그들의 지식을 철저히 보호했던 내용과 일치하며, 보기 F는 6~7단락에서의 연금술에 대한 긍정적 평가와 과학계에서 나뉘는 (과학적 응용이 가능하다 vs 종교적이다) 의견에 대한 설명과 일치한다.

PASSAGE 3 : The Periodic Table

1 [정답] **D**

[Sentence Simplification] 음영 표시된 문장 전체가 핵심내용으로서 "It is an attempt to categorize the known chemical elements according to a logical system and according to how they relate to each other"(주기율표는 알려진 화학원소를 논리적인 체계로 어떻게 서로 관련이 있는지를 고려해 정리하려는 시도이다)를 보기 D "주기율표는 논리적으로 정돈됐으며, 각각의 물질들은 주변 원소와의 관계를 고려해 위치한다"와 일치한다.

2 [정답] **B**

[Fact] 질문의 키워드는 Antoine Lavoisier이다. 그가 언급된 문장을 살펴보면 "Crucially to the development of the Periodic Table, Lavoisier grouped the known elements into four categories…"(주기율표를 만드는데 핵심이였던 Lavoisier는 알려진 원소들을 네 가지 카테고리로 분류하였다) 라고 나와 있다. 그의 역할이 중요했다는 게 포인트이기 때문에 보기 B가 정답이다.

3 [정답] **A**

[Negative Fact] 2단락에 나와 있지 않은 내용을 걸러내면 된다. 보기 B는 "…atomic weight of the second element was generally equal to the average of the first and third."(두 번째 원소의 원자량은 대게 첫 번째와 세 번째의 평균과 일치한다) 와 일치하고, 보기 C는 "…it did not apply universally to all of the chemical elements."(모든 화학원소에게 보편적으로 적용되지 않는다) 와 일치하며 마지막 보기 D는 "Döbereiner's work formed the foundation for the organization of the Periodic Table."(Döbereiner의 업적=the law of triads는 후에 주기율표를 만드는 데에 기반이 되었다)와 일치한다. 따라서 언급되지 않은 보기 A가 정답이다.

4 [정답] **C**

[Rhetorical Purpose] valency 설명 바로 다음 문장을 보면 "Both of these measurements were critical…"(둘의[원자량과 valency=원자가] 측정은 매우 중요했다) 라고 나온다. 따라서 both 중 하나인 valency ("another important factor)에 대한 설명이기 때문에 정답은 보기 C이다.

5 [정답] **B**

[Rhetorical Purpose] 음영 표시된 the law of Octaves가 나온 내용을 살펴보면 된다. 음악의 옥타브처럼, "Just as with an octave in a piece of music"이라고 비유가 시작되고, 문장 뒤를 보면 "John Newlands discovered that every eighth element was similar to the first when they were plotted from lightest atomic

weight to heaviest."(John Newlands는 원자량을 가벼운 것에서 무거운 순서대로 그렸을 때 매 8번째 원소는 첫 번째와 비슷하다는 것을 발견했다) 라고 나와 있다. 또한 이러한 발견을 통해 "…would lead to the publication of…"(후에 주기율표의 발행으로 이어졌다) 라는 내용은 보기 B의 "formation of future versions of the Periodic Table"로 서술했다.

6 [정답] **C**

[Inference] 5단락에서 Mendeleev와 Meyer가 비슷한 시기에 주기율표를 만들었음에도 불구하고 Mendeleev의 버전을 더 높게 평가하는 이유가 나와 있다. 그 이유 중 하나는 Mendeleev는 "left spaces for elements which had not yet been discovered but must exist"(Mendeleev 아직 발견되지 않은 원소 자리를 남겨두었다) 라고 나와 있다. 이 말은 Meyer 은 반대로 아직 발견되지 않은 원소에 자리를 남겨두지 않았다고 볼 수 있다. 따라서 정답은 보기 C이다.

7 [정답] **B**

[Sentence Insertion] 삽입문장의 키워드는 "He" 이다. "그"에 대한 설명이 나오기 때문에 (미국 화학자) 그의 소개가 먼저 선행이 되고, 나중 얘기가 나오면 자연스럽다. 그는 Horace Groves Deming 이라는 걸 알 수 있다. 따라서 정답은 보기 B이다.

8 [정답] **D**

[Vocabulary] 지문의 inevitably (필연적으로, 당연히)의 동의어를 찾으면 된다. 따라서 답은 보기 D이다.
* Exactly 정확하게　　　　　* Uncertainly 자신 없게
* Unfortunately 불운하게　　* Undoubtedly 확실히

9 [정답] **A**

[Structure] 전체 글의 구조(흐름)를 물어보는 질문이다. 1단락부터 마지막 단락까지 시간의 순서대로, 주기율표가 만들어지게 된 역사와 기여한 과학자들의 대한 설명으로 이루어진다. 2, 3, 4 문단의 내용을 충족시키는 보기 B도 충분히 매력적인 선택지이지만 지문 전체의 구조를 아우르는 보기는 A이다.따라서 정답은 A이다.

10 [정답] **A, B, F**

[Summary] 본문의 핵심내용은 오늘날의 주기율표의 탄생은 적어도 200년이 걸렸고, 화학의 발전에 큰 기여를 했다는 부분이다. 보기 A는 4단락의 "Law of Octaves" 관련된 핵심 내용이고, B는 Periodic Table의 중요성을 언급하였다. F는 2단락의 "Law of Triads"에 관한 핵심내용이다. 보기 C의 경우에는 끝난 것이 아니고 아직까지 찾고 있으므로 답이 아니다. 보기 D에서는 Predict 한다는 내용은 나오지 않았다.

✓ ANSWERS

PASSAGE 1

1 A	2 C	3 C	4 A	5 D
6 C	7 D	8 A	9 D	

10 B, C, E

PASSAGE 2

1 C	2 C	3 C	4 C	5 A
6 C	7 C	8 C	9 B	

10 A, B, F

PASSAGE 3

1 C	2 D	3 C	4 B	5 A
6 B	7 D	8 B	9 C	

10 A, C, E

Phenotype 표현형	Constipation 변비
Genotype 유전형	Eczema 습진
Peripatric 주변부의	Rosacea 빨간 코
Flora and fauna 동식물	Dwarfism 난쟁이증
Postulate 상정하다	Genocide 대량 학살
Purport 주장하다, 전반적인 뜻	Anemia 빈혈
Circumference 원주, 둘레	Encephalitis 뇌염

PASSAGE 1 : The Founder Effect

1
[정답] **A**

[Sentence Simplification] 음영 표시된 문장 전체가 핵심내용으로서 "Humans have a particular gene that determines eye color, but it is the variant of the gene, the allele, that determines what color the eye will be."(인간에게는 눈 색깔을 결정하는 구체적인 유전자가 있으나, 이 유전자의 변이인 –대립 유전자– 눈 색깔을 결정한다)를 보기 A의 "An allele is a variant of a gene, and it is responsible for eye color."(대립 유전자는 유전자의 종류이며 눈 색깔에 영향을 미친다)로 간략히 paraphrase 되었다.

2
[정답] **C**

[Fact] 음영 표시된 phenotypes에 관련된 문장을 살펴보면 된다. Phenotype(표현형)은 "an outwardly expressed, physical characteristic"(외적으로 표현된 신체적 특징) 라고 되었다. 따라서

보기 C가 정답이다.

3
[정답] **C**

[Negative Fact] 2단락에서 나와 있지 않은 내용을 고르면 된다. 보기 A는 2단락 마지막 문장의 "...could lead to speciation and ultimately the evolution of a new species."(새로운 종의 진화로 이루어질 수 있다) 와 일치하며, 보기 B는 founder effect가 처음 언급되는 문장에서의 정의 "...to the decrease in genetic variance that takes place when a new colony is established by a very small population from a larger, parent population." 와 일치한다. 마지막 보기 D는 앞서 언급된 보기 A와 B를 결합시켜 놓은 내용이다. 따라서 나오지 않은 내용은 보기 C이다.

4
[정답] **A**

[Vocabulary] 지문의 ceases (멈추다) 의 동의어를 찾으면 된다. 따라서 답은 보기 A이다.

* Stops 멈추다
* Continues 지속되다
* Start 시작회다
* Stands 일어서다

5
[정답] **D**

[Negative Fact] 3단락에서 언급되지 않은 내용을 고르면 된다. 보기 A는 "...bottleneck, when the size of a population is drastically reduced."(...은 병목현상 때문에 일어나는데, 이 현상은 개체 수의 크기가 급격히 줄어들 때를 말한다) 와 일치하고, 보기 B는 "This reduction is caused by external events such as famine, floods and drought." 의 내용을 environmental disasters 라고 표현했기 때문에 일치하고, 보기 C는 peripatric speciation 의 정의를 내린 내용 "Peripatric speciation is what can happen when a smaller element of a larger population finds itself cut off and isolated and ceases to share genetic materials with its parent population." 과 일치하므로 걸러낸다. 따라서 정답은 보기 D이다.

6
[정답] **C**

[Inference] 질문의 키워드는 scientist 이다. 과학자들의 노력에 대한 설명이 나온 문장을 보면 되는데, "scientists will introduce or re-introduce a species to an area in order to study its effects over a long period of time." 이 내용을 다르게 표현한 것이 보기 C이다.

7
[정답] **C**

[Rhetorical Purpose] 작가의 의도를 묻는 질문이다. Amish

---

population에게 나타나는 genetic disorder에 대해서 이야기하고 있는데 dwarfism, angelman's syndrome과 같은 유전병이 발생하며 "lower rates of cancer"을 언급하고 있다. 그리고 5단락의 서두에 "A good example of this…"에 따르면 The Founder Effect의 예시로 아미쉬 사람들의 유전적 고립에 의하여 특정 유전 질환이 발생하는 현상을 보여주고 있으므로 Genetic disorder을 언급하는 작가의 의도는 보기 D에 가장 일치한다. 보기 A는 The Founder Effect가 이러한 현상을 일으키는 요소라는 사실(fact)을 강화하고 있다고 설명하는데 작가가 둘 사이의 상관관계가 사실임을 명시하지 않았으므로 정답이 아니다.

보기 B는 아미쉬 사람들이 얼마나 고립되어 있는지에 대해서 보여준다고 이야기하는데 이는 작가의 의도에 맞지 않는다. 보기 너무 구체적(Specific)이어서 답이 아니다. 이 단락은 아미쉬인들이 다른 사람들과 어떻게 다른 유전적 구성을 가지고 있는지를 보여주기 위해 다른 genetic disorders 를 언급한다(특정 질병의 증가율과 암의 위험 감소).

8
[정답] **A**

[Inference] 질문의 키워드는 "first human migrations out of Africa" 이다. 6단락 마지막 문장을 보면 "This Serial Founder Effect is thought to have been at play during the first human migrations out of Africa."(Serial Founder Effect는 아프리카에서 이주가 일어났을 때 발생했던 것으로 생각된다) 라고 나와 있으므로 보기 A가 정답이다.

9
[정답] **D**

[Sentence Insertion] 삽입문장의 키워드 "Additionally" 이다. 추가적인 내용이라는 결정적 단서이며, 뒤에 내용을 보면 아프리카 대륙의 인구에 대한 내용이므로 6단락에서 African migration 내용이 나온 후 뒤에 연결되면 자연스럽다. 따라서 정답은 보기 D이다.

10
[정답] **B, C, E**

[Summary] 본문의 핵심내용은 새로운 군집(colony)을 초래할 수 있는 유전변이인 Founder Effect에 대한 설명이다. 보기 A는 본문에서 언급된 적이 없으므로 오답이다. 토플에서의 답은 추측이 아니라 본문에서 근거해서 답을 찾아야 한다. 보기 D에서 jar of marble analogy는 언급된 적이 없으므로 오답이다. 보기 F는 특히 아미쉬 사람들 내에서 더욱 고립된 공동체에 대한 언급이 없고 이들에게 유전 질환이 더욱 흔하게 나타난다는 내용이 없으므로 오답이다.

PASSAGE 2 : The Paleolithic Diet

1
[정답] **C**

[Inference] 질문의 키워드는 Paleo Diet이다. 1단락 마지막 문장을 보면 "Those who champion the Paleo diet claim this approach decreases the risk of chronic diet-related diseases and improves human performance."라고 나와 있는데, 이 식단을 옹호하는 사람들은 다양한 질병에 걸릴 위험을 낮춰준다라고 주장한다. 따라서 건강한 식이요법 "healthy diet"라고 표현할 수 있다. 따라서 정답은 보기 C이다.

2
[정답] **C**

[Vocabulary] 지문의 champion (지지하다, 옹호하다) 의 동의어를 찾으면 된다. 따라서 답은 보기 C이다.

＊Address 다루다, 해결하다
＊Accomplish 성취하다
＊Advocate 옹호하다, 지지하다
＊Preach 가르치다, 설교하다

3
[정답] **C**

[Negative Fact] 2단락에서 Paleo Diet에 대해 나오지 않는 내용을 고르면 된다. 보기 A는 첫 번째 문장에 "no dairy products(유제품)"에 대한 언급과 일치하고, 보기 B는 "because the human genome developed on this high-protein diet" 의 내용과 일치하며, 보기 D는 "grass-fed game protein from hunting and fishing. It was high in wild fruits, vegetables, and fungi, and low in starches and grains." 내용과 일치한다. 따라서 정답은 언급되지 않은 보기 C이다.

4
[정답] **C**

[Fact] 3단락에서 Paleo Diet에 대한 올바른 설명 문장을 고르면 된다. 마지막 부분을 읽어 보면 "…those with blood sugar regulation and weight loss issues do well on the Paleo Diet."(혈당과 체중감소에도 Paleo 식단은 도움이 된다)라고 나와 있다. 따라서 보기 C가 정답이다.

5
[정답] **A**

[Main Idea] 4단락의 핵심내용을 물어보는 질문이다. 4단락 첫 번째 문장을 보면 "Paleo Diet benefits include…"라고 시작이 되고, 이어지는 문장들에는 다양한 이점이 설명되고 있다. 하지만 심리적인 장점은 나와 있지 않고, 육체적 생리적 장점에 대해 언급이 나와 있기 때문에 보기 A가 정답이다.

6

[정답] **C**

[Sentence Simplification] 음영 표시된 문장 전체가 핵심내용으로서 "Eliminating sugar, processed foods, and unhealthy fats" 부분을 "If a person eliminates the poor foods from the diet"로 표현했고, "removes the sources of stress and inflammation from the digestive tract."를 "it will decrease inflammation in the digestive system"으로 표현한 보기 C가 정답이다.

7

[정답] **C**

[Negative Fact] 5단락에 Paleo 식단에 대한 단점과 일치하지 않는 문장을 고르면 된다. 보기 A는 "Eliminating entire food groups restricts variety and makes eating a balanced diet difficult." 내용과 일치하고, 보기 B는 "...so the Paleo Diet is likely to be hard on one's budget" 과 일치하며 보기 D는 ". Nutrient-dense and energy-providing foods to avoid on the diet include dairy products, oats, wheat, corn, rice, quinoa, soybeans, peanuts, lentils, potatoes, and chickpeas." 내용과 일치한다. 따라서 보기 C가 정답이다.

8

[정답] **C**

[Sentence Insertion] 삽입문장의 단서는 "This is…" 라고 시작하는 부분이 어떤 "this" 에 대한 내용일지 파악하면 된다. 문장 뒤의 내용은 '이것은 사람들이 이 식단을 그만두거나 유지하기 쉽지 않게 하는 중요한 요소이다' 이다. 앞에 budget=예산에 대한 부담감에 대한 내용이 나오고 사람들이 유지하기 힘든 이유로 설명이 나오면 자연스럽다. 따라서 정답은 보기 C이다.

9

[정답] **B**

[Inference] 마지막 6단락에서 첫 번째 문장을 보면 paleo diet는 "had significant improvements in glucose tolerance" 분명한 장점이 있다고 나와 있다. 이 부분이 보기 B의 "It is effective when used for short periods of time"를 설명하고 있고, 본문에서의 "no significant consequence on the muscle cell fat content" 이 내용을 보기의 "but it does not help reduce fat levels considerably." 로 대체했다. 따라서 정답은 보기 B이다.

10

[정답] **A, B, F**

[Summary] 본문의 핵심내용은 Paleo 식단은 오래전부터 내려오는 방법인데, 음식에 제한을 두면서 만성 질병의 위험을 높이지만 효율이 좋다는 내용이다. 보기 A는 3단락의 Paleo 식단이 건강문제를 도와줄 수 있는 설명내용이고, 보기 B는 4단락의 Paleo 식단이 정신건강에도 이롭다는 내용을 다루는 내용이고, 보기 F는 5단락의 Paleo 식단의 단점을 언급하면서 주의해야 할 내용에 관한 문장이다.

PASSAGE 3 : Parasites

1

[정답] **C**

[Fact] 1단락 두 번째 문장을 보면 "These opportunistic organisms get their food from or at the expense of their host."(기생충은 숙주로부터 영양분을 얻어낸다) 라고 나와 있다. 따라서 정답은 보기 C이다.

2

[정답] **D**

[Negative Fact] Protozoa 에 대한 설명으로 틀린 내용을 고르면 된다. 보기 A는 "...microscopic, one-celled organisms…" 부분에 작은 크기에 대한 언급과 일치하고, 보기 B는 전염성에 대한 ". A single organism can cause a serious infection because fecal-oral transmission…" 내용과 일치하며, 보기 C는 다른 곤충(모기, 파리)을 통한 전염성에 대한 내용 "Bites from a mosquito or a fly transmit the organism into blood or tissue in animals and humans."과 일치한다. 따라서 틀린 내용은 보기 D이다.

3

[정답] **C**

[Vocabulary] 지문의 thrive (번성하다) 동의어를 찾으면 된다. 따라서 답은 보기 C이다.

＊Reproduce 번식하다
＊Transcend 초월하다
＊Prosper 번성하다, 번창하다
＊Survive 생존하다

4

[정답] **B**

[Rhetorical Purpose] 본문에서 tapeworm이 왜 나왔는지 확인해보자. "Three main groups of helminths exist in humans." helminth에는 세 가지 부류가 있다는 설명에 이어 그중 하나인 Flatworms에 두 가지 종류가 있는데, 그 종류 중 하나가 tapeworms로 나와 있다. 따라서 정답은 보기 B이다.

5

[정답] **A**

[Main Idea] 4단락의 핵심내용을 파악해야 한다. 1단락에 기생충의 세 가지 종류가 언급됐었는데, 그 후 단락이 차례대로 각각의 기생충에 대해 설명한다. 4단락은 그중에서도 마지막 종류인 ectoparasite에 대한 내용이다. 따라서 보기 A가 정답이다.

6

[정답] **B**

[Sentence Simplification] 음영 표시된 문장 전체가 핵심내용으로서 "Ticks, mites, fleas, and lice … are also classified as ectoparasites" 내용이 "Ectoparasites are blood-sucking arthropods"로 서술됐고, "...that attach to the body or burrow into the skin, and remain there for relatively long periods of time,...." 내용이 "...that attach to the body or dig under the skin and live there for extensive periods."으로 paraphrase 되었다.

7

[정답] D

[Negative Fact] 기생충 접촉시 생기는 결과에 대한 설명이 틀린 것을 고르면 된다. 보기 A는 "First, a possible host can ingest contaminated food or water." 내용과 일치하고, 보기 B는 "Walking barefoot in the dirt or grass can also cause parasitic infestation." 내용과 일치하며 보기 C는 "Many parasites can be transmitted through exchange of saliva or through sexual contact" 내용과 일치한다. 따라서 언급되지 않은 내용은 보기 D이다.

8

[정답] B

[Sentence Insertion] 삽입 문장의 키워드는 "Next... can also be problematic"으로서, 추가적인 infestation에 대한 원인, 특히 음식을 통한 원인을 설명하고 있다. 앞에서 원인에 대한 언급이 나온 후 들어가면 자연스럽기 때문에 정답은 보기기 B이다.

9

[정답] C

[Rhetorical Purpose] 작가가 음영 표시된 표현을 사용한 의도를 물어보는 질문이다. 6단락 첫 번째 문장을 보면 "Many symptoms can help identify a possible parasitic infection…" 다양한 증상이 나타난다. "Especially after international travel" 특히 해외여행을 다녀온 후라고 감염에 걸리기 취약한 방법 중 하나를 제시하는 의도로 사용된 표현이라는 걸 알 수 있다. 따라서 정답은 보기 C이다.

10

[정답] A, C, E

[Summary] 본문의 핵심은 기생충이 기회주의적인 생물체이며 그 수는 거의 줄고 있지 않다는 내용이다. 보기 A는 기생충의 정의와 종류, 그리고 숙주에 미치는 영향에 대해서 이야기하므로 기회주의적인 생물체라는 핵심내용과 일치한다. 보기 B는 2단락 중 기생충의 전이에 해당하는 내용인데 지엽적인 내용이라 오답이다. 보기 C는 기생충의 전이가 오염된 음식이나 신체 접촉에 의해 이루어진다 5단락에서 언급된 포괄적인 내용을 언급하고 있다. 보기 D는 Ectoparasite에 대한 내용인데 "remain there"이라는 내용이 본문에서 언급된 적이 없기에 오답이다. 보기 E는 6단락에서 설명된 여러 증상 중 두 가지를 언급하고 있다. 보기 F는 기생충의 감염 이후에 국제 여행은 권고하지 않는다는 내용으로 본문에서 언급된 내용이 아니기에 오답이다. 따라서 답은 A, C, E이다.

✓ ANSWERS

PASSAGE 1

1 C	2 A	3 B	4 D	5 D
6 C	7 A	8 A	9 D	

10 Divergent Plates: 1;5 Convergent Plates: 6;7 Transform Plates:4.

PASSAGE 2

1 C	2 D	3 B	4 A	5 A
6 C	7 C	8 D	9 B	

10 Igneous: 1, 5 Sedimentary: 4, 7 Metamorphic: 6.

PASSAGE 3

1 C	2 D	3 A	4 B	5 B
6 A	7 C	8 D	9 A	

10 Hard Rock: 2, 5 Placer Deposit: 1, 4, 7.

Tectonic 구조상의	Sedimentary 퇴적층의
Divergent 갈래로 나뉘는	Cardinal 주요한, 추기경
Traction 견인, 견인력	Fissionable 핵분열의
Gargantuan 엄청난	Impervious 통과시키지 않는
Slab 평판, 조각, 바닥 판	Opulent 호화스러운, 엄청나게 부유한
Leach 침출되다, 침출시키다	Prospective 장래가 있는, 곧 있을
Igneous 화성의	Deposit 퇴적물

PASSAGE 1 : Plate Tectonics

1

[정답] C

[Sentence Simplification] 음영 표시된 문장 전체가 핵심내용으로서 그 중에서도 "The key observation that Wegener made was in recording how identical plant and animal fossils as well as rock formations were discovered on continents"(Wegener가 발견한 중요한 사실 중 하나는 식물과 동물의 화석이 똑같다는 점과 대륙에서 발견된 Rock formation과도 일치한다는 점이다) 이를 보기 C에서 간략하게 "Wegener noticed and recorded that identical rock formations and plant and animal fossils were found on different continents"로, "...which today are separated by hundreds of thousands of kilometers"를 "that are currently far apart from each other"로 paraphrase 한 보기 C가 정답이다.

2

[Fact] 질문의 키워드는 Wegener's explanation for finding the same fossils… 이다. 그의 이론이 어떤 근거로 비롯됐는지를 물어보는 거라 1단락 첫 번째 문장의 "…it is almost universally accepted that all of the world's continents were once joined together…" 오늘날 보편적으로 알려진 것은 지구의 대륙은 이전엔 하나로 이루어졌었다는 내용이다. 따라서 보기 A가 정답이다.

3

[정답] **B**

[Negative Fact] 질문의 키워드는 continental drift이고 틀린 설명을 걸러내면 된다. 보기 A는 "Wegener could never satisfactorily explain the mechanical process which led to the drifting of the continents." 내용과 일치하고, 보기 C는 "It was not until later in the century, in the 1950s and 1960s, that evidence was produced for the process of continental drift, and the theory of plate tectonics was advanced." 의 내용과 일치하며 보기 D는 "It was not until later in the century, in the 1950s and 1960s, that evidence was produced for the process of continental drift, and the theory of plate tectonics was advanced. A tectonic plate can be simply described as the vast tablets of rock that the continents lie on, and their interaction is known as plate tectonics." 내용에서 유추해 볼 수 있다. 따라서 정답은 보기 B이다.

4

[정답] **D**

[Vocabulary] 지문의 employed (사용되다) 글의 맥락상 이러한 기술은 세계 2차 대전 때 사용됐다. 따라서 답은 보기 D이다.

* Hired 고용되다
* Labored 일하다 (노력/노동) 하다
* Accepted 받아들이다
* Utilized 사용하다

5

[정답] **D**

[Fact] 보기 A는 "development of ocean floor mapping technology"에서 development가 아니라 employment로 고쳐야 본문과 일치하는 내용이다. 보기 B는 "move away from plate boundaries"가 아니라 "oceanic ridge"로 고쳐야 본문과 일치한다. 보기 C는 "took more than 20 million years to form"에서 형성(form)이 아니라 발달(develop)로 고쳐야 본문과 일치한다. 보기 D는 기술의 발전으로 인해 "the most important discovery they made was the processes at work around mid ocean ridges"라는 내용과 일치한다. 따라서 정답은 D이다.

6

[정답] **C**

[Rhetorical Purpose] 작가가 음영 표시된 San Andreas Fault 를 언급하는 이유를 생각해보자. 해당 문장을 보면 "A famous example of a transform plate boundary is the San Andreas Fault in California…" transform plate boundary으로 유명한 예시는 캘리포니아에 있는 San Andreas Fault 라고 transform plate boundary를 좀 더 시각적인 설명으로 뒷받치고 있다. 따라서 정답은 보기 C이다.

7

[정답] **A**

[Inference] 질문의 키워드는 San Andreas Fault인데 해당 내용 직전 문장을 보면 "The huge stresses created at these points means that chunks of the Earth's crust can break off, and earthquakes are frequent."(… 이 지점에서 지진은 흔하게 발생된다) 라고 나와 있다. 따라서 해당 '지점'에 대한 예시로 언급된 San Andreas Fault에서도 지진이 자주 발생한다고 유추해 볼 수 있다. 따라서 정답은 보기 A이다.

8

[정답] **A**

[Vocabulary] 지문의 leach (침출되다) 의 동의어를 찾으면 된다. 따라서 답은 보기 A이다.

* Leak (물 등이) 새다
* Filter 걸러내다
* Separate 분리하다
* Pour 붓다

9

[정답] **D**

[Sentence Insertion] 삽입문장의 단서는 문장 전체의 내용이다. 지질학자들은 이러한 과정이 생명이 없는 다른 행성에서도 발견되는지 궁금해한다. 여기서 말하는 이러한 현상 "this process" 는 앞에 나온 모든 내용을 일컫는 표면이기 때문에 보기 D가 정답이다.

10

[정답] **Divergent Plates: 1;5. Convergent Plates: 6;7. Transform Plates:4**

[Summary] Divergent Plates 보기 1번은 2단락의 내용과 일치하고 보기 5번은 3단락의 내용과 일치한다. Convergent Plate 내용인 보기 6, 7번은 모두 4단락의 내용과 일치하며 transform plate 내용인 4번 내용은 4단락의 내용과 일치한다.

PASSAGE 2 : Rocks

1 [정답] **C**

[Negative Fact] 1단락에서 나오지 않은 내용을 고르면 된다. 보기 A는 "The 'rock cycle' is a term used to describe natural, everlasting (영원한) geological process…" 와 일치하고 보기 B는 "…have no discernable(식별 가능한) beginning or end."와 일치하며 보기 D는 "we can pinpoint the beginnings and ends of various humanistic cycles and land-changes." 내용에서 유추해 볼 수 있다. 인간과 땅의 변화 (시작과 끝)은 식별할 수 있지만, 그 후에 보면 rock cycle은 그렇지 않다고 나와 있기 때문에 올바른 문장이다. 따라서 보기 C가 정답이다.

2 [정답] **D**

[Sentence Simplification] 음영 표시된 문장은 지구의 탄생 (=birth of our planet) 에서부터 지속되는 주기로 우리가 비롯되고 남길 모든 것들을 정의한다(="it defines where we came from and what we will leave behind")의 내용을 담고 있다. 이를 각각 "origins of life" 와 "continue even after all life has gone"으로 paraphrase한 보기 D가 정답이다.

언뜻 보기에 보기 C의 내용도 rock cycle이 인간 이전에 그리고 그 이후에도 지속될 것 이다라는 내용으로 음영 표시된 문장과 일치하는 것처럼 보인다. 하지만 보기 C는 인간에만 초점이 찍힌 문장으로 충분히 매력적인 답안임에도 보기 D는 음영 표시된 문장의 핵심 뉘앙스를 더 잘 보여주고 있다. 따라서 D가 정답이다.

3 [정답] **B**

[Rhetorical Purpose] 음영 표시된 building-block 가 언급된 내용을 이해하면 된다. 해당 문장을 보면 "These cardinal (= 가장 중요한) building-blocks allowed organisms to spawn (낳다, 초래하다) and begin a 4.5 billion-year evolutionary chain – ultimately leading to homo sapiens."이라고 나와 있다. 중요한 건 "building blocks"로 인해 호모 사피엔스가 태어나게 되었다는 내용이므로 보기 B가 정답이다.

4 [정답] **A**

[Inference] 질문의 키워드는 coal(석탄)이다. 3단락 두 번째 문장을 보면 Coal, a sedimentary rock from the Paleolithic-era, is not only the earliest known source of heat and energy for man but also the most infamous due to its prolific ability to pollute and destroy the natural world. 라고 나와 있다. 즉, 석탄은 오랫동안 사용되어 왔지만 infamous (악명이 높은) 하고 환경 오염의 주범이자 자연계를 망가트린다고 나와 있다. 따라서 정답은 보기 A 이다.

5 [정답] **A**

[Fact] 질문의 키워드는 rocks이다. 4단락 중간을 보면 "Sedimentary rocks are a common requirement for all public buildings"라고 나와 있으므로 정답은 보기 A이다.

6 [정답] **C**

[Vocabulary] 지문의 impervious(~의 영향을 받지 않는)의 동의어를 찾으면 된다. 따라서 답은 보기 C이다.
* Sturdy 튼튼한
* Resilient 회복력 있는, 탄력 있는
* Resistant 저항력 있는, 강한
* Robust 튼튼한

7 [정답] **C**

[Fact] 5단락 첫 문장을 보면 해당 단락은 metamorphic rocks 에 관한 내용임을 알 수 있다. 그리고 단락 중간을 보면 "When limestone is melted, calcites inside it recrystallize and transform into a dense, equigranular, crystal-filled rock."에서 Limestone 예시를 들고 있고, 그다음 문장에서도 "In a similar fashion, sandstone metamorphoses into quartzite." 마찬가지로 sandstone 예시를 들고 있다. 따라서 정답은 보기 C이다.

8 [정답] **D**

[Sentence Insertion] 삽입 문장의 키워드는 "the grains inside it"이다. 앞 문장에서 grain과 관련된 내용 "grainy texture"가 나온 후, "When melted…" 녹여졌을 때의 나타나는 현상에 대한 내용이 나오면 자연스럽다. 따라서 보기 D가 정답이다.

9 [정답] **B**

[Structure] 5단락과 6단락의 핵심내용과 구조를 이해했는지 물어보는 질문이다. 5단락에서는 'metamorphic rocks' 의 과정과 예시가 나오는 반면, 6단락은 해당 rocks가 "precious gemstone"(귀중한 보석의 원석)으로서의 단계에 대해 설명한다. 따라서 보기 B 가 정답이다.

10 [정답] **Igneous: 1, 5. Sedimentary: 4, 7. Metamorphic: 6**

[Summary] Igneous 보기 1, 5번은 모두 2단락의 내용과 일치한다. Sedimentary 보기 4번은 5단락의 내용과 일치하며 7번은 4단락의 내용과 일치한다. Metamorphic 보기 6번은 4단락의 내용과 일치한다.

PASSAGE 3 : Gold mining

1 [정답] **C**

[Fact] 질문의 키워드는 copper이다. 해당 문장을 보면 "Copper was mined for millennia to create weapons once it was combined with tin to form a bronze alloy."라고 나와 있고 가장 정확하게 paraphrase 한 문장은 보기 C이다.

2 [정답] **D**

[Sentence Simplification] 음영 표시된 문장 전체가 핵심내용 으로서 본문의 "Some materials are not mined for their practical applications," 은 "Not all materials we mine are used for something practical,"으로, "but purely on the basis of the value we assign to them based on their aesthetic (미적인) qualities." 는 " but solely for how they look."으로 간략하게 paraphrase 된 보기 D가 정답이다.

3 [정답] **A**

[Vocabulary] 지문의 in earnest (진심으로) 의 동의어를 찾으면 된다. 따라서 답은 보기 A이다.

＊devotedly 헌신적으로
＊Soberly 냉정하게
＊casually 우연히, 아무 생각 없이
＊Impatiently 성급하게, 조바심내며

4 [정답] **B**

[Negative Fact] 3단락에서 설명되지 않은 내용을 고르면 된다. 보기 A는 "...where heavier gold has settled at the bottom…" 금 이 더 무거워서 가라앉는다는 내용으로 유추할 수 있고, 보기 C 는 "...this kind of deposit is mined using water…" 내용과 일치하 며 보기 D는 "The exception to this is where the ground around the deposit is permanently frozen." 내용과 일치한다. 따라서 정 답은 보기 B이다.

5 [정답] **B**

[Inference] 질문의 키워드는 gold이다. 해당 문장을 살펴보 면 "...where heavier gold has settled at the bottom of loose deposits of alluvium." 보다 무거운 금이 헐거운 충적토 아래에 깔 려있다고 나와 있다. 따라서 정답은 보기 B이다.

6 [정답] **A**

[Structure] 4단락의 핵심내용이자 목적을 물어보는 질문이다. 3 단락 첫 번째 문장을 통해 핵심내용은 "...different types of gold deposits…" 임을 알 수 있다. 4단락에서는 "Panning, sluicing, dredging, and the rocker box…"를 통해 충적토에서 금을 캐낼 수 있는 방법들을 설명한다. 따라서 보기 A가 정답이다.

7 [정답] **C**

[Sentence Insertion] 삽입 문장의 키워드는 "Smaller enterprises" 이다. 비교급 smaller를 쓰기 위해선 비교 대상이 앞 에 나와야 하고, enterprises는 기업이라는 뜻이므로 "...by large companies due to the expertise and equipment required for its successful execution." 내용 뒤에 오면 자연스럽다. 따라서 정답은 보기 C이다.

8 [정답] **D**

[Fact] 6단락 첫 번째 문장을 보면 "Mercury extraction has almost stopped completely, and it is generally only used in smaller placer deposit mines…" 수은 추출은 거의 중단되었고, 대부분 작은 규모의 placer deposit 광산에서만 사용된다고 나와 있다. 따라서 정답은 보기 D이다.

9 [정답] **A**

[Rhetorical Purpose] 질문의 키워드는 child labor이다. 해 당 내용이 언급된 문장을 보면 "Unfortunately, many mines in developing countries tend to employ children to do a lot of the manual labor..."(불행히도 개도국의 많은 광산들은 아이들을 고 용하고 그들에게 힘든 노동을 시킨다) 라고 나와 있다. 그리고 나 중 문장을 보면 이를 개선하기 위한 노력 "Many organizations will now only sell gold that they can prove was ethically produced…"이 언급됐기 때문에 보기 A가 정답이다.

10 [정답] **Hard Rock: 2, 5. Placer Deposit: 1, 4, 7.**

[Summary] Hard Rock 보기 2는 6단락의 내용과 일치하고 보기 5는 5단락의 내용과 일치한다. Place Deposit 보기 1은 4단락의 내용과 일치하고, 보기 4, 7은 3단락의 내용과 일치한다.

TOEFL

Reading

Actual Test